D1276348

Due	Return	Due	Ret
		Date	

THE AUDIENCIA
OF NEW GALICIA IN THE
SIXTEENTH CENTURY

THE AUDIENCIA
OF NEW GALICIA IN THE
SIXTEENTH CENTURY

A Study in
Spanish Colonial Government

BY

J. H. PARRY

Fellow of Clare College
Cambridge

CAMBRIDGE
AT THE UNIVERSITY PRESS
1948
REPRINTED
1968

LIBRARY
EISENHOWER COLLEGE

Published by the Syndics of the Cambridge University Press
Bentley House, 200 Euston Road, London, N.W. 1
American Branch: 32 East 57th Street, New York, N.Y. 10022

PUBLISHER'S NOTE

Cambridge University Press Library Editions are re-issues of out-of-print standard works from the Cambridge catalogue. The texts are unrevised and, apart from minor corrections, reproduce the latest published edition.

Standard Book Number: 521 07394 4
Library of Congress Catalogue Card Number: 49–21037

First published 1948
Reprinted 1968

JL
1200
Z9
N83
1968

First printed in Great Britain at the University Press, Cambridge
Reprinted in Great Britain by John Dickens & Co. Ltd, Northampton

'Inasmuch as the kingdoms of Castile and of the Indies are under one Crown, the laws and the manner of government of the one should conform as nearly as possible to those of the other. Our royal Council, in establishing laws and institutions of government in the Indies, must ensure that those kingdoms are administered according to the same form and order as Castile and León, in so far as the differences of the lands and peoples will allow.'

Recopilación de Leyes de Indias, lib. ii, tit. ii, ley 13

CONTENTS

Preface   *page* ix

List of abbreviations   xi

Introduction   1

PART I. THE SUBORDINATE AUDIENCIA, 1548–72

Chapter I. The Conquest of New Galicia   14

   II. The Foundation of the Audiencia   35

  III. The Audiencia and the Indians   55

  IV. The Audiencia and the Conquistadores   84

   V. The Audiencia and the Church   97

  VI. The Reorganisation of the Audiencia, 1570–72   120

PART II. THE AUDIENCIA AND ROYAL CHANCELLERY, 1572–1600

  VII. Administration   133

 VIII. Jurisdiction and Procedure   150

  IX. Conflicts of Jurisdiction   167

Conclusion   185

Appendix A. Specimen Title of *Encomienda* in New Galicia   197

Appendix B. Specimen Appointment of a *Corregidor* in New   198
       Galicia

Map of Mexico showing New Galicia   *at end*

PREFACE

This study is concerned with the day-to-day government of a remote Spanish American province at the time when the disorders of conquest were giving way to a settled administration. Most of the material was collected in the course of visits to Mexico and Spain before the recent war. The first five chapters were written in 1939. The work had then to be laid aside, and did not emerge from its drawer until the beginning of 1946. Belated but none the less sincere thanks are due to Mr F. A. Kirkpatrick; to the distinguished historian of New Galicia, Sr. J. López-Portillo y Weber; and to Sr. J. de la Peña, of the Archive of the Indies in Seville. Especially I would wish to thank Professor C. H. Haring for his teaching and encouragement during a most happy year at Harvard before the war, and for his kindness in reading the manuscript since its completion.

1948   J. H. P.

LIST OF ABBREVIATIONS USED
IN THE REFERENCES

A.G.I.   Archivo general de Indias, Sevilla.

A.G.N.   Archivo general de la Nación, Mexico, D.F.

D.I.I.   *Colección de documentos inéditos relativos al descubrimiento, conquista y colonización de las posesiones españolas en América y Oceanía, sacados en su mayor parte del Real Archivo de Indias* (Pacheco and Cárdenas eds.). Madrid, 1864–81.

D.I.U.   *Colección de documentos inéditos relativos al descubrimiento, conquista y organización de las antiguas posesiones españolas de ultramar.* Madrid, 1886–7.

Orozco y Jiménez, *Colección.*   *Colección de documentos históricos inéditos o muy raros referentes al arzobispado de Guadalajara* (F. Orozco y Jiménez, ed.). Guadalajara, Jalisco, 1921–   .

Puga, *Cedulario.*   *Provisiones, cédulas, instrucciones de Su Magestad de esta Nueva España* (V. de Puga, ed. 1525–63). Mexico, 1878–9.

INTRODUCTION

Spain at the close of the fifteenth century had just completed a long process of unification, accomplished by a series of crusades, partly national and partly religious in character, within Iberian territory. Pride of race, skill in arms, and a truculent missionary catholicism characterised the leading elements of the new Spanish State, especially in Castile, the dominant partner of the union. With the completion of reconquest the Crown was able to bring this intractable aristocracy of swordsmen more and more under military discipline and the centralised rule of law. The monarchy was strong and national in character; under the Catholic monarchs it achieved effective supremacy in both Church and State. It commanded the services not only of able soldiers and administrators but also of able theologians and legal and political theorists, so that the nature and purpose of government, as well as its effectiveness, were matters of public concern.

It is not surprising, therefore, that when Columbus discovered in the New World a new outlet for the restless energy of Spanish swordsmen, a strong and self-conscious imperialism quickly grew up at the Spanish court. After the failure of Columbus as autonomous governor of Española, the Crown stepped in to check the private exploitation which had reduced the colony to chaos and which seemed likely in time to exterminate the natives altogether. It is true that under Ferdinand the sharpest conflict appeared to be between exploitation of the Indians by the colonists, and the even more disastrous system of exploitation by Aragonese concessionaires at court;[1] but this was a temporary tendency. The ultimate intentions of royal policy were plain: as soon as the armed conquest of any territory was complete, a judicial and ecclesiastical bureaucracy was to take over supervision of its government, to mould and educate the natives, to weld the Indies into a homogeneous empire governed from Castile and exploited for the benefit of the Crown. Jurists and theologians discussed, by royal command, the rights and duties which natural law and papal provision might assign to the Spaniards in the New World. Inspectors, judges, missionaries, sailed for the Indies. Decrees were

---

[1] See C. H. Haring, 'Genesis of royal government in the Spanish Indies', *Hispanic American Historical Review* (1927), vol. VII.

issued—the beginnings of a great body of statute law emphasising the rights of the Crown and of the Indians. Within thirty years of Columbus's first landfall, the general foundations had been laid of a centralised system of government which was to serve the whole of the Spanish empire and which, although designed honourably, and not unsuccessfully, to protect and preserve the mass of the American Indians, was to supplant their priests and shamans, to reduce their chieftains to a class of petty officials, and to weaken, in some places to destroy, their native cultures. Of this system the *audiencia* or court of appeal was the most essential and characteristic institution.

The gradual development of a centralised legal system had been one of the most important factors in the unification of Spain. The law of medieval Spain had been derived partly from the ancient Gothic laws—the *Fuero-Juzgo*—partly from the accretion of customary law, partly from many jealously-guarded *fueros* ranging from the model *Fuero Real* of Alfonso the Wise down to the various local *fueros* granting special liberties to particular places and particular classes of people. From the thirteenth century, Civil Law with its severe practice and authoritarian principles, and Canon Law its ecclesiastical counterpart, were superimposed more and more upon the mass of native law. The famous code known as the *Siete Partidas* (1256–65) bore the strong stamp of the Civil Law, though it drew largely also upon the native *fueros*.[1] The codes of the succeeding centuries showed the Civil Law gaining ground steadily, though not unopposed. The Laws of Toro of 1505 are usually considered to mark the triumph of Civil Law in Spain.[2] The permanence of its triumph, especially in matters of procedure and in legal theory, was assured by the great and growing influence of the law schools of the Spanish Universities, which turned out year by year a class of professional lawyers thoroughly grounded in Roman jurisprudence. It was characteristic of Spanish legal development, however, that the earlier codes, particularly the *Siete Partidas*, remained in force, being emended but not superseded by the later compilations. Privileged classes and municipalities, moreover,

[1] F. Martínez Marina, *Ensayo histórico crítico sobre la legislación y principales cuerpos legales de León y Castilla* (Madrid, 1834); F. W. von Rauchhaupt, *Geschichte der spanischen Gesetzesquellen* (Heidelberg, 1923), pp. 112 ff.

[2] F. W. von Rauchhaupt, op. cit. p. 174; F. Sánchez Román, *Estudios de derecho civil...e historia general de la legislación española* (Madrid, 1889–1900), vol. 1, p. 372.

clung tenaciously to their ancient *fueros* in the teeth of the growing autocracy of the sixteenth century.

The sixteenth century added to the existing tangle of law a long series of royal decrees (*cédulas*), the whole being collected and published in 1567 as the *Nueva Recopilación de Leyes de España*. This collection went through nine editions, down to 1774.[1] It was followed in 1680 by a separate collection of decrees relating to the government of the Indies—the *Recopilación de Leyes de Indias*.[2] These *recopilaciones* were collections of Statute Law, some of general application, others applying to particular places and circumstances. They, too, supplemented but did not supersede the mixture of *fueros* and Civil Law rules which was being enforced by the courts at the beginning of the sixteenth century. Throughout the colonial period, therefore, the Empire was governed not by one but by several codes of law, all to some extent valid, and often conflicting one with another.

The interpretation of these various codes in Spain lay in the hands of a numerous and powerful judiciary, at whose head stood the king. Spain carried over from the age of feudalism into the age of sovereignty the notion of jurisdiction as the essential function of authority. Though he legislated continually, the king was still regarded primarily as a judge, the chief of judges. His authority was most directly and characteristically represented by the high courts of justice and in the government of his dominions the school-trained lawyer was his most useful servant.

The professional lawyer was an admirable agent of centralised government. Though not always devoid of adventurous qualities, he had no excessive family pride, and as a rule no great ambition for military glory. His training gave him a deep respect for authority and for the forms of authority, and a habit of careful attention to detail, while it discouraged any tendency towards rash or unauthorised action. A judge, moreover, representing the jurisdiction of the monarch, preserved a certain impersonality, which enabled him to hold in check turbulent *hidalgos* who would have resented the authority of one of their own caste. The chancelleries of Valladolid, Cuidad-Real (later Granada) and Galicia, courts of appeal representing the royal jurisdiction in their

---

[1] Subsequent references are to the edition of 1772.

[2] Subsequent references are to the edition of 1841. For an account of the *Recopilaciones* see F. Sánchez Román, op. cit. vol. I, cap. xix.

localities, had rendered valuable service in the unification of Spain under the Catholic monarchs.[1] The conquest of the Indies represented to the legal mind an immense expansion of the area requiring unification, and offered, besides, special problems of its own. A connecting link was needed between a paternal royal authority and a subject people of alien culture, who were regarded as the direct subjects of the Crown and who were unprotected by capitulations such as those made with the Moors of Granada in 1492. The link must be sufficiently strong to resist the centrifugal tendencies of an avaricious and disorderly colonial society. The task of forging the link was naturally entrusted to benches of professional judges.

The Council of the Indies, established in 1511 as a permanent committee of the Council of Castile, and constituted as a separate organ of government in 1524, was a predominantly legal body. The composition of the Council in its early days was variable, as was its place of residence—it followed the peregrinations of the Court; but the records of the first ten years show the payment of salaries to a president, four or five councillors, a secretary, a *fiscal*, a *relator*, and a porter. In the first year for which a complete list is available, the president was a prelate and four of the five councillors were professional lawyers.[2] The council combined, in the manner characteristic of Spanish institutions, the functions of a supreme court of appeal in important cases with those of an advisory council and a directive ministry for the supervision of colonial affairs. The power of legislation, also, though legally reserved for the king, must often have been exercised by the council with little more than a purely formal royal assent,[3] so that the council, sitting as a court of appeal, frequently faced the task of interpreting and enforcing its own legislative enactments.

The other organ of colonial government in Spain, the *Casa de Contratación* in Seville, though established for the regulation of commerce and emigration, was enlarged by a decree of 1583 to

[1] M. Danvila y Collado, *El poder civil en España* (Madrid, 1885), vol. I, p. 533.
[2] E. Schäfer, *Der Königl. Spanische Oberste Indienrat* (Ibero-Americanische Studien, No. 3, Hamburg 1936), pp. 64–78. C. H. Haring, *The Spanish Empire in America* (New York, 1947), p. 103.
[3] *Cédulas*, or formal decrees, were always signed by the king and all the members of the Council of the Indies. The king, on the other hand, might issue royal orders, signed only by himself and his secretary; but these usually referred to minor matters.

contain within itself a *Sala de Justicia*, with two (later three) qualified judges and a *fiscal*.[1] This audiencia—for so in form it was—heard appeals concerning the economic activities for which the *Casa* was responsible, so that even in day-to-day economic affairs the 'togado' class exercised a considerable influence.

In the Indies, the absence oi colonial precedents and the wholesale concessions made to the Columbus family, delayed the establishment of a supreme royal jurisdiction for a number of years. The first judicial arrangements in Española, drawn up probably at Columbus's own suggestion, made no provision for professional judges; Columbus was empowered in 1492 to appoint judges of first instance (*alcaldes*) and to hear appeals from their decisions himself.[2] In 1507 the towns of Española, fourteen in number, sought and obtained the privileges of municipal incorporation, with nominated councils (*cabildos*) empowered to elect municipal judges (*alcaldes ordinarios*) according to the common custom in the towns of Spain. In 1511, after three successive governors had failed in the hopeless task of pleasing both missionaries and colonists, and numerous petitions had been received begging for the establishment of an appellate jurisdiction in the island, the Crown appointed an independent royal tribunal, consisting of three qualified professional judges, each with the title of *alcalde mayor*, collectively empowered to hear appeals from the decisions of the governor and of his *alcaldes* and *tenientes*.[3] The court was modelled upon the audiencias of Spain, and may be regarded as the direct predecessor of the audiencia of Santo Domingo (Española), formally established fifteen years later.

The audiencia of Santo Domingo, which developed from the 1511 tribunal, became a royal Chancellery in 1526.[4] It consisted of a president, who was also governor and captain-general, four *oidores*[5] and a *fiscal*,[6] together with the staff of lawyers—

---

[1] *Recopilación de Leyes de Indias*, IX. i. 2. Cf. R. B. Merriman, *Rise of the Spanish Empire*, vol. IV, p. 206.

[2] M. Fernández de Navarrete, *Colección de Viages—Título expedido por los Reyes católicos*, vol. II, pp. 9–11; cf. C. de Lannoy and H. Vanderlinden, *L'Expansion coloniale des Peuples européens* (Portugal et Espagne), pp. 277–83, 338.

[3] C. H. Haring, *The Spanish Empire in America*, p. 18.

[4] *Recopilación de Leyes de Indias*, II. xv. 2.

[5] An *oidor* was a justice of appeal in either the Council of the Indies or an audiencia. He was always a professional lawyer, with the degree of Licentiate or of Doctor in Law.

[6] The *fiscal's* chief duty was to safeguard the royal interests before the audiencia; he acted, therefore, as public prosecutor. A discussion of this office follows in ch. VIII.

advocates, notaries, clerks—which the cumbrous procedure of all Spanish courts made necessary. The services of such a tribunal, in checking the ill-treatment of natives by the colonists, in keeping watch upon the activities of colonial governors, and in sending home reasonably impartial reports and recommendations, proved so valuable that the institution was quickly extended from the islands to the mainland. Ten audiencias were created in the sixteenth century, representing royal authority in the more important and populous provinces.[1] These courts varied considerably in size, importance, and constitutional organisation.[2] The two 'viceregal' audiencias of Mexico and Lima (after 1535 and 1542 respectively) exercised only judicial authority, administrative and military power being in each case in the hands of the viceroy, as governor and captain-general. The viceroy also presided over the audiencia, though unless he happened to be a qualified lawyer, he had no vote in its judgements. The decision of what matters fell within the sphere of *gobernación* lay with the viceroy, though in taking any important step he was required to seek the advice of the audiencia, sitting in *acuerdo*.[3] During an interregnum, or a prolonged absence of the viceroy, the audiencia temporarily exercised all his powers. At all times the audiencia might hear appeals against the viceroy's actions, and might draw up corporate complaints against his administration. The viceroy, on the other hand, might complain to the Crown against the conduct of any of the *oidores*, an arrangement which fostered the mutual tale-bearing so characteristic of the official correspondence of the Indies.

In the districts of the lesser audiencias, the three offices of governor, captain-general, and president of audiencia might be combined, as they were for instance in Santo Domingo and New Granada,[4] so that the arrangements of the viceregal audiencias

[1] Santo Domingo, 1526; Mexico (New Spain), 1527; Panamá 1535; Lima (los Reyes), 1542; Santiago de Guatemala (los Confines), 1543; New Galicia, 1548; Santa Fe (New Granada), 1549; La Plata (los Charcas), 1559; San Francisco de Quito, 1563; Manila (los Filipinos), 1583. *Recopilación de Leyes de Indias*, II. xv. For general studies, see C. H. Haring, op. cit. ch. VII; E. Ruiz Guinazú, *La Magistratura Indiana* (Buenos Aires, 1917).

[2] E. Ruiz Guinazú (op. cit.) gives an elaborate classification of the audiencias.

[3] The phrase *casos de gobernación* covered all matters of administration within the competence of the colonial authorities, including public works, the appointment of officials, and all actions involving the expenditure of royal revenue, other than the income expressly appropriated to the courts. An *acuerdo* was a special meeting of an audiencia, sitting not as a court but as an advisory body to a governor in his administrative capacity.   [4] *Recopilación de Leyes de Indias*, V. i. 1.

were reproduced on a smaller scale. In other provinces, the president of the audiencia held the office of governor, but not that of captain-general, as in los Charcas after 1563.[1] In yet other audiencias the president was merely the senior of a bench of justices, as in New Galicia for a short period after 1572, when the administration of the province was entrusted to the viceroy of New Spain.[2] A president was not always appointed upon the creation of a new audiencia. The audiencia of los Charcas, founded in 1559,[3] exercised purely judicial functions until 1563, when the office of president was created to deal with the administration of the province. In New Galicia, an audiencia of four *oidores*, without a president, held both judicial and administrative authority from 1548 to 1572, being subordinate in certain administrative matters to the viceroy, and in judicial matters to the audiencia of Mexico.

New Galicia furnished the one example in sixteenth-century colonial organisation of appeals from the decisions of one audiencia being heard in another. Officially the audiencias held an equal jurisdiction under the Council of the Indies. In practice, however, a variety of combinations of judicial, administrative and military authority existed, and the audiencias differed widely from one another in their power and degree of independence, according to their importance and the extent of their geographical isolation.

The importance of geographical situation in determining the powers of colonial institutions was emphasised by Juan de Solórzano, the greatest of all the writers upon Spanish imperial administration, in his *Política Indiana*.[4] After pointing out that the great distance separating the Indies from Spain made complete centralisation impossible, Solórzano described the inevitable difference between the audiencias of the Indies and the purely judicial chancelleries of Valladolid and Granada. Many special powers, reserved in Spain for the royal councils, were delegated in America to the courts. The audiencias there exercised a general supervision over the conduct of inferior justices; they were empowered to review the routine inquiries (*residencias*) into the records of retiring *corregidores* and other judges, which the law required. They might send out special commissioners (*jueces pesquisidores*) to make

---

[1] R. Levillier, *Correspondencia de la Audiencia de Charcas* (Buenos Aires, 1916), p. 574.
[2] *A.G.I.* Auda. de Guadalajara 230: 'Registro de Reales Cédulas', lib. Z 1, fol. 257 verso.
[3] R. Levillier, op. cit. pp. 530 ff.
[4] Juan de Solórzano Pereira, *Política Indiana* (Madrid 1647), lib. v, cap. iii.

additional investigations whenever necessary. They were to guard the royal prerogative, patronage and revenue, giving priority to suits concerning these matters, and investigating all usurpations of royal authority; they were to maintain the boundaries of the various jurisdictions, and to issue writs of *recurso de fuerza* in restraint of illegal extensions of the ecclesiastical jurisdiction. All legal fees, the fees charged by ecclesiastics for the administration of various sacraments, the tributes paid by the Indians, were to be assessed by the audiencias, and the assessments enforced. Each audiencia was to sit regularly in *acuerdo* to discuss and propose measures concerning the administration of its province, and in *acuerdo de hacienda*, jointly with the royal treasury officials, to determine urgent questions of financial administration. Finally, the supervision of Indian affairs was laid under the especial care of the audiencias.

This last constituted the most urgent and most difficult task which confronted the audiencias. The Spaniards who travelled to the New World were not settlers seeking an empty land, but adventurers, soldiers, missionaries, lawyers—a governing class. They could not survive without Indian labour; but the support of a large number of economic parasites was impossible, without a drastic modification of the Indian way of life, organised as it was within self-sufficient agricultural communities. The Indian would not willingly accept the life of a wage-earning labourer, and the Crown from the first refused to countenance a general reduction to slavery. This was the same problem, which in our own day has become familiar in African administration. The commission appointed for the protection of the natives of the Congo, for instance—a body composed largely of Roman Catholic missionaries—reported in 1912 that 'it is necessary to impose labour on the blacks in order to secure the modification of their mentality and to bring them to realise their duty as civilised people do'.[1] Similar opinions were prevalent among Spanish colonial administrators, and the Spanish system of forced labour invites analogy with the methods employed to secure labourers in the early days of the Kenya coffee plantations or the copper mines of Northern Rhodesia; occasionally even with those formerly used in the rubber plantations of the Congo basin.

[1] *Diocesan Magazine* (West Equatorial Africa, July 1912), p. 13; cited by F. D. Lugard, *The Dual Mandate in British Tropical Africa* (London, 1920), p. 418.

The Spanish system was based upon the complementary institutions of *encomienda* and *repartimiento*. An *encomienda* was a native settlement, or part of one, or a group of settlements 'commended' to the care of an individual Spaniard—an *encomendero*—whose duty it was to protect the inhabitants, to appoint and maintain missionary clergy in the villages, and to undertake a share in the military defence of the province. The *encomendero* was required, accordingly, to reside in the province in which his *encomienda* lay, but outside the Indian settlements.[1] In case of unavoidable absence (for which the permission of the governor was necessary) he might appoint a paid champion (*escudero*); if a minor inherited an *encomienda*, his tutor appointed the champion, with the governor's approval. The *encomendero* was entitled to support his household by levying tribute from the villages under his care—tribute which, in the earlier history of the institution, often took the form of free forced labour. Not all the villages of any province were granted in *encomienda*; some were always retained as crown tributaries— *en cabeza de Su Majestad*. The grant of *encomienda* involved no cession of land or jurisdiction. The initial right to commend Indians was in theory reserved to the Crown, but was usually delegated to *adelantados*—officers in command of new conquests. In established colonies the right to commend was delegated to the viceroy of Peru. In New Spain special authority for this purpose was given to the first viceroy but not expressly to his successors.[2] Solórzano considered that no special authority was needed.[3] In fact the viceroys of New Spain did regularly commend Indians, and royal decrees implicitly acknowledged the right by ordering them to confer *encomiendas* upon favoured individuals.

A grant of *encomienda*, however it originated, was officially limited in duration to the lives of the grantee and (after 1535) of one successor.[4] If the successor were a woman, she was required to marry within a year, so that her husband might perform the obligations of military service. From 1555 the viceroys were permitted to extend existing *encomiendas* to a third, and later to a fourth and fifth 'life' in the holders' families.

---

[1] For duties of *encomenderos* in general, cf. *Recopilación de Leyes de Indias*, vi. ix. 1–23. A specimen *cédula* of *encomienda* in New Galicia is appended (Appendix A).
[2] A. de León-Pinelo, *Tratado de confirmaciones de reales cédulas de encomiendas de Indios* (Madrid, 1630), pt. i, cap. vii.
[3] Solórzano, *Política Indiana*, iii. v. 1, 2; v. xiii. 13.
[4] *Recopilación de Leyes de Indias*, vi. viii. 2, 48; vi. xi. 1–

9

Encomienda was an exact legal term. *Repartimiento* on the other hand means simply *division*—either the act of dividing[1] or the thing divided. The administrative act of allotting Indians;[2] a grant of land;[3] the allotment—actually the forced sale—of commodities to the Indians by the *corregidores*, in the later colonial period—all might be described by the word *repartimiento*. The word was often used loosely, also, as a synonym for *encomienda*,[4] or for a village or group of villages of the appropriate size, whether granted in *encomienda* or not.[5] This use dated from the early island period, before the *encomienda* had received any sort of legal definition. At that time a rough and ready method was employed of allocating Indians to the most necessary tasks of cultivation and building, for the benefit of members of the Spanish community. Later, when the *encomienda* had become a recognised institution and was losing its connection with forced labour, the primitive labour-*repartimiento* remained in existence and in its turn acquired a certain degree of legal definition. All Indians, whether held in *encomienda* or not, were subjected to the labour-*repartimiento*. In this sense, therefore, *repartimiento* was a synonym for the Peruvian word *mita*;[6] in New Spain the word *tanda* was also sometimes used. Each village was called upon to provide a fixed quota of labourers every week. A local magistrate, detailed to act as *juez repartidor*, assigned the labourers to their tasks—whether to necessary public works or to the service of private employers. The *repartimiento* was not strictly a labour-tribute, for in New Spain at least the employers—whether private individuals or public bodies—paid their Indians daily wages at a rate fixed by law.

[1] Cf. *D.I.I.* vol. XXXI, p. 309. *Capitulación* of 1505 authorising Vicente Yáñez Pinzón to settle the island of Puerto Rico and to make 'repartimiento de las caballerías y tierras y árboles y otras cosas de la dicha isla'.   [2] E.g. Puga, *Cedulario*, vol. I, p. 479.

[3] The common terms for grants of land, however, were *peonia* (a grant of about 100 acres) and *caballería* (500 acres or rather more)—theoretically the estate necessary to support a foot-soldier and a horseman respectively. A building-plot and garden in a town was called *solar*.

[4] Cf. Las Casas, *Historia de las Indias*, bk. II—Argumento: 'Se introdujo el repartimiento de los Indios a los Españoles, que después llamaron encomiendas, en todas las Indias.' Cf. also J. de Solórzano, *Política Indiana*, lib. III, cap. i; F. A. Kirkpatrick, 'Encomienda-Repartimiento', *Hisp. Amer. Hist. Rev.* (August 1939).

[5] J. López de Velasco, in *Geografía de las Indias 1571–1574* (1894), says that New Galicia contained '104 repartimientos de Indios, la mitad de su Magestad y la otra mitad de particulares'. Cf. also *Recopilación de Leyes de Indias*, VI. viii. 40.

[6] *Recopilación de Leyes de Indias*, VI. xii. 20, 21, 22, 23, 24, 25, 27, 29, 30, 33; VI. xv. 3, 4, 5, 6. See L. B. Simpson, 'The *Repartimiento* system of native labour in New Spain and Guatemala', *Ibero-Americana*, no. 13 (Berkeley, California, 1938).

Neither *encomienda* nor *repartimiento* was intended to affect the titles by which Indian *pueblos* held their lands.[1] Spanish colonial legislation embodied from the first the principle laid down in our time, 'from which no civilised government would think of departing—that in countries acquired by conquest or cession, private property, whether of individuals or communities, existing at the time of the cession or conquest, is respected'.[2] *Peonías* and *caballerías* of land were granted to Spaniards in fee simple (*en dominio propio*) from unoccupied areas in the colonies.[3] The Spanish Crown also respected the communal aspect of Indian economic life, both in New Spain and in Peru, wherever it survived the shock of conquest. Each village was corporately responsible for its *corvée* or its tribute. *Personal* servitude was always discouraged and after 1549 expressly condemned.[4]

Even with all these qualifications, both the labour-*repartimiento* and the *encomienda*, with its quasi-feudal implications and its possibilities of abuse, remained a source of anxiety and distrust on the part of the Crown and the missionary Orders. Numerous legislative attacks were made, especially on the *encomienda*, but with only partial success. In the early days, when royal administration was in embryo, some such system had been indispensable if the colonists were to support life at all. Later, at the time when the audiencias were established, the *encomienda* had already struck deep roots, as even its enemies admitted.[5]

The only successful modification achieved in the sixteenth century was the commutation of labour dues into tribute payments, accomplished in New Spain, at least in law, between 1545 and 1550. In the tripartite programme proposed by the Crown for the Indians—the inculcation of law, industry, and the Christian religion—the *encomienda* was expected to provide for the second and third items, while local judges, *corregidores* and *alcaldes*, attended to

[1] *Recopilación de Leyes de Indias*, iv. xii. 7, 9, 17, 18; vi. iii. 9. See S. Zavala, 'La propiedad territorial en las encomiendas de Indios', *Universidad*, vol. iv, no. 20, pp. 24–37 (Mexico, 1937).

[2] Lord Lugard, *The Dual Mandate*, p. 288. See also judgement of the Privy Council in the Oleuwa land case, July 1921.

[3] Cf. G. M. MacBride, *The Land Systems of Mexico* (New York, 1923).

[4] *Recopilación de Leyes de Indias*, vi. xii. 1, 5, 7, 49.

[5] '...El remedio se intentó tardamente, y a ésto se debió que la encomienda creciera y echara tantas y tan arraigadas raíces...que ya el Rey con todo su poder no ha podido en algunos tiempos extirparla.' Las Casas, *Apologética Historia*, cited by S. Zavala, *La Encomienda Indiana* (Madrid, 1935).

the administration of the law. These minor judges were themselves drawn, for the most part, from the same class as the *encomenderos*. The audiencias, charged with the general supervision of the whole system, were compelled to steer a delicate course between the vested interests represented by the *encomienda*, and the direct control of the Indians which the policy of royal paternalism demanded. To offend the *encomenderos*, always an influential body in any province, meant creating serious trouble within the Spanish community, and might mean the cessation of work in the ranches and mines; on the other hand, the abuses associated with the *encomienda*, if allowed free play, led to discontent and rebellion among the Indians, and determined agitation from humanitarian missionaries of the Las Casas school. In either event, the *quinto*[1] of the silver—that royal barometer of good administration—might suffer, and disagreeable inquiries might be made at home. To add to the difficulty of the situation, both Spaniard and Indian displayed an inordinate fondness for litigation, which at times brought into prominence the worst features of the Spanish judicial system—cumbrous procedure, and meticulous concern with unimportant detail.

The special powers which Solórzano attributed to the audiencias of the Indies, if not all strictly judicial in character, lay on the borderline of judicial authority. He wrote, however, in the seventeenth century, when the more serious problems confronting the audiencias had been to some extent solved. At least the danger of rebellion was less. In the sixteenth century, the more remote audiencias, to function as successfully as they did, must have exercised, in practice if not in law, a much greater measure of discretionary authority than Solórzano would admit. Certainly the audiencia of New Galicia from time to time exercised independent powers of legislation in minor matters, controlled public works, made emergency appropriations for military and executive needs, provided for exploration and defence, created new offices to meet new necessities and appointed candidates to vacant offices already existing. The study which follows is concerned with this one audiencia, and with the government of an area comprising, at its greatest extent, the modern Mexican States of Jalisco, Nayarit, Colima, and Aguascalientes, and parts of Sinaloa, Zacatecas, Durango, Guanajuato, Querétaro and San Luis Potosí.

[1] A proportion of all silver produced in the Indies—usually one-fifth—was claimed by the Crown.

This district presented, of course, many problems peculiar to itself; but the story of the audiencia is probably characteristic— the story of a judicial institution, composed of professional lawyers, which steadily acquired executive power and became, for a time at least, the supreme representative of royal authority within its jurisdiction.

The burden of imperialism is often heavy and at the time unprofitable for the conquered and for all but a few of the conquerors—'a vast system of outdoor relief for the upper classes' as James Mill cynically called it. The credit for the attempts which were made to lighten the burden in the Spanish Indies, as most contemporary students of colonial government admitted, must be shared between the more enlightened missionaries and the royal audiencias. Solórzano (though, as an *oidor* himself, his testimony is suspect) truly described the aim and ideal of the Spanish royal jurisdiction overseas, in his eulogy upon the audiencias: 'Our kings have earned the lasting thanks of all, for the blessings they conferred upon the Indies by the foundation of the royal audiencias; for no man can deny that they are the rock and defence of those kingdoms, where justice is done, where the poor find their defence from the oppression of the great and powerful, and where every man may claim his own in truth and in law.'[1]

---

[1] Solórzano, *Política Indiana*, lib. v, cap. iii, § 7.

PART I

THE SUBORDINATE AUDIENCIA, 1548–1572

CHAPTER I

THE CONQUEST OF NEW GALICIA

The whole story of the conquest of Spanish North America is coloured by the genius of its greatest hero, Hernán Cortés. Every *conquistador* sought to emulate Cortés in his meteoric rise to fame. None equalled him in his diversity of talents—his military ability; his capacity for retaining the loyalty not only of his own men, but of his conquered foes; his skill in placating and reassuring Charles V, that most jealous of monarchs.

Cortés's defeat of the Aztec confederacy, however, and his capture of the capital city of Tenochtitlán-Mexico in 1521, marked only the beginning of the conquest of New Spain. West of Anáhuac, the Mexico of the Aztecs, were great mountain ranges, their valleys inhabited by independent peoples speaking alien tongues. Beyond them lay the South Sea and the way to China. To the north were endless barren hills; beyond the hills, deserts; and beyond the deserts another region inhabited by settled village-dwellers. Native rumours of these northern *pueblos* gave rise, in the Spanish imagination, to golden tales of Gran Quivira and Cíbola of the Seven Cities.

Most of the area of northern Mexico (the name being used, for the moment, in its modern sense) is a high table-land, becoming less elevated, less broken, and progressively more arid towards the north. The table-land is bounded on the west by a chain of high mountains—the Sierra Madre Occidental—some hundred miles wide and running north and south. In the modern states of Jalisco and southern Nayarit the mountains reach nearly to the coast, and the cluster of volcanic peaks in the south-west corner of Jalisco includes one of the highest in the Sierra Madre—the shapely Nevado de Colima. Further north, however, in central and northern Nayarit, a hot and formerly fertile coastal flood-plain separates the mountains from the sea. This low country stretches northward through Sinaloa into Sonora. The passes through the

Sierra Madre down to the coastal plain are few and widely separated, and their position naturally determined the route of Spanish penetration in that direction.

The road to Cíbola, as first reported to the early conquerors,[1] lay first through Michoacán, outlying and independent kingdom of the great Mexican plateau; through the extensive and relatively fertile upland area of central Jalisco and south-western Nayarit; through Aztatlán in the hot coastal flood-plain, from which the Aztecs of Anáhuac traditionally migrated; through Chiametla, Culiacán and the arid wastes of Sonora, into the region of the *pueblo* cultures of Arizona and New Mexico. This route was marked before the Spaniards came, by well-used Indian trails, which were to develop later into the *camino real*—the royal road, connecting the missions and *presidios* of the New Mexico frontier with the capital city of Guadalajara. Out of the search for the road to Cíbola was to grow the kingdom of New Galicia—Chimalhuacán, the 'land of shield bearers', to give it its native name[2]—to which was added later, as a result of the search for silver, a great inland tract in the modern States of Zacatecas, Guanajuato and Aguascalientes.

The area is divided geographically, but not ethnographically, by a big river, the Santiago or Tololotlán, which rises in Lake Chapala in the north-west corner of Michoacán and flows north-west through the uplands of Jalisco, passing close to the site of modern Guadalajara. Leaving the State of Jalisco, the Santiago cuts through the Sierra Madre by way of a canyon some four thousand feet deep, which gave to the river its sixteenth-century Spanish name—Río Grande de la Barranca. This great Barranca is only the largest among many; the whole escarpment is seamed with such chasms. The country on the left bank of the Barranca is passable; the Spanish armies marched through it, and the railway from Guadalajara to Tepic and Culiacán now runs that way. On the right bank the land rises steeply into the wild and rugged Sierra de Nayarit, a deeply folded mountain range with parallel ridges and valleys running north and south. This is the most

[1] See C. Sauer, 'The road to Cíbola', *Ibero-Americana*, no. 3 (Berkeley, California, 1932).
[2] The translation of the name in J. Dávila Garibi, *Los aborígenes de Jalisco* (Guadalajara, Jalisco, 1933), p. 7. The *oidor* Hernán Martínez de la Marcha, in his *visita* of 1550, commented on the gaily painted wooden shields used by the Caxcanes. See ch. II, below.

continuous and most impassable section of the Sierra Madre Occidental, and effectively prevents direct communication between northern Jalisco and the coast. Below the Barranca, the river flows through the flood-plain of modern Nayarit, ancient Aztatlán, to the Pacific.

The ethnography of the region before the arrival of the Spaniards is extremely difficult to trace in detail. Rough boundaries can be drawn, however, between the settled agricultural peoples of the uplands and coastal plain, and the non-agricultural or semi-agricultural tribes of the mountains and barrancas.[1] The upland area of Chimalhuacán (central and southern Jalisco, southern Nayarit, and Colima) was inhabited by an extensive sub-Mexican group of tribes including Teules, Tecuexes, Caxcanes, and probably other sub-tribes whose names have disappeared. These peoples lived in settled villages and practised agriculture. Many of the cultural characteristics of Anáhuac occurred also in this region—irrigation; the cultivation of maize, beans and the alligator pear; the use of cotton armour; stone and adobe dwelling-houses; temples and temple-mounds. Unlike the Aztecs of Anáhuac, these western Mexicans had no sort of unity among their many towns and villages, and no political centre. Their principal spiritual centre seems to have been the great temple-pyramid El Teul in the hills near Nochistlán, north of the Santiago. Archaeologists differ over the question of whether human sacrifices were offered at El Teul, but agree that none of the religious observances of Chimalhuacán equalled the ritual savagery of the State religion of Aztec Mexico. El Teul was simply a temple; it had not developed into a political capital or an important centre of population; in this respect also it differed from the Mexican temples to which the Spaniards were accustomed.

A second group of settled agricultural peoples existed in the coastal lowlands of northern Nayarit and Sinaloa. The tribes of this region, the Totorames and Tahues, had fewer obviously Mexican characteristics.[2] They built few temple-pyramids. Their houses were of mud and wattle, thatch, or palm mat, not of stone or adobe. Though maize was their principal crop, its cultivation

---

[1] See R. L. Beals, 'The comparative ethnology of northern Mexico before 1750', *Ibero-Americana*, no. 2 (Berkeley, California, 1932).
[2] R. L. Beals, op. cit. C. Sauer and D. Brand, 'Aztatlán, prehistoric Mexican frontier on the Pacific coast', *Ibero-Americana*, no. 1 (Berkeley, California, 1932).

does not appear to have included the elaborate ritual of corn-dance and rain-dance which played so important a part in the agricultural life of the plateau. They did not practise human sacrifice. Their villages were grouped loosely into four leagues or kingdoms— Aztatlán, Chiametla, Culiacán and Sentispac;[1] but they had no real political cohesion. Their military organisation was designed to ward off local raids, not to repel a disciplined and desperate army. They had no fortified sites comparable to the *peñoles* of the Caxcanes. In general, both Tahues and Totorames seem to have been remarkably peaceful people. Their country, now arid and inhospitable except in the larger river valleys, was both populous and prosperous at the time of the Spanish invasion, and had regular trade connections both with the northern *pueblos* and with Anáhuac.[2] Turquoise and buffalo-skins came from the north, the plumage of parrots and other tropical birds from the south—feathers being objects of ceremonial value all over north America. Maize also was probably an article of barter in times of crop failure. The *relaciones* of the conquest constantly remark on the density of population and the abundance of food. Often a single *pueblo* sufficed to billet the entire Spanish army with its thousands of auxiliaries.

East of the coastal plain, the Sierra de Nayarit was inhabited by more primitive, more formidable tribes—Coras, Huicholes, Tepehuanes—living in tiny settlements high up on the ridges, practising only the most rudimentary seasonal agriculture on the barranca floors and making intermittent war upon the more settled peoples. Their cultural affinities were chiefly with the Caxcanes; they practised human sacrifice; they maintained their warlike independence and their practice of raiding, although surrounded by conquered peoples, throughout the greater part of the colonial period. Their mountain fastnesses were penetrated by very few Spaniards until the eighteenth century and were never extensively colonised, with the result that the Huicholes have retained their language and their tribal identity to this day.[3]

Farther inland, north of Michoacán and Jalisco, the semi-arid hill country of Zacatecas and Aguascalientes was sparsely inhabited

[1] C. Sauer, 'Aboriginal population of north-western Mexico', *Ibero-Americana*, no. 10 (Berkeley, California, 1935).

[2] C. Sauer, 'The road to Cíbola', loc. cit.

[3] For an account of the primitive hill tribes, see J. Dávila Garibi, *Breves apuntes acerca de los Chimalhuacanos* (Guadalajara, 1927).

17

by still more primitive peoples. These were the Zacatecos, and farther east the cannibal Guachichiles, non-agricultural nomads, hunters and gatherers of roots, to whom the Spaniards gave the general name of Chichimecas—the 'wild people'. Their territory had at first sight little to offer; but it was there that the richest silver mines were found. The country was too dry for agriculture, without extensive irrigation; apart from mining, it could only be used by the Spaniards as rough cattle range. Both miners and ranchers maintained a constant guerrilla warfare with the intractable savages who surrounded them, throughout colonial times.

The languages of the area were as diverse as the peoples. Nahuatl, however, the Aztec language, was widely used as a *lingua franca* from Durango to Nicaragua in colonial times, and many of the languages spoken by independent tribes before the conquest may have been dialects of Nahuatl.[1] Nahuatl-speaking Indians from Anáhuac also migrated into New Galicia in large numbers in the wake of the Spanish armies, to fill the gaps created by an exceptionally destructive conquest. These Mexicans were settled in *encomiendas* all over the cultivated areas, and as a result of their presence the local languages died out in many places. Pre-conquest linguistic boundaries cannot therefore be traced with any certainty. Nahuatl was the language regularly used by Spanish missionaries and official interpreters throughout New Galicia; comparatively few friars mastered the more barbarous Cora, Zacateco or Guachichile speeches. A college was founded at Guadalajara in 1583 for instructing clergy in the 'Mexican' language.[2]

The conquest of New Galicia was accomplished in 1531, ten years after the capture of Mexico. The southern part of the region had, however, been explored some years before that date. Cortés, as governor of New Spain, was aware of the importance of the possession of the Pacific coast, and during the years between his

[1] The standard works on this subject are: M. Orozco y Berra, *Geografía de las lenguas y carta etnográfica de México* (Mexico, D.F., 1864); C. Thomas and J. R. Swanton, *Indian languages of Mexico and central America* (Washington, D.C., 1911). Both books describe the language of the whole region on the left bank of the Santiago, and the whole coastal plain of Tepic and Sinaloa, as 'Mexican' or 'Aztec'. Sauer, correcting these authors, considers that the state of affairs which they describe arose only after the Spanish conquest. C. Sauer, 'The distribution of aboriginal tribes and languages in north-western Mexico', *Ibero-Americana*, no. 5 (Berkeley, California, 1934).

[2] A. Tello, *Crónica miscelánea de la santa provincia de Jalisco*, 1643 (Mexico, D.F., 1898), cap. ccxiv; G. Guerra, *Arte de la lengua mexicana según la acostumbran hablar los indios en todo el obispado de Guadalajara* (1692), A. Santoscoy, ed. (Guadalajara, Jalisco, 1900).

capture of Mexico and his first journey to Spain in 1529, dispatched several expeditions to the west. Cristóbal de Olid
conquered Michoacán up to its northern boundary, the Lerma
river, in 1522; his lieutenants, Alvárez Chico and Alonso de Avalos,
added the coastal provinces of Zacatula and Colima, and the wedge
of inland territory in southern Jalisco known as the 'pueblos of
Avalos'. In 1524 the conqueror's cousin, Francisco Cortés de San
Buenaventura, explored the coast lands up to the mouth of the
Río de Santiago, and much of the territory on the south bank.
At the time of Cortés's departure for Spain, in the hope of justifying
himself before his suspicious sovereign, most of the land south of
the Río Grande had been roughly explored by his agents, and all
to the south-east of a line drawn roughly between Ayutla and
Navidad Bay had been settled and granted in *encomienda*. Between
this line and the lower reaches of the Santiago, therefore, was
debatable ground, and everything north of the Santiago and
Lerma rivers was quite unknown. The work of conquering both
the debatable and the unknown, and welding all into one kingdom, fell to one of the most sinister figures in the story of the
Spanish conquest—Beltrán Nuño de Guzmán, who was to be-
queath a tradition of savagery to the whole government of New
Galicia.[1]

Nuño de Guzmán was a natural gangster. Such men flourish in
times of violence, and the annals of the conquest are full of them.
Nuño had certain advantages over his fellow adventurers; he
claimed to be a qualified lawyer, though his letters betray small
knowledge of law; and he bore an illustrious name, though his
right to use the arms of the house of Guzmán was far from clear.
He had none of Cortés's statesmanship, certainly none of his
charm. His dominant characteristic was a sombre ferocity,
a demonic energy which enabled him to command and hold
together whole armies of lesser scoundrels. He had a great love of
public ceremonial, and this no doubt contributed to the terror
with which the Indians regarded him. Nuño's rise to high public
office, and the decision of the Council of the Indies to promote
him and his associates, are hard to explain. As governor of the

[1] For an account of Nuño de Guzmán, see J. López-Portillo y Weber, *Conquista de la
Nueva Galicia* (Mexico, 1935). The various *Relaciones* written by members of the expedition are printed in *Documentos para la historia de México*, J. García-Icazbalceta, ed.
(Mexico, 1858–66), vol. ii, and in *D.I.I.* vols. xiii and xiv. See López-Portillo 'Los
cronistas de la Nueva Galicia', *Mem. Acad. Mex. Hist.* vol. ii, 1943.

ill-defined region of Pánuco in eastern Mexico, during Cortés's disastrous expedition to Honduras, he had amassed a considerable fortune by shipping slaves to the islands. He was a personal enemy of Cortés, and a trusted adherent of Velázquez, the governor of Cuba, who had done all in his power to thwart the conqueror since 1519. Possibly these facts weighed with the Crown, when in 1527 Nuño was appointed president of the first audiencia of New Spain, and empowered to conduct an inquiry into the truth of the charges brought against Cortés at the Spanish court—an inquiry which dragged on for years, with many petty recriminations, and which no doubt contributed to Cortés's decision to return to Spain.[1] Nuño was disliked and distrusted upon all sides. The followers of Cortés hated him and resisted all his attempts to detach them from their leader. The Indians were helpless victims of the slave-hunting activities pursued by the *oidores*, in the vast *encomiendas* which they assigned illegally to themselves and their friends. Fray Juan de Zumárraga, bishop (later archbishop) of Mexico, and official protector of the Indians, though himself not very well disposed towards Cortés, conducted a furious campaign against the audiencia, culminating in a general interdict, upon the seizure in sanctuary of two missionary friars who had preached against Nuño's conduct. Nuño attempted to silence Zumárraga, by intercepting the bishop's correspondence with Spain. His orgy of power could not continue long, however, without the Council of the Indies becoming aware of the disastrous results of the recent appointments. Cortés was in Spain, establishing himself once more in the confidence of the emperor; one of Zumárraga's letters, which had eluded Nuño's vigilance, reached the court, and in the same year, 1529, the decision was taken to replace all the members of the audiencia, and the treasury officials, and to send Cortés (now Marquis of the Valley of Oaxaca) back to Mexico as captain-general. Nuño, meanwhile, warned perhaps by early rumours, or finding Mexico already too hot to hold him, pushed ahead with plans, which he had always held in his mind, to explore to the north-west, and conquer a new kingdom of his own.

Nuño's following consisted of his own colleagues, none of them men of distinction; the treasury officials Salazar and Chirinos, whose feud with Cortés led them to support Cortés's most powerful

---

[1] H. H. Bancroft, *History of the Pacific States* (San Francisco 1883–8), vol. v, p. 289, and references there.

enemy, and whose venality and incompetence was certain to lead sooner or later to disgrace; and a host of poor *hidalgos*, out-at-elbows adventurers who had arrived in New Spain too late to receive a share of the *encomiendas* which went to Cortés's followers. Most of them were from the north of Spain, Basques, Asturianos and Montañeses. They made formidable fighting material. With the financial resources which Nuño commanded as president of the audiencia, he was able to assemble a powerful force, consisting of about three hundred well-armed Spaniards,[1] many of them mounted, and some thousands of native auxiliaries. With this following he left Mexico at the end of 1529, taking the overseer Chirinos with him, and leaving his colleagues Matienzo and Delgadillo in charge of the audiencia.

Nuño's route took him through Toluca and Ixtlahuaca, then west through Michoacán as far as Tzintzunzán, where the army turned to the north and marched towards what is now the State of Guanajuato. Upon crossing the Lerma river, Nuño, entering unoccupied territory for the first time, performed one of those wordy ceremonies to which he was addicted, and built a shrine at the place of the crossing. Here occurred the death of Caltzonzín, the 'king of Michoacán', a Christian convert who had rashly trusted himself in Nuño's power, and who was tortured and executed for refusing to disclose the whereabouts of an imaginary treasure. The murder of Caltzonzín, and the failure of the murderer, in spite of repeated royal orders, to send home the 'case' against his victim, added yet another count to the reckoning against Nuño.

After crossing the Lerma near Conguripo, the army penetrated to the north, according to Mota-Padilla,[2] as far as modern Guanajuato, but finding the mountains bare and sparsely inhabited, turned south-west through the province of Cuitzeo, to the southern half of which Francisco Cortés had previously laid claim. Reaching the shores of lake Chapala, Nuño crossed the Río de Santiago near its source, and marched westwards, into the Caxcane country around the site of modern Guadalajara. Here he fought his first battle; the 'ruler' of the country, a woman, had decided to receive

---

[1] According to J. López-Portillo y Weber. Tello says five hundred. *Crónica miscelánea*, vol. xxx.

[2] M. de la Mota-Padilla, *Historia de la Conquista de la Nueva Galicia*, 1742 (Mexico, 1856), cap. xxvii.

the Spaniards in peace. Her warriors, however, exasperated by the demands for supplies and services which Nuño made upon them, resisted his entry into the capital village; only after a day of hard fighting were they defeated by superior numbers and armament. Nuño had little military skill. Almost all his battles were fought against inferior forces, and on many occasions he deliberately provoked resistance, in order to justify the plunder and enslavement of peaceful natives. His difficulties arose from flood, plague, famine, or the superior strategy of his opponents—never because the Spaniards and their allies were overwhelmed by numbers.[1]

In the Guadalajara neighbourhood Nuño apparently heard of the temple of El Teul, and thinking perhaps to find another Tenochtitlán, he once again crossed the Santiago—now the Río Grande de la Barranca, a formidable obstacle—and struck north as far as Nochistlán, driving the Caxcane army which opposed him to seek refuge in the fortified *peñol*. El Teul lay a short distance to the west; Chirinos, sent out upon a reconnaissance with a body of Mexican troops, discovered it first, and the main army reached the temple-pyramid early in April 1530. Even Nuño was impressed by this solemn and lonely place; though its sanctity did not save it from desecration:

It consists of a great mound, the strongest place we have yet seen, built of blocks of hewn stone, and is evidently a centre of great impor-tance, being covered with ornate buildings and shrines, each main-tained by a local chief, for the purpose of sacrifice. The natives say that the greatest of all their idols lived there, and that he was made of gold, but was destroyed in a war long ago.... It resembled the temples which used to stand in Mexico.... The overseer said that it was a wonderful sight when he first arrived, but the auxiliary troops destroyed every-thing.[2]

No hope remained, after that destruction, that the Caxcanes would settle down contentedly under Spanish rule.

At Teul, Nuño divided his forces; he himself crossed the river and marched through the uplands of central Jalisco to the town of Tepic, burning and plundering the Caxcane villages upon his way. At Tepic he paused to rest his troops and to await Chirinos. The overseer had been sent from Teul with a body of troops to search for

---

[1] J. López-Portillo y Weber, op. cit.
[2] *D.I.I.* vol. xiii, p. 380: 'Carta a S.M. de ...Nuño de Guzmán. 8 de Julio, 1530.'

a city of 'Amazons' to the north—a persistent legend throughout the conquest. He discovered only barren hills inhabited by primitive tribesmen; and turning south-west in order to rejoin his leader, found his way blocked by the precipitous Sierra de Nayarit. The march of Chirinos and his companions, without sufficient food or water, leading and dragging their horses for fifteen days over the crests of the Sierra, was perhaps the only heroic episode in the whole conquest of New Galicia; and native mythology soon provided magical explanations of their dramatic appearance at Tepic.

At Tepic, the army was still in territory explored by Francisco Cortés. Crossing the Santiago once more, this time in the teeth of desperate resistance, Nuño entered the tropical flood-plain of Aztatlán, the 'place of waters', a land thickly settled, peaceful, prosperous and hitherto unknown to Europeans. Here Nuño performed once more the ceremony of taking possession, giving to his conquests the name of 'Greater Spain', and dispatched a long and pretentious letter to the emperor,[1] giving account of the expedition and asking royal confirmation of the conquest. In Aztatlán, however, serious difficulties began to overtake him for the first time. Resistance led by the able chieftan Ocelotl and largely provoked by Spanish looting; floods (during the season of rain, the late summer of 1530); pestilence; mutiny among the auxiliaries, all combined to decimate the Spanish army in the 'kingdom' of Aztatlán. Here, too, Nuño received definite news of his removal from the office of president, of the return of Cortés to Mexico and of the appointment of the second audiencia. The anxious letter which Nuño sent to the emperor in January 1531[2] reflected his fear that the new *oidores* would listen to the accusations of Zumárraga and others. Indeed, the statesmanlike Ramírez de Fuenleal, the able Salmerón, the saintly Vasco de Quiroga were little disposed to show mercy to Nuño and his kind, and in this matter they were supported by the jealousy and the genius of Cortés. To add to his anxieties, Nuño learned of revolts in his rear, in Jalisco and southern Nayarit. Chirinos was sent in haste to Mexico, to try to save Nuño's interests there; Nuño himself hanged his mutineers, abandoned his sick, and dragged his army out of the swamps of Aztatlán towards the north, leaving behind him a trail of burning villages. The adjutant Gonzalo López rushed south to

[1] Ibid. vol. XIII, p. 356.   [2] Ibid. vol. XIII, p. 406.

Tepic, crushed the Jalisco revolt with speed and great brutality (he and Cristóbal de Oñate were perhaps the two best soldiers in Nuño's army) and persuaded some of the Spaniards of Colima to join the depleted expedition. Seizing a number of Indians from the *pueblos* of Avalos to serve as porters (despite the protests of their *encomenderos*) López returned north to rejoin Nuño in Chiametla (southern Sinaloa). His arrival with reinforcements and supplies saved the expedition, which continued its march north as far as Culiacán. Here, finding neither gold nor populous cities, Nuño attempted to climb the scarp of the Sierra de Durango, hoping perhaps to regain the central plateau and to connect Culiacán with his old province of Pánuco. Failing in this, he decided at last to turn back. He founded the settlement of San Miguel de Culiacán as the northern outpost of his conquest, leaving there such of his men as were tempted by grants of *encomienda* in that region, and returned to Tepic in the autumn of 1531 to attend to the organisation of the new kingdom.

The second audiencia of New Spain held authority to take *residencia*[1] of Nuño and his associates for the many crimes and irregularities committed during the tenure of office of the first audiencia. However, the arrest of the conqueror of a new kingdom, in command of a formidable army, was a different proposition from the mere trial of a venal and incompetent president. Cortés's offer to lead troops in person against Nuño[2] was declined, presumably for fear of civil war; Cortés himself was not entirely trusted. The *oidores* therefore confined themselves to seizing Nuño's goods, and to collecting evidence of the uselessness and rashness of his expedition, and the danger to which he had exposed the kingdom of New Spain by deserting his post.[3] The charges were all zealously forwarded to Spain. Nuño persistently ignored writs summoning him to Mexico, preferring to negotiate directly with the emperor, in the hope of ingratiating himself at court and so escaping his *residencia*. Though deprived of his presidency and of the title of governor of Pánuco, he received confirmation of the conquest of the new kingdom, now more modestly styled, by royal

---

[1] For definition of *residencia* see ch. III, below.

[2] *D.I.I.* vol. XIII, p. 193: 'Carta del Lic. Salmerón.'

[3] *D.I.I.* vol. XVI, p. 363: 'Información sobre los acaecimientos de la guerra que hace el gobernador Nuño de Guzmán a los Indios, para con los pareceres de las personas examinadas, tomar resolución, 1531.' The witnesses differed widely in their opinions of Nuño's venture. The missionaries were united in condemning it.

command, New Galicia. An emissary of Cortés, at the head of an armed force and bearing a commission from the audiencia to expel Nuño from the land south of the Santiago, was captured and sent back empty handed. This act of contempt eventually swelled the indictment against Nuño, but its immediate and practical result was to confirm to New Galicia the region between the Santiago and the strongly-held *pueblos* of Avalos.

To the legal proceedings in Mexico, Nuño replied by granting *encomiendas* and founding towns. At that time, any group of colonists might seek recognition as a corporate town, and claim the jurisdiction and other privileges attached to such recognition.[1] New 'towns' sprang up in all parts of the Indies, including New Galicia. Compostela, established near the *pueblo* of Tepic, and named after the capital of Galicia in Spain, remained for thirty years the capital of New Galicia and the safeguard of the Tepic region. Purificación, to the south, founded by Nuño's order, guarded a long strip of coast stretching south to the boundary of Colima. More important than either, Guadalajara was founded at the end of 1531 as a Spanish garrison in the middle of the dangerous area of Chimalhuacán; it occupied three successive sites, the first near Nochistlán, the second in the valley of Tlacotlán;[2] in 1542, after the Mixton rising, it was finally established in its present position, to the south of the river, where it quickly outstripped Compostela in prosperity and importance. Municipal councils set up in all these settlements, in imitation of Cortés's own procedure at Vera Cruz in 1519, received royal recognition and gave a faint colour of legality to Nuño's actions.

Nuño, however, had neither the character necessary to retain the loyalty of his adherents, nor the skill—possessed so abundantly by Cortés—to justify illegal acts by legal arguments. His own cold tenacity of purpose never failed him; but as soon as the common dangers of the expedition were past, his friends fell away. He had little to offer them; the *encomiendas* of New Galicia did not become valuable prizes until later, when rich silver mines had been discovered; the eagerly sought permission, to take slaves in the new provinces, was sternly refused by the emperor. The charges against Nuño were serious enough to hang a far more popular leader,

[1] The 'Ordenanzas sobre Descubrimiento' of 1573 first laid down general rules regulating the foundation of towns. *D.I.I.* vol. XVI, p. 142, cap. xc.

[2] J. Iguíniz, *Biblioteca Histórica Jalisciense* (Guadalajara, Jalisco, 1921), vol. I, p. 218.

including as they did, the murder of Caltzonzín and other chiefs, the devastation of towns, the enslavement of Indians alike in peace and in war, persistent disregard of royal writs, and the illegal use of royal revenue to finance a private conquest. As early as 1533 Nuño had been ordered to exercise his powers as governor under the authority of the audiencia of New Spain, instead of corresponding directly with the emperor.[1] In 1536 he was definitely superseded. A new governor, the licentiate Diego Pérez de la Torre, came from Spain with instructions to take *residencia* of Nuño and of all officials appointed by him in New Galicia.

The government of New Spain had been immensely strengthened in the previous year by the arrival of the first viceroy, Antonio de Mendoza, who was to preside over the audiencia as a court of appeal, and to take over the administrative authority which it had exercised. Nuño, having taken in 1536 the desperate decision to go to Spain, as Cortés had done, to justify himself before the emperor in person, stopped in Mexico on his way, in the hope of ingratiating himself with Mendoza. He was arrested by the newly arrived De la Torre in the viceregal palace itself. His trial, after dragging on for two years in Mexico, was removed to Spain in 1538. He died in obscure confinement at Torrejón de Velasco six years later.[2] Even the charitable Tello, in recording his achievements, could find no good word for Nuño. He had conquered, more or less, an immense territory to the north of the Santiago, extending along the coast almost to the gulf of California; a narrower belt of land along the left bank of the river, running from Lake Chapala westward to the Pacific; and a coastal strip stretching from the river mouth south-east to Navidad Bay. He had handed over the people of this great area almost entirely to a clique of rapacious *encomenderos*. He had made no provision of crown Indians; this was one of his worst mistakes, and his own *encomiendas* and later those of Coronado were confiscated to remedy the omission. He had established no government, except a few scattered town councils and a group of treasury officials, creatures of his own whom the Council of the Indies quickly replaced. In all his conquest he had set an example of greed, savage egoism, and ill-considered destruction which was to remain uncomfortably vivid in the minds of Indian and Spaniard for many years.

De la Torre, whom all the chroniclers describe as a just and able

[1] Puga, *Cedulario*, vol. I, p. 308.   [2] M. de la Mota-Padilla, *Conquista*, vol. cv.

governor, could do little to remedy the condition of the province; he held office only for two years before being fatally injured by a fall from his horse in one of the interminable Indian campaigns. Upon his death-bed he appointed Cristóbal de Oñate, now a leading *encomendero* and a member of the town council of Guadalajara, to succeed him; but the viceroy, wishing to establish a firmer hold over the frontier provinces, rescinded the appointment, and granted the office to an adherent of his own, Francisco Vázquez Coronado.

Coronado is chiefly remembered, not for his administration of New Galicia, which was short-lived and uneventful,[1] but for the fruitless expedition which he led to New Mexico, under the viceroy's commission. Mendoza had become infected by 1539 with the general excitement over reports of the seven cities of Cíbola, or Quivira, excitement fostered by the tales of Cabeza de Vaca and his companions, and of Fray Marcos de Niza, who combined a propensity for wandering with a fertile imagination. Coronado was instructed to search for the fabulous golden provinces in the north, and received every help from the viceroy in collecting a numerous and well-equipped following. The settlers of New Galicia, surrounded by sullen and resentful Indians whom Nuño had driven into the more inaccessible Sierras, saw with misgivings the departure of many of the best fighting men of the province, upon an exploration of doubtful value.[2] Their objections were set aside, however,[3] and Coronado set out with his men early in 1540, leaving Cristóbal de Oñate as deputy-governor.

The Mixton rising, of which all the chroniclers wrote extensive accounts, seems to have been well planned beforehand among what was left of the priesthood and military nobility of the Caxcanes;[4] the departure of Coronado provided a suitable occasion. Hostilities began in the spring of 1540, with the murder of Juan de Arce, by the Guaynamota Indians of his *encomienda*. Other risings quickly followed in the hills round Teul and Nochistlán, and in the coastal region from Tepic to Purificación; everywhere friars and *encomenderos* were attacked by their

---

[1] See A. S. Aiton, 'Coronado's first report on the government of New Galicia', *Hisp. Amer. Hist. Rev.* (August, 1939).
[2] García-Icazbalceta, *Documentos*, vol. II, pp. 63–4: 'Petición de Cortés contra Mendoza.' [3] *D.I.I.* vol. XIV, pp. 373–84. 'Informaciones. 1540.'
[4] H. H. Bancroft, *Pacific States*, vol. V, p. 490. J. López-Portillo y Weber, *La rebelión de la Nueva Galicia.* Pub. del Instituto pan-Americano de Geografía e Historia, no. 37, Mexico, 1939.

half-subdued charges, supported by the wild tribes of Zacatecas. The *peñoles* of Mixton, Nochistlán, Acatic and Cuinao, fortified and prepared to withstand siege, became bases for operations which threatened simultaneously all the Spanish towns in the province. Oñate, fortunately for his countrymen, realised from the first the serious character of the revolt, and concentrated his energies upon the defence of Guadalajara and the dispatch of urgent appeals to the viceroy. Guadalajara was successfully defended, and the unexpected arrival of Cortés's lieutenant, the renowned Pedro de Alvarado, with four hundred men destined to man an expedition to the Spice Islands, placed the Indians in their turn upon the defensive. Alvarado, however, underrating the military skill of the Caxcanes, insisted against Oñate's advice on leading a direct attack against the *peñol* of Nochistlán; his forces were disastrously routed, and he himself received the wound from which he died. Only the arrival of the viceroy in person, with four hundred and fifty Spaniards and some thousands of Aztec auxiliaries saved a critical situation.[1] The *peñoles* were taken one by one; Coronado, returning empty handed with a disorganised and mutinous army, found the rebellion crushed everywhere except in Culiacán and the Sierra de Nayarit. The rising had lasted two years and had seriously endangered not only the frontier settlements, but the whole Spanish government of New Spain; a corresponding revolt in Mendoza's rear might indeed have proved fatal to the Spanish cause. New Galicia was perhaps the only province, besides Araucania, in which the conquest ran serious danger of failure; this danger inevitably produced lasting nervousness on the part of the colonists, and uncompromising harshness in their attitude towards the Indians.

The Mixton war was followed by widespread enslavement of the natives, except in a few villages where the *encomenderos* contrived to retain their Indians on the terms of previous grants. The rebellious spirit of the Caxcanes was broken; only the savage Chichimecas—the hunting tribes of the sierras—remained untamed. Recurring epidemics of plague continued the ravages which war had begun, and the economic development of New Galicia, with its ever-increasing demand for labour, laid fresh burdens upon the native population. In 1543 the silver mine of Espíritu Santo was discovered near the town of Compostela, which enjoyed in consequence

[1] H. H. Bancroft, *Pacific States*, vol. v, p. 505. Bancroft gives the number of auxiliaries as 30,000, following Tello.

a brief period of prosperity. In 1548, Cristóbal de Oñate and three companions, Diego de Ibarra, Juan de Tolosa and Baltasar Temiño de Bañuelos, came upon still richer deposits in the barren country of the Zacatecas, and founded the settlement of Nuestra Señora de los Zacatecas, destined to become one of the greatest centres of wealth in Spanish North America. As prospectors flocked to Zacatecas from all over New Spain, prosperity receded from Compostela. Guadalajara, on the other hand, lying on the road between Mexico and Zacatecas, profited by the concentration of Spanish inhabitants in the eastern half of the province, and became a rendezvous for travelling merchants, who bought European goods in Mexico or Vera Cruz, and sold them in the mining camps. The settlers of Guadalajara also, assured of a constant market for food in the crowded camps, applied themselves to farming and stock-raising in the valleys of Jalisco, using, of course, the labour of the Indians of their *encomiendas*. All this economic activity involved more hardships for the natives. Stock farms encroached on the cultivated land of the *pueblos*; more and more porters were needed to carry goods to the mines. *Encomenderos* who owned mining claims drove their Indians wholesale into the mines to die of exposure, or later from the effects of the mercury process of silver extraction, while those miners who held no *encomiendas*, and could not afford to purchase negroes, organised slave-hunts in the sierras, in defiance of all the decrees issued by royal authority for the protection of the native races.

Legislation upon the Indian question had for some years been growing steadily more severe, up to the promulgation in 1542 of the New Laws, which were designed to abolish within a generation the whole economic structure based on the *encomienda*—forced labour, compulsory hospitality, the use of carriers and the payment of tribute to individuals. Francisco Tello de Sandoval, the *visitador* entrusted with the task of enforcing the code in New Spain, bore instructions to dispatch one of the *oidores* of the audiencia of Mexico upon a similar errand in New Galicia. Accordingly, in the summer of 1544, the licentiate Tejada arrived in Guadalajara, and proceeded to take *residencia* of Coronado and his associates, and to audit the accounts of the royal revenue and the *bienes de difuntos*.[1]

---

[1] Property of men who died in the Indies leaving heirs in Spain. The royal officials in the province were responsible for selling such property and sending its value to the *Casa de Contratación*, for payment to the heirs. See ch. v, below.

Coronado was censured and fined for negligence and corruption in the administration of justice; he resigned from his office in 1545, leaving the government of the province in the hands of an *alcalde mayor*, a judge of first instance appointed by the audiencia of Mexico.[1] Oñate, for his conduct as deputy-governor in Coronado's absence, received warm praise. The proceeds of the *residencia* and the *cuenta* were delivered to Sandoval, who held commission to receive them.

In dealing with the questions raised by the New Laws, Tejada observed greater caution. The laws were duly proclaimed by his order in Guadalajara, Compostela and Purificación. The Indians of the *encomiendas* of Coronado and Nuño de Guzmán were forfeited, and placed under the Crown; and other *encomenderos* were ordered to remove their Indians from the mines. No charges were made, however, for reasons which Tejada explained in his report: 'Your Majesty has been consulted many times about this matter [of forced labour] but has refused until now to give a clear answer, to permit or to condemn. If infractions of the law were to be punished now, every Spaniard in the province would be affected, and probably ruined. All we can do is to make provision for the future.'[2] The prevalence of slavery Tejada diplomatically ascribed to the activities of native slave-dealers, several of whom he caused to be flogged and driven in irons round their villages. His general conclusion was equally diplomatic: 'New Galicia is one of the valuable provinces of new Spain, but sadly lacks both religion and justice, owing both to the inadequate supply of missionary teachers, and to the incompetence of former governors.'[3]

In spite of his anxiety not to create unrest among the colonists of New Galicia, Tejada perceived one thing very clearly: legislation of the type of the New Laws could only be enforced, if at all, by servants of the king, with sufficient authority and adequate salaries, who might hold themselves entirely aloof from the economic activities of the Spanish colony and maintain a judicial impartiality.

Your Majesty must provide a bishop, preferably a friar of one of the Orders, in this province, and create an audiencia, having jurisdiction over Colima, Zacatula and the pueblos of Avalos, which march with

---

[1] *A.G.I.* Auda. de México 68: 'Carta del Lic. Lorenzo de Tejada. 1545.'
[2] Ibid.　　　　　　　　　　　　　　[3] Ibid.

New Galicia and are too far from the audiencia (of Mexico)....A single
governor is powerless, however able he may be; but a royal audiencia
would exercise an unquestioned authority and would command far
greater respect than an individual. Would to God that Your Majesty
had done this in all the troubled provinces of these Indies!...[1]

The policy adopted by Sandoval upon Mendoza's advice, and
the partial revocation of the New Laws by the *Cédula* of Malines
in 1545,[2] set the seal of official approval upon Tejada's conduct.
His 'buena diligencia' was commended, and his advice, eventually,
adopted. In January 1548 the king in the Council of the Indies
issued ordinances establishing an audiencia in Compostela, which
should consist, like the audiencia of Galicia in Spain, of four
oidores alcaldes mayores, empowered to hear appeals from all the
inferior justices of New Galicia, but themselves subordinate to the
audiencia of New Spain. A second set of regulations dated
19 March in the same year, conferred administrative authority
also upon the new audiencia.[3]

The administration of justice at the time of the creation of the
audiencia lay in the hands of the *alcalde mayor*, Baltasar de Gallegos,
the municipal judges of the Spanish towns, and the *corregidores* of
the Crown *pueblos*. The *corregidor* in Spain had been an important
royal justice, exercising in his district 'jurisdicción alta y baja y
mero y mixto imperio'. The Catholic monarchs had, for the first
time, entrusted him with administrative powers and turned him
into a local governor; and as a mixture of magistrate and governor
he made his appearance in the Indies. The big *corregimientos*,
which were retained in the gift of the Crown, became valuable
offices—Manuel Romero de Terreros says that the *corregidor* of
Mexico City 'could consider himself the most important person in
New Spain, after the viceroy and the members of the audiencia.'[4]
In New Galicia, however, at least until the establishment of the
corregimiento of Zacatecas in 1580, the *corregidores* merely served as
minor governors and judges of first instance in those groups of
Indian villages which were not held by Spaniards in *encomienda*.
For this, they were paid a modest salary ranging from 100 to about

[1] Ibid.   [2] *Recopilación de Leyes de Indias*, VI. viii. 4.
[3] J. H. Parry (ed.), 'The Ordinances of the Audiencia of New Galicia', *Hisp. Amer.
Hist. Rev.* (August 1938).
[4] Manuel Romero de Terreros, *Los Corregidores de México* (Madrid, 1917), p. 3. See
C. Castañeda, 'The Corregidor in Spanish Colonial Administration', *Hisp. Amer. Hist.
Rev.* (1929), vol. IX.

380 *pesos*, and were required upon taking office, to furnish guarantees that they would submit to the *residencia* held by their successors and pay such fines as might be imposed upon them for misconduct by the audiencia. They were not required to be qualified lawyers, since the most serious cases lay outside their jurisdiction, and appeals against their decisions might always be carried to an audiencia. Besides judicial work, their duties included a general supervision of the steps taken to instruct the Indians in European religion and customs; the protection of the Indians in the peaceful possession and working of their lands; and the collection of tribute. Although repeated decrees forbade the *corregidores* to collect their salaries out of the tributes of their own districts or to reside within Indian settlements, the *corregimiento* offered many opportunities for peculation and oppression. As the royal policy became more effective in curtailing the number of villages granted in *encomienda*, and in abolishing the labour dues and restricting the tributes which the *encomenderos* might exact, the *corregimiento* came to be regarded as a convenient means of rewarding and supporting indigent conquerors and settlers, frequently at the expense of the Indians under their jurisdiction.

Corregidores were not appointed in the Spanish settlements in New Galicia until after the establishment of the audiencia. In the early days, therefore, the chartered towns were virtually autonomous republics. Only four towns in New Galicia—Compostela, Guadalajara, Purificación. and San Miguel de Culiacán—held charters of incorporation in 1548. Each was governed by a town council (*cabildo*) of six or eight councillors (*regidores*), usually, but not always, prominent house-holders. In newly-founded town settlements in the Indies, the first *regidores* were nearly always appointed by the conquerors who founded the towns,[1] and held office for one year. The mode of subsequent appointments varied greatly; the retiring *regidores* might elect their successors, or the governor might appoint new *regidores* each year. In all important towns, however, the Crown itself, following its custom in Spain, early exercised the right of appointing life-members of these municipal bodies.[2] From appointment to sale was a short step.

[1] *Recopilación de Leyes de Indias*, IV. iii. 10. On the *cabildos* in general see C. H. Haring, *The Spanish Empire in America*, ch. IX.

[2] The first grant by the crown of a *regimiento* for life in Mexico was made in 1525 in favour of Bernardino Vázquez de Tapia. He arrived in Mexico three years later. *Actas del Cabildo de México* (Mexico, 1877), vol. I, p. 140.

An important decree of 1554,[1] the first to deal generally with the matter, implies that sale was the normal method of appointing *regidores*, while recognising that in certain cases the town councils might appoint householders to fill vacant *regimientos* for which no purchasers could be found. The wording of this decree seems to indicate that by that date the right to appoint *regidores* was as a general rule reserved to the Crown, which sold the posts, and no longer delegated to its representatives in the Indies, who had granted them;[2] but in the small and remote towns of New Galicia there can have been no ready sale of *regimientos*, and irregular appointments and elections must have been frequent.

The *regidores*, sitting under the presidency of the local governor, formed the governing body of each municipality. There was nothing democratic about these bodies; they were irresponsible and virtually irremovable, and they deliberated in secret.[3] The *regidores* had the right to elect annually—subject to the governor's confirmation—two municipal magistrates (*alcaldes ordinarios*). *Regidores* might not themselves be elected as *alcaldes*;[4] this prohibition being the only constitutional safeguard possessed by the townspeople in general against the power of the municipal oligarchy. The *alcaldes* held first-instance jurisdiction in all secular cases arising within the neighbourhood of the towns, without, however, the power to inflict sentences of death or mutilation. Their office was principally judicial; but in towns—such as those of New Galicia in the early years—which had no governor, the senior *alcalde* presided in the town council. In 1573 the *alcaldes* were legally excluded from the *cabildos* 'except where custom may have introduced the contrary';[5] but their exclusion was not consistently enforced. They were always included in the *regimiento y justicia* in whose name municipal petitions were presented to the Crown or its agents. Appeals from their decisions lay to the local governor, *corregidor* or *alcalde mayor*, where one existed, and from him to the provincial audiencia.

None of the justices of New Galicia in 1548, then, were

---

[1] *Recopilación de Leyes de Indias*, IV. x. 6.

[2] For details of the sale of municipal offices see ch. VII, p. 141.

[3] In 1531 the town clerk of Mexico was imprisoned by the *cabildo* for disclosing details of its deliberations to outside persons. *Actas del Cabildo de México*, vol. II, p. 73.

[4] Solórzano, *Política Indiana*, v. i. 9.

[5] *Recopilación de Leyes de Indias*, v. iii. 14.

professional lawyers.[1] *Corregidores, alcaldes ordinarios,* and the *alcalde mayor* (who, though he held jurisdiction over the whole province, was primarily a judge of first instance) all belonged to the class of 'conquerors and settlers'. Most of them regarded their offices as personal property from which a maximum profit might be drawn. Many held *encomiendas;* all were committed to the system of Indian labour and tribute of which the *encomienda* was the central institution. The audiencia which was to control the inferior judges, to supplant the single *alcalde mayor* and to appoint others, represented paternal royal authority and the rule of professional judges fresh from Spain. It would be unwelcome at first among the colonists; its subsequent degree of popularity would depend upon the extent to which it consented to relax the letter of its instructions in the interests of the Spanish community.

---

[1] *Alcaldes ordinarios* were required to be able to read and write. *Recopilación de Leyes de Indias,* v. iii. 4.

CHAPTER II

THE FOUNDATION OF THE AUDIENCIA

It was the fixed policy of Spanish imperial government to entrust to its agents in the Indies the minimum of independent authority compatible with effective administration. The Council of the Indies was particularly suspicious of new and untried institutions, and in placing an audiencia in the wild and remote ranges of New Galicia it made use of every possible device to ensure that all important decisions of the new court should be reviewed by the existing authorities in Mexico City or in Spain. The coupling of the title of *oidor* with the less dignified one of *alcalde mayor* in itself emphasised the subordinate status of the newly appointed justices. There was a close analogy in this respect with the organisation of Galicia in Spain, where the judges of the audiencia held the title of *alcalde mayor* and where appeals from their decisions lay to the *oidores* of the audiencia of Valladolid.[1] The composite title was peculiar to New Galicia. Like the audiencia of Galicia in Spain, the New Galicia court held no royal seal—was not a chancellery.

The district assigned to the new audiencia—assigned, of course, after consultation with the viceroy and *oidores* of New Spain—was much smaller than that suggested by Tejada in 1544. The ordinances of 1548[2] mentioned only the new kingdom of Galicia—that is, the territory actually conquered by Nuño de Guzmán and governed by his successors, with the acquisitions added by mining prospectors in the north. The older settlements in the coastal provinces of Zacatula, Colima, and the *pueblos* of Avalos, remained within the jurisdiction of Mexico, despite constant protests from Guadalajara, until 1574.

Royal treasury returns—the *quinto*, tributes, and proceeds of the sale of offices—supplied the measure of the relative importance of the various American provinces. Both the Council of the Indies and the audiencia of Mexico regarded the administration of New Galicia in 1548 as a comparatively slight responsibility; the

---

[1] *Nueva Recopilación de Leyes de España* (Madrid, 1772), III. i. 1.
[2] J. H. Parry (ed.), 'The ordinances of the audiencia of New Galicia', *Hisp. Amer. Hist. Rev.* (August 1938). The text of the ordinances, taken from the Archivo General de la Nación, Mexico, D.F.: Ramo de Duplicados, tit. I, fol. 26.

35

corregimientos and *encomiendas* of the province were poor, the land wild, the Indians savage and intractable. For these reasons, probably more than on account of geographical remoteness, the new audiencia was allowed the exercise of administrative authority within its district. The whole business of administration was relegated, as it were, to a footnote. The ordinances of 13 January made no mention of administration; only in the supplementary regulations of two months later was it laid down that the audiencia should exercise the same authority in matters of government as was enjoyed by the audiencia of Guatemala, including the right to appoint *corregidores*. The office of *alcalde mayor* which, under the audiencia, involved duties similar to those of a *corregidor*, but which in New Galicia existed only in districts settled or held by Spaniards,[1] received no mention in the ordinances. In practice, the audiencia interpreted its instructions to include the appointment of new *alcaldes mayores* also; the Crown endorsed this interpretation by issuing numerous letters of favour, requesting the audiencia to appoint the bearers to offices when vacancies occurred.[2] Beyond this, the administrative duties of the court were vague. It certainly held no military authority, though in practice it was sometimes to usurp the viceroy's powers in times of emergency. It exercised no lawful control over the appointment of the municipal magistrates.[3] It had no power to grant Indians in *encomienda*.[4] Its effectiveness in carrying out public works and maintaining general order was restricted, since it had no power to make extraordinary appropriations from royal funds, without the previous consent of the Council of the Indies. Apart from the general analogy with the audiencia of Guatemala, relations with the viceroy were uncertain, and it was left for subsequent cases and decrees to define the scope of viceregal supervision in matters of administration.

In marked contrast, the judicial functions of the audiencia were very carefully specified in the ordinances, as was indeed to be expected. Not only was an exaggerated emphasis upon juris-

---

[1] See ch. vi, below.
[2] See *A.G.I.* Auda. de Guadalajara 230, Z 1: 'Registro de Reales Cédulas.' About one-third of the entries in the register consist of private *cédulas* of this type.
[3] See *A.G.I.* Auda. de Guadalajara 230, Z 1, fol. 38, 7 de Feb. 1560. Decree confirming right of *cabildo* to elect magistrates without interference. The audiencia to confine itself to confirming the elections.
[4] A. de León Pinelo, *Tratado de confirmaciones de reales cédulas de encomiendas de Indios* (Madrid, 1630), Parte I, cap. vii, § 32.

diction characteristic of all Spanish constitutional arrangements at that time; there was the additional consideration, that increased litigation involved more legal fees, and presented opportunities for enrichment to the advocates and hangers-on round the courts, and even to the judges themselves. 'Justitia magnum emolumentum est.' Both the audiencia of New Spain and the Council of the Indies were far more suspicious of a new and independent jurisdiction, than of a new centre of administration, and both strove to set definite limits to the judicial authority of New Galicia. The audiencia was to hear and decide all cases, civil and criminal, brought before it in appeals from the decisions of minor justices— *corregidores*, *alcaldes mayores*, and *alcaldes ordinarios*—throughout the kingdom; in addition, it was to exercise first-instance jurisdiction in cases concerning the royal prerogative, and in major criminal cases (*casos de corte*) throughout the kingdom; and might hear in first instance cases of every class, arising within a radius of twelve leagues from the capital city—its jurisdiction in these cases overlapping but not superseding that of the municipal judges. Only in minor matters were its decisions final. In civil cases involving sums of 300 *pesos de oro de minas* or more and in criminal cases involving sentence of death, aggrieved parties might appeal from its decisions, not to the Council of the Indies, but to the audiencia of Mexico. The sum of 300 *pesos* was comparatively small—much smaller than any of the varying sums over which litigants might normally appeal to the Council of the Indies;[1] a decree of 1550 raised the level to 500 *pesos*,[2] but the arrangement remained a grievance in the eyes of the *oidores alcaldes mayores* and tended seriously to weaken their authority in their district. The audiencia, however, though forbidden to hinder lawful appeals, might offer for the choice of the parties the alternative of a re-trial *en grado de suplicación*, at which all four *oidores alcaldes mayores* should be present;[3] and some provision was made against the inevitable delays of the appeal system, by an ordinance which laid down that orders of restitution or sequestration issued by the audiencia in connection

[1] The *Cédula* of Malines of 1545 had fixed the minimum at 10,000 *pesos*; Puga, *Cedulario*, vol. I, p. 469. A law of 1620 permitted appeals to the council over sums exceeding 6,000 *pesos* (*Recopilación de Leyes de Indias*, v. xiii. 1).

[2] Puga, *Cedulario*, vol. II, p. 99; Tello, *Crónica miscelánea*, cap. clxiv.

[3] General decrees fixed a minimum sum over which litigants might demand this second hearing. In 1545 the sum was fixed at 6,000 *maravedises* (*Recopilación de Leyes de Indias*, v. xii. 29), in 1563, at 200 *pesos* (ibid. v. x. 3).

with notorious cases of force or fraud were to be executed temporarily, pending the hearing of an appeal in Mexico City. All these arrangements were closely analogous with those in force in the audiencia of Galicia in Spain.

Further duties, principally judicial but involving possible administrative action, were assigned to the *oidores alcaldes mayores* by the provisions for *visitas* and *cuentas*. The *visita* was a general tour of inspection, in which the travelling justice, or *visitador*, temporarily superseded the minor justices through whose area he passed, dispatched the cases pending before them, investigated their conduct and heard complaints against them. The *visita* was thus distinct from the *residencia*—a routine investigation of the conduct of a particular judge or official at the end of his tenure of office—and from the *pesquisa*, an 'extraordinary' investigation made by special royal order in cases of notorious scandal or serious denunciation. It was a common feature in most of the audiencias, that the *oidores* should serve in turn as *visitadores*, so that one of them should always be away upon *visita*. The *oidor* so occupied received an extra payment to cover his expenses. *Oidores-visitadores* in New Galicia were especially charged to investigate the treatment meted out to the Indians of the kingdom, whether held in *encomienda*, or under the Crown, and to enforce the numerous decrees which regulated Indian affairs. They held full judicial powers, except that their decisions in all criminal cases and in civil suits involving more than 30,000 *maravedíses*[1] might be carried in appeal before the audiencia. In matters which called for the issue of administrative orders, they were to report the facts, in order that the audiencia, sitting in *acuerdo*, might make such provisions as it thought necessary.

The *cuenta*, or audit of the accounts of the royal *hacienda*, came in later times to be demanded annually. The ordinances of 1548

[1] Professor Haring, in his article 'Ledgers of the Royal Treasurers in Spanish America in the sixteenth century' (*Hisp. Amer. Hist. Rev.* vol. II, 1919), gives the following table of approximate values of the different types of gold *peso*, in *maravedíses*:

Peso de Oro	Mrs.
de Tipuzque	= 272
común	= 300
común con tres quilates añadidos	= 360
de ley perfecta	= 450
de minas	= 450

The silver *peso* was worth 272 *mrs.*, the ducat (= 11 *reales*—a sum of money, not a coin) 374 *mrs.*

merely commanded the audiencia to take the *cuenta* of the existing treasury officials in New Galicia, to see that deficits were made good and to impose fines for past negligence or misconduct. The task of taking *cuenta*, like the conduct of *visitas*, was usually delegated to one *oidor* at a time, in each audiencia, the *oidores* serving in rotation; and in a province disorganised as was New Galicia, where no *cuenta* had been taken for some years, the task might prove a very heavy one.

Finally, the new *oidores alcaldes mayores* were instructed to take *residencia* of all who held judicial office at the time of their arrival—*corregidores, alcaldes mayores* and *alcaldes ordinarios*; a task which, if performed thoroughly, would have occupied the time of the whole audiencia for many months. In fact, these *residencias* were eventually taken in a very perfunctory manner as a part of the first *visita* conducted under the new regime.

Of the institution, to which were entrusted such mixed and arduous duties, the chief members were, of course, the four justices. They, together with the bishop, occupied the principal dignities of the kingdom—a squalid splendour! The laws of the Indies prescribed a semi-monastic life for the *oidores* of each audiencia, in the interests of impartiality. They lived together, as a rule in a house adjoining the audiencia building. They were forbidden not only to take gifts and fees, but also to hold land or Indians, to engage in trade, and to take any part in enterprises of discovery or new settlement. The presence of the *oidores* at bull-fights and other public amusements, or even the exchange of visits with neighbours, might lead to the forming of friendships and the perversion of justice. Their very dress was prescribed.[1] In strict law, the only relaxation permitted to them was the attendance at religious festivals. Those not occupied with *visitas* or other special commissions were required, in New Galicia, to attend in court for three hours every morning, and when necessary, for two hours on Monday, Wednesday and Friday afternoons (a characteristic example of the meticulous detail of Spanish legislation)—and were to inspect the prisons—that of the audiencia and that of the municipality—every Saturday afternoon. Each week one of the

---

[1] A portrait of Francisco Gómez de Mendiola, in the possession of the archbishop of Guadalajara, shows the official costume of an *oidor*—black doublet and breeches, white ruff and full-sleeved gown. The portrait is reproduced in Orozco y Jiménez, *Colección*, vol. III, p. 246.

oidores, serving in turn, was required to be constantly available for the issue of writs of course. For this rather dreary round, the *oidores alcaldes mayores* received each a yearly salary of 650,000 *maravedises*[1] a considerably larger sum than that paid to the officials of the royal treasury in New Galicia, and a little larger than the salaries of the *oidores* of the audiencia of New Spain.[2] This unexpected generosity in the payment of the subordinate audiencia was overset by the fact that prices in New Galicia were usually much higher than in New Spain owing to the abundance of silver and the shortage of all other commodities. The *oidores* complained continually of the inadequacy of their salaries.[3]

Besides the *oidores*, the ordinances made provision for a number of minor officials. All the notaries (*escribanos*) who practised in the audiencias were in a sense officials. They prepared the pleas (*procesos*) with the supporting evidence in writing, in due form for presentation before the court. Any of them might be required to perform public duties, such as accompanying the *oidores* upon *visitas*, and witnessing the *autos* issued by the court. Their fees were prescribed in the *arancel* or rate-book of the audiencia, and they purchased their practices for life from the Crown. There were certain other offices entrusted to lawyers, which, while still saleable, carried with them special duties and special fees. The ordinances provided for four *receptores* and one *relator*.[4] These officials received, in addition to litigants' fees, a salary of 1 *peso de oro fino* for every full day's work.

Only three audiencia offices might be held by men without legal training. The *alguacil mayor* or chief constable (not to be confused with the municipal constable) was a person of some dignity, usually a *vecino* of the capital city. He purchased his office for life and received a percentage of the fines imposed upon the delinquents whom he arrested.[5] He might, if he chose, appoint and pay

<hr>

[1] *A.G.I.* Auda. de Guadalajara 230: 'Registro de Reales Cédulas', lib. Z 1, fol. 4 verso.
[2] 600,000 *mrs.* according to Professor Haring, op. cit. The treasurer, auditor and factor of New Galicia each received 300,000 *mrs.*, the overseer 200,000, by a *cédula* of 24 January 1545. Puga, *Cedulario*, vol. 1, p. 47.
[3] See for example, *A.G.I.* Auda. de Guadalajara 5: 'Información...por el audiencia ...sobre los gastos y costas que tienen. 13 de Enero 1560.'
[4] For the duties of these officials see below, Part II, ch. VIII.
[5] See *A.G.I.* Auda. de Guadalajara 51: 'Oidores alcaldes mayores al Rey. 28 de Noviembre 1549.' This letter announced that the first *alguacil mayor* had resigned because his fees were not sufficient to live on; and begged the king to allow a regular salary for the office.

deputy constables. Finally, the audiencia employed a janitor and a crier—probably a negro—who also served as executioner. The last two were appointed by the judges and received a salary fixed by them; the executioner being commanded, for no obvious reason, to live in the same house as the judges.

Four *oidores alcaldes mayores* were appointed in 1548—the licentiates Hernando Martínez de la Marcha; Lorenzo Lebrón de Quiñones; Miguel Ladrón de Contreras y Guevara; and Dr Juan Meléndez de Sepúlveda. Only Lebrón de Quiñones had been in the Indies before. He came of a family distinguished in the colonial service, and had himself spent part of his youth in Española. His father, Cristóbal Lebrón, went there as *Juez de Comisión* in 1515; his brother Gerónimo had been governor of Santa Marta[1] where he had shown the same characteristics that Lorenzo was to display in New Galicia—a genius for winning the confidence of the Indians, and a tendency to irritate the Spanish colonists.[2] Lorenzo Lebrón was thirty-four years of age at the time of his appointment. Little is known of the previous history of his three colleagues, except that Martínez de la Marcha, the senior of the four, claimed to have had fifteen years' experience of judicial work in Spain. Sepúlveda does not enter into the story of New Galicia; he died in the city of San Domingo, on his way to Mexico. De la Marcha missed the ship which carried his colleagues from Spain, and arrived several months after them. Contreras contracted a fever on the voyage, and arrived in a critical condition at Mexico City, where he was compelled to spend three months in convalescence. The duty of establishing the new audiencia and of proclaiming its ordinances fell therefore to Lebrón alone.

Lebrón presented his credentials in the *acuerdo* of the audiencia of New Spain at the beginning of November 1548. In the same month he wrote to the king[3] explaining the situation of his colleagues and reporting the gossip concerning New Galicia, which was current in official circles in Mexico. Compostela was considered

[1] Herrera, and the editors of the *Colección de documentos... de América y Oceanía (D.I.I.)*, in vol. x, p. 52, assume these three men to be one and the same. Lorenzo Lebrón, however, explains his family history in a letter to the king, asking promotion, dated 10 September 1554. *A.G.I.* Auda. de Guadalajara 51.

[2] See Herrera's account of Gerónimo's exploits in Santa Marta. *Décadas*, vol. vi, pp. 73 and 190.

[3] *D.I.I.* vol. x, p. 52: 'Carta a S.M. del Licenciado Lebrón de Quiñones, sobre las disposiciones que conviene tomar para la buena administración de la justicia. 20 de Noviembre 1548.'

an unsuitable capital for the audiencia, situated as it was in the extreme west of the province, far from the principal centres of Spanish population, without hope of expansion in the future. Whatever the conditions had been in Nuño's day, Guadalajara was now the natural centre of the kingdom; though New Galicia as a whole, within its existing limits, formed a highly inconvenient administrative area—'un girón de tierra que entra en atravesía', poor, barren, and sparsely populated. The viceroy had received no specific decree commanding him to relinquish the government of any part of the viceroyalty of New Spain and would not acknowledge, without a special order, the administrative authority given by the ordinances to the new audiencia, although he himself admitted the difficulty of governing New Galicia from so distant a centre as Mexico City. In the light of this information, Lebrón made a series of recommendations; he asked that the viceroy be instructed clearly in the matter of the administration of New Galicia; that the area of the kingdom be extended to include all the territory west and north of Jacona in Michoacán;[1] that the audiencia be confirmed in its administrative powers, and be allowed to select its own administrative capital; and that he himself be given authority to discharge in person all the functions of the audiencia, until the other *oidores alcaldes mayores* should come to his assistance. All these suggestions were disregarded at the time, except one: Luis de Velasco, who succeeded Mendoza as viceroy, rarely attempted to interfere in the internal administration of New Galicia.

His official business in Mexico City concluded, Lebrón set out for his district, and reached Guadalajara towards the end of December. According to Father Tello's chronicle, he was given a cool reception.[2] The Spanish householders, between twenty and thirty in number, assembled at the new bishop's house to hear the ordinances of the audiencia proclaimed, and after expressing perfunctory thanks for the honour which the king intended for them, informed Lebrón that their country was too poor to support an audiencia and a bishop. His inquiry, as to where the audiencia might most usefully be placed, elicited the insolent reply 'in Cíbola, for that is five hundred leagues from here'.[3] It became clear, however, when Lebrón announced his intention of establishing his

---

[1] Now a suburb of Zamora, Michoacán.　　[2] Tello, *Crónica miscelánea*, cap. clxii.
[3] Ibid.

court at Compostela, that the *vecinos*[1] of Guadalajara deeply resented the proposal to make the rival city the administrative capital of New Galicia, and to divert to Compostela the traffic which a press of litigants might bring. On 29 December a petition from the *vecinos* was presented to Lebrón, informing him of the disadvantages of Compostela as an administrative centre, and calling upon him to set up the audiencia in Guadalajara at once.[2] Guadalajara stood in the most populous region of New Galicia, within convenient distance of the other Spanish towns of the region—Compostela, Colima, La Purificación, Michoacán, Zacatecas—and connected with them by passable roads (a doubtful statement, even to-day). Compostela, on the other hand, stood at the edge of the territory, unconnected with any other town except Guadalajara. Above all, Compostela was most inconveniently distant from Zacatecas, where the silver mines had attracted by far the largest Spanish community in the province. Zacatecas, according to the petitioners, sorely needed the attention of government; the turbulent mining community contained no representative of the Law and was faced with starvation, owing to the lack of arrangements for carrying food into the barren sierras where the silver veins lay. In the interests of the mining industry and of the royal revenues, the audiencia, conveniently established at Guadalajara, should appoint an *alcalde mayor* to restore order in Zacatecas, and should issue orders to commute labour and other tributes owed by Indians under the Crown administration, into a regular contribution of corn for the support of the miners.

Other petitions followed, to the same end, from the principal mine-owners themselves.[3] To them all, Lebrón replied that 'His Majesty had given instructions for the audiencia to reside in the city of Compostela, and that he could not set aside the royal command; but that he would investigate the matter himself, and would advise his Majesty as to the most suitable capital for the audiencia'. Then, leaving the *vecinos* of Guadalajara to collect

---

[1] The *vecinos* were the Spanish householders. All statements of population of towns and provinces in New Spain in the sixteenth century, gave the number of *vecinos*—not the total number of human beings. The same principle was applied to estimates of Indian population, the number of tax-paying males being counted.

[2] Orozco y Jiménez, *Colección de documentos históricos inéditos o muy raros referentes al arzobispado de Guadalajara*, vol. I, p. 99: 'Petición...al Lic. Lorenzo Lebrón de Quiñones. 9 de Diciembre 1548.'

[3] Ibid. p. 104.

evidence and draw up yet more emphatic petitions, Lebrón moved to Compostela and proclaimed there the foundation of a new royal audiencia.

Contreras reached Compostela in the spring, de la Marcha in the autumn, of 1549. The audiencia was received there with even less enthusiasm than at Guadalajara. The little settlement seemed, indeed, at the end of its resources, and in a letter to the king of 1 November 1548,[1] its municipal councillors had already asserted that only the most vigorous methods could save them from starvation:

> ...The Indians of this country are so few and so weak, that we have been compelled to endure great poverty, and live under the most miserable conditions, in order to save them from hardship. If now, the audiencia and the bishop are to establish themselves here, and build a cathedral, royal houses, law courts, and all the other necessary buildings, the miserable natives will all be killed by the labour of it, and we shall be forced to desert the place; for besides our other misfortunes, we have no food here; there is no one to till our land, and we cannot keep cattle in this hot climate.

All the economic helplessness of an 'hidalgo' community was evident in their complaints; they begged, among other relief measures, the reduction of the royal 'fifth' of the silver to one-twentieth, license to import two thousand negro slaves at reduced prices, and the appointment of Cristóbal de Oñate as governor and captain-general.

For complaints such as these, a bench of inexperienced, school-trained lawyers was expected to find remedies. The first official report from the audiencia[2] analysed the situation clearly; Compostela contained twenty householders, who, in spite of a reduction of Indian labour (effected presumably by Tejada's *visita*) had made some progress in the cultivation of cacao and other crops suitable to the lowland climate. In addition, there were in the town a dozen or more *conquistadores*, who held neither land nor houses, but who were waiting in the hope of being appointed to *corregimientos* or other offices. It would be impossible to find places for so many; they could never be persuaded to till the soil themselves; the only

---

[1] *A.G.I.* Auda. de Guadalajara 51: 'A. Su Magestad la justicia y regimiento de Compostela. 1º de Noviembre 1548.'

[2] Ibid.: 'Oidores alcaldes mayores de Compostela al Rey. 28 de Nov. 1549.'

solution was to enforce a decree of 1546 empowering the viceroy to carry out a general redistribution of *encomiendas*;[1] the Crown *pueblos* should be included in the distribution, and *encomenderos* should receive a promise of security of tenure for themselves and their heirs. Restless *conquistadores* might thus be induced to settle down, to interest themselves in the development of the land, and to bear arms for the defence of the province.

Except for this not very original suggestion the *oidores* were chiefly concerned, in their first official report, with the limits of their own authority. They reiterated Lebrón's demands for permission to move the audiencia to a more suitable place, and to extend its district—demands which furnished a refrain to all the letters of the audiencia for the next decade.[2] They asked that the minimum sum in civil suits, over which appeals might be carried to the audiencia of Mexico, be raised from 300 to 3000 *pesos*, in order to avoid the trouble and expense of frequent appeals; and inquired what procedure was to be followed in cases in which they themselves could not agree upon a decision. For the benefit of the province as a whole, they asked that the opening of new silver mines be encouraged by a temporary reduction of the royal tax from one-fifth to one-tenth, as had been effected already in New Spain; and recommended various fiscal reforms. A mint, they asserted, was badly needed, as coin was very scarce. A subsidiary royal chest, also, might with advantage be placed either in Zacatecas or in Guadalajara, under a separate official, who should be empowered to assay, stamp and tax the silver on the spot. The existing arrangement, by which all silver had to be brought to Compostela for stamping, inflicted great inconvenience upon law-abiding miners, and led to the illicit removal of unstamped silver to Mexico, where it paid a tax of one-tenth instead of one-fifth, and swelled the treasurer's returns in Mexico at the expense of those of New Galicia.

Of positive achievements the report said little, except that *alcaldías mayores* had been created by the audiencia in Zacatecas, los Llanos, and Tepeque, the first with a salary of 300 *pesos de oro común* and a *corregimiento*, the others with 365 *pesos* a year ('atenta

---

[1] Puga, *Cedulario*, vol. I, p. 479. See ch. III, below.

[2] *A.G.I.* Patronato 181, R⁰. 13: 'Pareceres de la audiencia de Nueva Galicia sobre cuál de las dos ciudades, Guadalajara o Compostela, era más a propósito para poner este tribunal...y informaciones hechas en virtud de Real cédula, acerca del distrito que debía tener la jurisdicción de esta audiencia.'

la carestía de por allí'). The king was asked to authorise the payment of these salaries.

The report produced some effect. The salaries of the *alcaldes mayores* were paid. To the recommendations for fiscal reform, the Council of the Indies replied, with characteristic deliberation, by demanding a more detailed statement of the conditions, and by ordering the viceroy to investigate and report on the matter.[1] The silver tax was eventually reduced, after much consultation, to one-tenth.[2] The requests of the *oidores* concerning their jurisdiction elicited two new decrees: one of 8 December 1550 raised the minimum sum in appeals to Mexico to 500 *pesos*;[3] the other, of 19 December in the same year, laid down that cases in which the *oidores alcaldes mayores* failed to reach agreement should be referred to the audiencia of Mexico.[4]

Opportunities for the employment of this second decree were to arise very shortly. A few days after signing the audiencia's report, Hernán Martínez de la Marcha, the senior *oidor*, set out upon the general *visita* of the kingdom, which the ordinances required. Lebrón and Contreras remained behind to carry on the work of the audiencia and to hear appeals from de la Marcha's decisions—an arrangement which was sure to produce quarrels between the *oidores*.

The situation of the justices at Compostela was far from satisfactory. By their insistence in establishing themselves there in obedience to the strict letter of their instructions, and, in general, by their reluctance to take any action not expressly authorised by the king, the *oidores* had lost much of the authority which they might have exercised in a more suitable place. Few litigants came to Compostela, and bitter criticism of the audiencia filled the reports sent home to Spain by the leading colonists. The town council of Guadalajara blamed the *oidores* for taking no steps to check the rush to the mines of Zacatecas, which, they said, was depopulating the other towns of New Galicia.[5] The royal treasury officials,

[1] Tello, *Crónica miscelánea*, cap. clxvi: 'Carta que S.M. escribió al virrey mandándole que le avise si la caja de tres llaves estaría en Compostela o en Guadalajara.'
[2] *A.G.I.* Auda. de Guadalajara 230, Z 1, fol. 18, 1556.
[3] Puga, *Cedulario*, vol. ii, p. 99; Tello, op. cit. cap. clxiv.
[4] Tello, op. cit. cap. clxv.
[5] *A.G.I.* Auda. de Guadalajara 51: 'Justicia y Regimiento de Guadalajara al Rey 1° Sept. 1550.' The rush to Zacatecas did not, in fact, prevent the growth of the other towns. Lebrón de Quiñones gave the following list in 1554: Zacatecas 300 *vecinos*; Guadalajara 80; Guachinango 80; Compostela 40; Purificación 30. *A.G.I.* Auda. de Guadalajara 51: 'Lebrón de Quiñones al Rey de Tlaximoroa en Michoacán, 10 Sept. 1554.'

writing from Compostela,[1] complained of the unwarranted interference of the *oidores* in the sale of produce brought in by the
Indians, as tribute to the Crown, and of their reluctance to allow
appeals from their decisions, especially in Indian affairs, to go to
Mexico, as the ordinances provided; the *oidores*, inexperienced as
they were, could not even agree upon a common policy without
the leadership of a president or governor who might restrain their
quarrels. The *contador*, Juan de Céspedes, writing under separate
cover six months later, was even more explicit than his colleagues
in his denunciations of the audiencia:[2] the *oidores*, though instructed
to take *cuenta* of the treasury officials, had not done so, and Céspedes
suggested that some responsible person be sent from Mexico to
carry out that duty. By refusing to place the royal chest at
Guadalajara, the *oidores* were conniving at the illicit removal of
silver from the kingdom. In judicial matters, their appointment
had served no useful purpose. 'No one ever wished before, to
appeal from the ordinary courts of this province, to Spain. We had
no need of further provision of justice, and now the *oidores alcaldes
mayores* are here, drawing large salaries for doing nothing.' In
administrative affairs they could not agree:

Certain appeals came before the audiencia, against provisions made
by the Licentiate de la Marcha in his *visita*; the *oidores alcaldes mayores*
decided these matters as they thought fit...and sent administrative
orders to the Licentiate de la Marcha, who took offence, and appealed
against them, and swore publicly that they were not his judges, and that
if the king did not quickly remedy such a disgraceful state of affairs, the
province would be lost.

Even the bishop, Pedro Gómez Maraver, with whom the
audiencia was required to hold the closest correspondence, did not
spare the *oidores* in his letters, and described contemptuously their
life in Compostela (he, unlike the *oidores*, had from the first refused
to live there):

The *oidores alcaldes mayores* have been in Compostela for two years.
They hold audiencia in a straw hut, and lodge in the houses of the
neighbours, for they have there neither the material nor the labour
necessary for constructing new buildings. There are no attorneys or

[1] *A.G.I.* Auda. de Guadalajara 51: 'Oficiales Reales del nuevo reino de Galicia al
Rey. Compostela. 20 de Diciembre 1549.'
[2] Ibid.: 'Juan de Céspedes al Rey. Guadalajara. 25 de Agosto 1550.'

advocates, only the *oidores*, who have no one upon whom to exercise their jurisdiction. The town has suffered greatly since their arrival and of its few inhabitants some have already left, owing to the shortage of food; or, some say, to the indignities which they have received. The whole kingdom has begged the *oidores* to move to Guadalajara where they are needed...and they have refused, so denying justice to many Spaniards, who preferred to suffer injustice rather than bring suits in so remote and inaccessible a place as Compostela. For these reasons no benefit whatever has been derived from the establishment of the audiencia; on the contrary, the whole kingdom is divided by disorders and disquieting rumours, and will soon become depopulated, through the work of partial and inexperienced judges.[1]

Probably the 'disquieting rumours' to which the bishop referred, concerned the possibility of the *oidores*' interpreting too literally the royal decrees in favour of the Indians. Maraver had little sympathy with the Indians. During the Mixton war, and later, he had advocated the general reduction of hostile natives to slavery,[2] and might be trusted to sanction no attack upon the interests of *encomenderos* and slave-owners.

The audiencia was a 'new broom', and was suspected and feared by most of the colonists and miners. One of its members, however—that one who quarrelled so readily with the others, the *oidor-visitador* de la Marcha—stood from the first upon the side of the colonists. De la Marcha returned from his *visita* in December 1550, having travelled more or less continuously for a year, sometimes on horseback, sometimes in a litter carried by Indians (a mode of travel which drew forth a royal inquiry and a severe rebuke),[3] hearing suits, taking *residencias* and *cuentas*, making provisions for local administration, investigating and reporting. He visited in the course of the year all the important Spanish settlements in the kingdom, except Culiacán in the extreme north-west. The various reports and letters which he dispatched to Spain—some of which have been published—contain valuable information about the conditions under which the settlers were living at the time.

---

[1] Orozco y Jiménez, *Colección*, vol. i, p. 211: 'Interesante relación del Ilmo. Sr. Maraver. 12 de Diciembre 1550.'

[2] *D.I.I.* vol. viii, p. 199, 'Carta del Presbítero Gómez Maraver, 1544.'

[3] See M. Cuevas (ed.), *Colección de documentos del siglo XVI para la historia de México* (Mexico, 1914): 'Carta de Don Luis de Velasco, el primero, a Felipe II. De México. 7 de Febrero 1554.' This method of travel was expressly forbidden. *Recopilación de Leyes de Indias*, vi. x. 17.

In Guadalajara, the first Spanish town upon his route, de la Marcha heard and determined some thirty civil suits pending before the local magistrates, and received a number of petitions from the municipality, from the miners of Zacatecas and Guachinango, and from some of the neighbouring Indian headmen, asking for the audiencia and royal chest to be transferred to Guadalajara. The petitions were supported by a series of attested statements of leading Spaniards in the neighbourhood, given in answer to an inquiry held by de la Marcha at the request of the municipal authorities;[1] all these documents were forwarded to Spain, with the *visitador's* recommendation that the petitions should be granted.[2]

Another important investigation made by de la Marcha in Guadalajara concerned the prices of foodstuffs.[3] The influx of Spaniards into New Galicia after the Zacatecas discoveries, the scarcity of provisions, and the abundance of unminted silver[4] had sent prices soaring. The *visitador* obtained from a number of independent witnesses lists of prices in the year of the *visita*, and estimates of prices three or four years before. The contrast was startling. Wheat had risen from 4 *reales* (136 *mrs.*) to 2 silver *pesos* (544 *mrs.*) per *fanega* (a little more than an English bushel); maize, the staple cereal of the country, produced almost entirely by Indians, rose in the same period from 1 *real* (34 *mrs.*) to 1 silver *peso* (272 *mrs.*) per *fanega*—an eloquent illustration of the fact that the Indians could not, or would not, increase production to meet an increased demand. Commodities imported from Spain showed a less spectacular, though still considerable rise; wine and oil each rose from 6 *pesos* (1632 *mrs.*) to 10 *pesos* (2720 *mrs.*) per *arroba* of four gallons—an alarming price for commodities which Spaniards regarded as necessities. Livestock, of which large quantities were being imported into New Galicia, and which was to contribute

---

[1] Orozco y Jiménez, *Colección*, vol. I, pp. 74 ff.: 'Poderes, peticiones, presentación de testigos.'

[2] *A.G.I.* Auda. de Guadalajara 5: 'Carta del Lic. de la Marcha 18 de Feb. 1551.'

[3] Orozco y Jiménez, *Colección*, vol. V, p. 7: 'Información hecha por el...Lic. Martínez de la Marcha acerca del precio de venta de varios alimentos. Guadalajara 1550.'

[4] See *A.G.I.* Auda. de Guadalajara 230, Z 1, fol. 115. 8 de Nov. 1562. An order to the royal officials to pay salaries in coin whenever possible: 'porque no es justo que anden quebrando pedazos de plata para el gasto ordinario, pues no había en esa provincia casa de moneda para labrar la plata en que se les pagase...y en cada marco se pierde por el trueco de tomines un peso.'

49

greatly to the prosperity of the province in later years, was cheap, and had risen comparatively little in price—bullocks only from 4 to 4½ or 5 *pesos*, sheep from 2 to 3 or 4 *reales*. Pigs, however— rather a rarity in New Galicia—had risen from 10 to 24 *reales* (3 *pesos*), while domestic fowls—then as now an important article of food in Mexico, and one raised almost entirely by Indians under Spanish encouragement—cost 4 or 5 *mrs.* each in 1546, 16 *mrs.* in 1550; the price of eggs rose correspondingly. Prices in Zacatecas were said to be even higher than in Guadalajara. These figures should be considered together with the assessments of Indian tributes[1] and the salaries paid in New Galicia.[2] The wages paid to Indians rose from 2 *reales* a month in 1546 to 4 *reales* in 1550, though this figure was still far below the official wage laid down, and as far as possible enforced shortly afterwards, under the orders of the viceroy Luis de Velasco.[3] It will be seen that difficult economic conditions[4] in New Galicia gave the colonists every incentive to extort as much tribute and as much unpaid labour as possible from the natives, in defiance of the royal regulations. If de la Marcha hoped for a relaxation of the regulations or an increase in the salaries of the officials of the audiencia as a result of his report, he was doomed to disappointment.

His investigations at Guadalajara completed, de la Marcha travelled down the Río Grande to Copalá, then east to Teul and Tepinchán, and north to Tlaltenango, where he settled a long-standing dispute over the possession of the *encomiendas* of the Río de Tepeque, and attempted without success to call the unsubdued Indians of that region to obedience. Zacatecas was the next important settlement upon his route, and there he found much to do; the mining camp—for despite its large size the place was as yet little more than a camp—had attracted prospectors from all over New Spain; mines quickly opened were as quickly abandoned, many mines were unregistered, and consequently paid no *quinto* upon their product; 'claim-jumping' was rife, and provision for

---

[1] See p. 70, below.

[2] See p. 40, above. It is, of course, impossible accurately to express these amounts in terms of modern money. The silver *peso* (piece of eight *reales*) was nominally one ounce of silver.

[3] 12 *mrs.* a day. See ch. III below.

[4] These lists of wages and prices may be compared with those current in Spain; cf. E. J. Hamilton, *American Treasure and the price revolution in Spain* (Harvard, 1934).

public order non-existent. De la Marcha made a thorough inspection of the claims which were being worked, and forwarded a list drawn up by the *alguacil mayor*,[1] which revealed Zacatecas as a thriving, if disorderly, community. About fifty separate owners, including six companies, were working mines, reduction works and refineries. Cristóbal de Oñate 'and company', for instance, owned a number of mines, thirteen engines for crushing and smelting the ore, buildings to accommodate slaves, a dwelling-house, and a church. Oñate, relieved of public office, was busily occupied in making himself the richest man in Spanish North America. Besides the mine-owners, there were about a dozen householders who held no mines, but engaged in other trades; such were the 'compañía de los Toledanos', general merchants. At the bottom of the white social scale were a number of hangers-on who owned neither houses nor mines. All the more prosperous miners employed the labour of slaves or of *naborias*—a class of serfs, of pre-Spanish origin, occupying a position between that of slaves and that of Indians held formally in tribute-paying *encomienda*.[2] At least one household of slaves was owned by a priest. De la Marcha did nothing, or very little, to remedy the forced labour situation, in spite of the well-known views of the home government. He did, however, issue a rough code of mining regulations[3] to be enforced by the *alcalde mayor* appointed by the audiencia, prohibiting the sale of unstamped silver, and the working of mines by Indians or negroes for their own profit;[4] and providing for the formal registration of claims, the definition of their extent and the immediate stamping and taxing of the silver produced. These ordinances, together with those concerning the treatment of Indians in the mines drawn up by the Licentiate Mendiola in 1567,[5] and a supplementary set issued by the Licentiate Riego in 1576,[6] were to form the 'corpus' of mining law in New Galicia, similar to but distinct from the famous code given to New

---

[1] *A.G.I.* Auda. de Guadalajara 5: 'Carta del Lic. de la Marcha. 18 de Febrero 1551.'

[2] Compare the status of the *presos* in Mozambique under Portuguese rule. For the native status of the *naborias* see Ch. III, below.

[3] *A.G.I.* Auda. de Guadalajara 5: 'Averiguaciones del Lic. Contreras y Guevara, sobre lo tocante a la visita del Real Consejo de Indias', fols. 105–21.

[4] Compare the colour-bar regulations introduced at Kimberley, *c.* 1870.

[5] *A.G.I.* Auda. de Guadalajara 5: 'Averiguaciones...', loc. cit.

[6] *A.G.I.* Patronato 182, R°. 52.

Spain by Antonio de Mendoza.[1] For the better enforcement of the law, de la Marcha made provisional arrangements, subject to the royal approval, whereby all silver in future, instead of going unstamped to Compostela or to Mexico, should be stamped and taxed at the mines, under the supervision of the royal overseer, who was to reside in Zacatecas, and to be assisted by representatives of the treasurer and the auditor.[2] The royal fifth was then to be sent to the chest at Compostela every six months under armed escort— a very necessary provision, for shortly before de la Marcha's arrival, a silver train had been set upon and scattered by the Zacateco Indians. Diego de Ibarra alone had lost fifty horses on that occasion.

From Zacatecas the *visitador* returned south to Nochistlán, scene of the defeat and death of the great Alvarado during the Mixton campaign; and to Guachinango. The miners of Guachinango were engaged in guerrilla warfare with the mountain Caxcanes, and de la Marcha noted with alarm that these redoubtable warriors had lost their fear of cavalry. He recommended that the old Indian rock-fortresses of Mixton and Nochistlán be reoccupied by the Spaniards, and fortified with cannon.

From the high sierra, to the hot coast-lands—de la Marcha, struck by the fertility of the country round Purificación, and the abundance of timber suitable for ship-building, became interested in the possibilities of Navidad Bay, nearby, as a harbour-base for Pacific exploration. He failed, however, to arouse a corresponding interest at home—the days of the Manila trade had not begun— and Purificación never attained any considerable prosperity, despite de la Marcha's patronage.

De la Marcha returned to Compostela, via Guadalajara, in December 1550. In spite of his energy in travelling, his *visita* had accomplished little—least of all in the direction of a solution of the Indian problems which were exercising the minds of the Council of the Indies. Either de la Marcha felt no concern over the fate of the Indians, and the effectiveness of the royal authority over them; or else he would not, or dared not, take any action which might endanger the interests of the *encomenderos* and mine-owners. His

---

[1] See A. S. Aiton: 'The First American Mining Code', *Michigan Law Review*, vol. xxiii, no. 2, p. 107. Santiago Ramírez, *La propiedad de las minas* (Mexico, 1883). pp. 86–104.

[2] *A.G.I.* Auda. de Guadalajara 5: 'Carta del Lic. de la Màrcha. 18 de Febrero 1551.'

reports indeed contained many references to the danger of attack, to which settlements were exposed, and to the necessity of retaining the allegiance of the conquered Indians, by protecting their fields from the incursions of their wilder relatives. His attitude to the mountain Indians was frankly that of a slave-hunter. Of the military situation he wrote:[1]

Ever since the time of Nuño de Guzmán, of Cristóbal de Oñate, and of other captains, whenever the Indians have shown similar signs of hostility, our people have hesitated to make war upon them, and the same disastrous results have followed, as we may see to-day....I am certain that nothing can be achieved, by attempts at persuasion. In order to raise troops, it will be necessary for Your Majesty to permit those who serve to reduce the rebels to slavery, or at least to the condition of *naborias*. The appalling crimes committed by the Indians supply ample justification for sacrificing the rules of law to the necessities of the case. We cannot make war with paid troops; for here, pay of three, ten, twenty, even fifty ducats, would not attract a drummer-boy. The only way to obtain soldiers is to pay them with slaves as I have suggested...that is the only method by which we can put a stop to the outrages of which we are the daily victims, and stamp out sodomy, idolatry, and cannibalism among the natives. This policy is made all the more necessary, by the attitude of those who refuse to submit to Your Majesty unless they are crushed and who say that they wish to see for themselves what manner of men the Christians are.

This was not the advice which de la Marcha had received from those who knew the Indians best. The Franciscan, Fray Gregorio de Beteta, perhaps the most successful missionary in the north of New Spain at that time, wrote to de la Marcha from Xuchipila, in August 1550, announcing his intention of attempting a missionary expedition from Culiacán towards the north in the hope, eventually, of reaching Florida:[2]

I have one obstacle to face, and that a serious one: it is, that certain Spaniards are planning an expedition through the same country in search of mines and other profitable undertakings. Some have already started; the Indians are greatly alarmed at the prospect of receiving in their country and in their houses a people so much more powerful than they, who have behaved so brutally in the past, and who show no sign

---

[1] H. Ternaux-Compans (ed.), *Recueil de documents et mémoires originaux sur l'histoire des possessions espagnoles dans l'Amérique* (Paris, 1837–41), pp. 171 ff.

[2] H. Ternaux-Compans, loc. cit. The name Florida at this time covered the whole of the north shore of the Gulf of Mexico.

of wishing to repair the damage they have done. These independent natives see daily the evidence of the oppression and extortions suffered by their conquered neighbours, at the hands of the Spaniards. . .and if any Spaniard goes into their country now, he will be resisted and treated as an enemy. I beg your lordship to put a stop to the ill-treatment of the natives, so that we may yet hope to win them over by peaceful means; and for the time, to forbid any fresh expeditions, as these are prohibited by the New Laws. In the name of Jesus Christ I beg you to restore peace to these provinces; for the Indians will be faithful to a peaceful sovereign, even though now they are so suspicious.

De la Marcha's comment upon this communication was non-committal: 'The proposed enterprise is very dangerous. . . .it is useless to try to dissuade the friars from these undertakings, especially when their vows and their faith are involved. They have indeed rendered valuable service.'[1]

De la Marcha's attitude towards the Indians did not pass unnoticed by his superiors. The viceroy, writing in 1554 in answer to a Royal question, reported unfavourably: 'I am informed that he (de la Marcha) cares little for the Indians and is at loggerheads with the religious. In the *visita* which he conducted, he made no effort to lighten the burdens of personal servitude, or to give slaves their freedom, though many begged it of him, or to regulate the tributes of the villages.'[2] Evidently, if the wishes of the Crown with regard to the Indians were to be given effect in New Galicia, little reliance could be placed upon the senior *oidor*. De la Marcha's failure to co-operate in this matter probably prompted Velasco to add, later in the same letter, that the audiencia of New Galicia was useless and obstructive, and that its work could be done more effectively by a single *alcalde mayor*.

[1] H. Ternaux-Compans, loc. cit.
[2] Mariano Cuevas, *Colección de documentos*, p. 205: 'Carta de don Luis de Velasco, el primero, a Felipe II, 7 de Febrero 1554.'

CHAPTER III

THE AUDIENCIA AND THE INDIANS

The Spanish settlements in the New World could not survive without Indian labour; the Indians, accustomed to a life of communal subsistence farming, would not willingly work, even at a high wage, for an outside employer. Those were the hard facts which confronted the humanitarian reformer and the agent of royal paternalism. The colonial authorities were required to suppress the abuses of the *encomienda*, slavery and personal servitude, without infringing the rights of deserving conquerors and settlers; to ensure an adequate supply of hired labour for the Spanish settlements, while protecting the Indians in their possession of land, which relieved them of the necessity of working for wages. The task was an impossible one. The ultimate solution lay in the disappearance of the Indian holdings, the ubiquitous growth of capitalist *haciendas*, and the reduction of the Indian, by the process of debt-slavery, to the condition of a landless *peón*. These developments lay in the future; in the sixteenth century the Crown and the audiencias strove continually to enforce the principle that the peaceful Indian retained his land and freedom according to his ancient customs, even if he lived within an *encomienda* grant; and that Spanish claims upon him were limited and might be defined by law.

Indian custom, however, admitted various forms of landholding and different degrees of personal freedom; and among the widely various tribes of New Spain there was naturally a corresponding variety of custom. In describing the ancient Mexicans and the sedentary peoples related to them some rough generalisation is possible.[1] The normal form of social organisation was the tribe or village (*pueblo*) of free husbandmen (*maceguales*) holding land in common. The village usually comprised a number of kinship groups or clans, each clan living together and holding a permanent

[1] See A. F. Bandelier, 'The art of war and mode of warfare of the ancient Mexicans', 'The distribution and tenure of land and the customs with regard to inheritance among the ancient Mexicans', 'The social organisation and mode of government of the ancient Mexicans', *Reports of the Peabody Museum of American Archaeology and Ethnology*, vol. II, 1876–9 (Cambridge, Mass., 1880). G. M. McBride, *The Land Systems of Mexico* (New York, 1923), pp. 111 ff.

share of the arable land of the village. How permanent these clan-divisions were, may be guessed from the fact that the Indian 'wards' of Mexico City—the ancient clans—retained their separate existence and their holdings of common land until the end of the eighteenth century. In so far as any notion of ownership existed, the ownership of land was vested in the clan, and many óf the operations of agriculture were performed by the clan in common. A strictly limited form of ownership, conditional upon effective cultivation, was delegated to the married males of the clan. These smaller, less permanent holdings usually descended from father to eldest son among the Aztecs (matrilineal succession was the rule in some tribes), though an individual might be deprived of his land for various offences, and every free male, upon reaching marriage-able age, might claim an allotment, if he were prepared to cultivate it, so long as sufficient land remained—a custom which still survives among many tribes, especially in New Mexico and Arizona.

The public affairs both of clan and of tribe were conducted by council meetings which seem to have been democratic in character, though great weight was attached to the words of the *caciques* or shamans—the 'old men'—and in military matters, to those of the war-chiefs of clan and of tribe.

Among the tribes of the Aztec confederacy this typical organisa-tion was already much modified before the Spanish invasion. The Aztec preoccupation with war gave special prominence to the office of head-war-chief—so much so that the Spaniards were led naturally into the mistake of regarding Montezuma as a despotic ruler. The war-chiefs were not rulers; but they had come to form, by the time of the conquest, a powerful aristocracy. Both they and the *caciques* were sufficiently important for considerable tracts of land to be set aside for their support. These tracts, together with the lands appointed for the upkeep of the temples and other public institutions, were tilled in some *pueblos*—perhaps originally in all—by the common labour of the *maceguales*. Among the more powerful tribes, however, there was a large class of persons who, though not slaves, stood outside the kinship groups. These unprivileged people (*mayeques* or *tlalmaites*) were the labourers of the villages. They worked the lands of the chiefs and of the community houses, and might also be employed by private members of the kins—by those, for instance, who followed the honourable and dangerous calling of

56

merchants and so could not maintain their tenant rights by culti-
vating personally their holdings of land. Probably the labour
exacted from the *mayeques* took other forms besides agriculture—
work as couriers and porters for example. They enjoyed the use of
small plots of land, upon which to support themselves, by way of
wages. The *naborias* or *tapias* mentioned in the laws of the Indies
and in official correspondence were these same *mayeques* set to
work for Spanish masters. Their status was interpreted in feudal
terms by the Spaniards, who called them *vasallos patrimoniales*.

Below the *mayeques* were the slaves proper. Slavery seems to
have taken a mild form among the ancient Mexicans; it was not
hereditary, nor did it preclude the owning of property. The slave
class was recruited mainly by sale; a man might sell himself or his
children for debt, or to escape the consequences of flood or famine.
Prisoners of war were usually sacrificed, so that recruitment from
that source was exceptional—another point at which Spanish
practice departed from Indian custom. The Spaniards deemed it
just to enslave prisoners of war.

Such was the social organisation of the Aztecs. A further modification of the typical organisation had taken place among the
numerous tribes conquered by the confederates; this was the
institution of tribute land, set aside to provide the tributes in kind
demanded by the conquerors. The only regular relations between
the conquerors and the conquered consisted in the collection of
tribute, or if tribute were withheld, in the dispatch of punitive
expeditions. To that extent only, the tributary tribes might be
described as forming part of the Mexican 'empire'. The tribes
of Michoacán and Chimalhuacán were of course completely
independent.

In the territory subject to Mexico, the *encomienda* was probably
the most serviceable institution which could be devised to enable
Indians and *conquistadores* to live together in peace. Under favourable circumstances, the Indians merely exchanged one conqueror
for another; their economy already provided for the payment of
tribute to chiefs and overlords, and for the performance of ordinary
labour services. The Spaniards who received *encomiendas* were
well content to live comfortably upon their tributes; usually they
preferred to live in the towns; they were not at first interested in
agriculture or industry, and so had little motive for seizing native
lands or for interfering with the Indians, except to the limited

extent of making a perfunctory provision for religious instruction. The system lent itself to abuses, of course. No adequate supervision was possible, and *encomenderos* naturally tended to regard themselves as feudatories possessing not only a right to a specified tribute in kind and labour, but also lordship over the lands and persons of their Indians. In provinces such as Michoacán, Colima, and New Galicia, where the *encomiendas* were small and poor and where (in contrast with the Anáhuac tribes) no native arrangement existed for furnishing tribute for a conqueror, extortion and heavy forced labour were inevitable. Moreover, the *encomienda*, though selected by Las Casas and others for special attack, represented only a part of the problem; the *encomenderos*, though powerful, were comparatively few in number. Other Spaniards had to seek their living in other ways, as miners, ranchers or merchants. Without the easy livelihood of the *encomenderos*, they had every reason to covet Indian lands. For their labour supply they depended on the labour-*repartimiento* and (whenever the law could be evaded) on slavery. The *repartimiento*, though theoretically more equitable than the *encomienda*, in practice probably caused far more hardship to the Indians. Constant complaints were made of Indians being cheated of their wages by their employers or by their own *caciques*; of excessive *repartimiento* assessments, leaving the Indians insufficient time to till their own lands; of overloading of Indian porters; of overcrowding, starvation and plague,[1] especially in the mining settlements. The only protection of these Indians was the vigilance of the overworked judges.

The general intentions of the Crown with regard to the economic life of the Indians have already been stated: to accustom them to working for wages, while preserving their personal freedom and protecting them in possession of their lands. The particular objects of colonial legislation were therefore clear: control of the alienation of Indian land and prevention of forcible seizure by Spaniards; delimitation of arable and pasture areas; rigid separation of *encomienda* from Spanish *hacienda*; limitation of tributes and services due to *encomenderos*—or preferably the abolition of services within the *encomienda*; strict supervision of *repartimientos* and of labour conditions generally; and the abolition of Indian slavery.

---

[1] For the ravages of plague among the Indians, cf. J. García-Icazbalceta, *Documentos*, vol. II, p. 198: 'Carta de Fray Domingo de Betanzos.' A decree of 1546 provided relief from taxation for *pueblos* attacked by plague. *Recopilación de Leyes de Indias*, VI. v. 45.

One of the greatest difficulties in dealing with the land question arose from the peculiar forms of land-holding customary among the Indians. Spaniards never understood that absolute ownership of land was unknown; that land belonged to the clan and that individuals owned merely the use of their holdings. On the other hand, an Indian who accepted a purchase price for his plot often had no notion that the land was thereby lost to his tribe forever. Much land changed hands through misunderstandings of this sort. Tribute lands, lands of the chiefs, lands of the temples or community houses—all common lands set aside for definite public purposes— were wrongly regarded by Spaniards as 'domain', to be confiscated upon the death without heir, or the deposition, of a native chief and transferred to a Spanish overlord, whether the Crown or a private person—a proceeding just and intelligible according to feudal law and custom, but plain confiscation in the eyes of the Indians. Indian agriculture, moreover, was bound up with social and religious observances. The Indians had no ploughs, no wheeled vehicles, no beasts of burden; their tools were of wood or of stone. Individually, with such tools they could have made little impression on the land. They could support themselves in reasonable comfort only by a highly organised system of communal labour. The organisation of this communal labour lay in the hands of the *caciques*, who marked each muster of labour by the appropriate seasonal ritual. Corn-dance and rain-dance thus had their proper and essential place in the year's work, along with digging, sowing, and all the other operations of primitive agriculture.

The coming of the Spaniards inevitably weakened the authority of the *caciques*, despite the attempts of government to maintain them in office and to employ them as minor native magistrates and as organisers of forced labour.[1] The consequent loosening of tribal and village organisation, the weaning of the Indians from their ancient beliefs and customs, the very prohibition of ritual dances,[2] all helped to weaken the hold of the Indians upon their land and to reduce the efficiency of their farming.

The Spanish authorities were aware of some of the difficulties of the situation and in legislation at least made genuine attempts to meet them. As early as 1530 colonial governors were instructed to respect the organisation and customs of the Indian

---

[1] *Recopilación de Leyes de Indias*, VI. vii. 1, 7, 8, 11, 13.
[2] Ibid. VI. i. 38.

communities, except in matters of pagan religion and barbarous practices.[1] *Oidores* when conducting *visitas* were to see that every village had sufficient common land and cultivated it effectively, planting trees where necessary—a surprisingly modern enactment.[2] Numerous decrees suggested improvements in the holdings, the introduction of European crops and cattle and the instruction of the Indians in new textile industries such as the growing, spinning and weaving of flax.[3] No reservation laws hindered the use of unoccupied fertile land by Indians, and the colonial officials were commanded to provide land and seed for the wild mountain tribes, if by such means the wanderers could be persuaded to settle in established villages.[4]

The granting of Indians in *encomienda* legally made no difference in the titles by which they held their lands. It was never intended that *encomiendas* should become feudal manors. It is true that an early decree of the island period laid down that a ranch in the neighbourhood of an Indian village must be owned by the *encomendero*, so that the Indians might not serve two masters;[5] but this law was never enforced on the mainland. *Encomenderos*, and indeed all Spaniards, were forbidden to reside or to quarter their servants in Indian villages, even within their own grants.[6] Stewards might be employed in *encomiendas* only with the consent of an audiencia, and might in no case assume judicial powers.[7] The land of Indians who died without heirs was to return to their *pueblos* and was not to be seized by *encomenderos* under the colour of a feudal escheat.[8] Later, in the seventeenth century, *encomenderos* were forbidden altogether to acquire land, to pasture stock or to establish factories within their *encomiendas*.[9]

The forcible seizure of Indian lands, whether by authority or by private individuals, was repeatedly forbidden.[10] The allotment of

---

[1] *Recopilación de Leyes de Indias*, v. ii. 22 (1530); II. i. 4 (1555).

[2] Ibid. II. xxxi. 9.

[3] Ibid. IV. xviii. 20, 21; IV. i. 22.

[4] See Tello, *Crónica miscelánea*, cap. ccxxiv.

[5] *D.I.U.* vol. XXII, p. 55: 'Gobernación espiritual y temporal de las Indias', tit. III, 12 and 174.

[6] *Recopilación de Leyes de Indias*, VI. iii. 21; VI. ix. 14, 15. From 1583 the *encomenderos* of New Galicia were ordered by royal decree to reside in Guadalajara. Tello, *Crónica miscelánea*, cap. ccxvi.

[7] *Recopilación de Leyes de Indias*, VI. iii. 27, 28.

[8] Ibid. VI. i. 30.

[9] Ibid. VI. ix. 17, 18, 19; IV. xvii. 10.   [10] Ibid. IV. xii. 7, 9; VI. iii. 9.

unoccupied land to Spaniards in newly settled areas was to be carried out in the first place by the *adelantado* responsible for the settlement, and subsequently by the viceroy or governor, acting upon the advice of the local town councils. An elaborate procedure was prescribed for all the forms of allotment.[1] Recipients of grants were required to take possession of their land within three months and to carry out improvements in the form of building and planting, under pain of confiscation.[2] All conveyances of land were to be witnessed by the *fiscal* of the nearest audiencia, so that titles might be examined and seizures of Indian land detected[3] (this enactment must have been impossible to enforce, in view of the large area which each audiencia had to control). The viceroys and travelling justices held the responsibility for preventing the encroachment of stock farms upon the cultivated fields[4]—probably a more serious Indian grievance, in the sixteenth century, than actual seizures of land.

As might be expected, much of this legislation was only occasionally effective, and even in strict law a serious weakness remained throughout the sixteenth century; nothing prevented a Spaniard from purchasing land from an Indian by free, or apparently free contract. Laws of 1571 and 1572 required Indians to seek permission from the local magistrates before selling property,[5] but—as in the case of most legislation of this type— the majority of Indians probably never knew of the existence of the law, and the local magistracy was notoriously the least effective section of the colonial administration in dealing with native affairs. Indian land was in fact regularly purchased by Spaniards.[6] Although Spaniards at first had little direct interest in agriculture, the Indians in general would not bestir themselves to produce a saleable surplus of food; and since the Indians already occupied most of the land suitable for agriculture, the Spanish ranchers were compelled either to plough up part of their pastures or acquire Indian land. Not until the seventeenth century did the Crown finally and totally prohibit the alienation of village lands,[7] and even if that prohibition could have been enforced, it came too late.

---

[1] Ibid. IV. xii. 1, 2, 4, 5, 6, 8.   [2] Ibid. IV. xii. 3, 11.
[3] Ibid. IV. xii. 16, 17.   [4] Ibid. IV. xii. 12, 13; IV. xvii. 10.
[5] Ibid. VI. i. 27.
[6] A law of 1546, repeating former enactments against Spaniards residing in Indian villages, added the clause 'even if they [the Spaniards] have bought land in the villages.' *Recopilación de Leyes de Indias*, VI. iii. 22.   [7] Ibid. IV. xii. 18.

The process of expropriation went on, often under colour of seizure for debt, and led in time to the development of self-contained *haciendas* cultivated by the labour of semi-servile landless *peones*.[1] The process was slow, however, and did not reach anything approaching completeness until the nineteenth century, when the restraining influence of the Spanish Crown had been removed; only the beginnings of the movement were perceptible in the sixteenth century.

The employment of Indian labour by Spaniards presented an even more difficult problem. Throughout the reign of Charles V there was a steady stream of protest by missionaries against the system which permitted *encomenderos* to exact labour from the Indians in their grants, and many missionaries favoured the total abolition of *encomiendas*. The New Laws of 1542–3, which reflected Dominican influence at Court, provided that upon the death of their present holders all *encomiendas* should revert to the Crown and should not be granted in future.[2] *Encomenderos* who ill-treated their Indians or who held them without lawful title were to be deprived immediately, and unduly large grants were to be reduced in size. The laws also re-enacted earlier decrees forbidding the sale or enslavement of Indians and their employment as *naborias* or as porters;[3] slaves held without lawful title were to be released. The exaction of services within *encomiendas*, while the *encomiendas* lasted, was not forbidden; the audiencias were ordered to assess the tributes and services which the Indians could provide without hardship, and to see that no exactions were made without the authority of such assessment.

Article XXX of the New Laws provoked such fierce opposition among the colonists that the Crown consented three years later to its repeal. The *cédula* of Malines of 1545[4] re-established the old rules concerning the succession to *encomiendas*: in most provinces the titles were for the lives of the recipient and of one successor, after which they were to revert to the Crown and to be granted afresh to 'deserving conquerors and settlers'. The colonists remained dissatisfied and pressed for further concessions, in particular for a *repartimiento general y perpétuo*—the permanent division of

[1] See G. M. McBride, *The land systems of Mexico* (New York, 1923), p. 25.
[2] J. García-Icazbalceta, *Documentos*, vol. II, p. 215: 'Leyes y Ordenanzas nuevamente hechas....'
[3] *Recopilación de Leyes de Indias*, VI. i. 16; VI. ii. 1, 2; VI. xii. 6.
[4] Puga, *Cedulario*, vol. I, pp. 472–5. *Recopilación de Leyes de Indias*, VI. viii. 4.

the whole territory of New Spain into *encomiendas* to be held in perpetuity as *mayorazgos*—entailed estates, not to be surrendered to the Crown after the second 'life'; the Crown *pueblos* being divided among those who held no *encomiendas*. This demand continued to be made at intervals for the next twenty or thirty years. It occurred frequently in petitions of the town council of Mexico, presented to the viceroy for transmission to the Crown.[1] Such petitions appear to have been forwarded with favourable comment by Mendoza. In 1546 the king authorised the viceroy to make an equitable redistribution of *encomiendas* and hinted that the new grants might be made heritable in perpetuity.[2] The *repartimiento general* was never carried out, however, and in 1549 the attack on the *encomienda* was renewed in a different form, in a series of decrees which abolished the old type of services to private individuals altogether, and further forbade the employment of Indians as porters or as labourers in the mines, unless they agreed to serve and received proper wages.[3] In 1550 it was again decreed that *encomiendas* which escheated to the Crown should not be granted anew to individuals.[4] It seemed possible, therefore, that the *encomiendas* might after all disappear within two or three generations. Even while the institution survived—as in fact it did for another two centuries—it had lost its original character of a charter to extort forced labour. No doubt *encomenderos* did extort illegal services, but in law they were entitled only to the tribute of their Indians[5]—tribute paid partly in money and partly in produce, which might either be consumed

[1] E.g. *Actas del cabildo de México*, vol. vii, p. 326: '...Que S.M. sea servido de hacer merced a esta tierra del repartimiento general y perpétuo della, de suerte que sucedan en los indios que tienen particulares en encomienda, los hijos o hijas a los padres... dando facultad a cada uno para que pueda hacer mayorazgo para siempre jamás del repartimiento de sus indios.' Vol. vii, p. 457: '...el repartimiento general...no solo para los encomenderos que al presente gozan, mas lo mismo para los...que han estado o están o estuvieren sin encomiendas....'   [2] Puga, *Cedulario*, vol. i, p. 479.

[3] *Recopilación de Leyes de Indias*, vi. xii. 1, 6, 8; vi. ix. 22; Puga, *Cedulario*, vol. ii, pp. 7, 14.

[4] Ibid. vol. ii, p. 70. Herrera (*Década*, vii, lib. x. cap. 13) indicates that this order merely re-enacted a secret instruction sent to Mendoza at the time of the promulgation of the *cédula* of Malines. Mendoza received several conflicting orders. See S. Zavala, 'Las encomiendas de Nueva España y el gobierno de Don Antonio de Mendoza.' *Revista histórica americana*, vol. i, pp. 59–75; 'Una instrucción secreta a Don Antonio de Mendoza', *Boletín del Archivo General* (Mexico, D.F.), vol. ix, no. 4.

[5] See Solórzano, *Política Indiana*, vol. iii, cap. i, §§ 24, 25: 'No se pueden conceder Indios en propiedad y vasallage a ningún particular....Quando solo se conceden los tributos de ellos, como sucede en las encomiendas ya reformadas, no se contraviene a la dicha ley.'

by the *encomenderos*' households or sold like the produce of the Crown *pueblos*. In many districts the enforcement of this law was rendered easier by circumstances; owing to the spread of a money economy in the colonies, the time was ripe for replacing tribute-labour by hired labour. The *encomienda* accordingly became a mere pension, with which the Crown might reward *conquistadores* for their services. In some cases the Crown even adopted the method of pensioning off deserving persons with annuities charged upon *encomiendas*, instead of granting the *encomiendas* themselves.[1]

The problem remained of inducing the Indians to work and to contribute to the economic life of a community wider than a single *pueblo*. The legislation of 1549, accordingly, while prohibiting personal servitude, permitted the colonial authorities to compel Indians to seek employment. In future, instead of waiting to be summoned in definite relays for labour, all unemployed Indians, whether held by the Crown or by *encomenderos*, were to offer themselves for hire in the public places of their districts, 'without molestation or pressure except such as should be necessary to make them work'[2]— a large exception, as events proved. They were to work for such employers as they chose, for the length of time agreed upon by free contract, and were to be paid wages according to a scale fixed by the viceroy or local governor. Only for certain (usually public) purposes were the compulsory *repartimiento* gangs to be employed. Subsequent legislation defined these purposes; the construction of roads, bridges and public buildings was naturally included; silver mining and the production of crops of special local importance also counted as 'public purposes' and qualified for *repartimiento* labour at the discretion of the colonial authorities.[3] The particular *repartimiento* requirements in each district came to be defined in local assessments issued by viceroys, governing audiencias or *visitadores*.[4]

---

[1] *Recopilación de Leyes de Indias*, VI. viii. 29, 30. For examples of this type of grant see 'Documentos del virrey Toledo' (L. Ulloa, ed.), *Revista Histórica*, vol. III (Lima, 1908).

[2] *Recopilación de Leyes de Indias*, VI. xii. 1; Puga, *Cedulario*, vol. II, p. 14.

[3] *Recopilación de Leyes de Indias*, VI. xii. 19, 20; VI. xiii. 1, 3; VI. xv. 1, 5. See also L. B. Simpson: *Studies in the administration of the Indians in New Spain*, vol. III: '*The repartimiento system of native labor in New Spain and Guatemala* (Berkeley, California, 1938). A survival of the type of *repartimiento* here described may perhaps be detected in the national *corvée* of Guatemala, by means of which the coffee production of that country is maintained. Cf. J. H. Jackson, *Notes on a Drum* (New York, 1938)—a study of contemporary Guatemala.

[4] See S. Zavala and M. Castelo, *Fuentes para la historia del trabajo en Nueva España*, vol. I (Mexico, 1938)—a collection of documents of the years 1575-6, chiefly viceregal

These assessments, infrequently revised, tended to grow into bodies of local custom as complex as those which in former times governed feudal labour-dues in the villages of Europe. Complaints concerning illegal *repartimiento* exactions were very frequent. Later, general legislation limited the number of Indians to be included in these gangs at any one time to four per cent of the total number of labourers available.[1] The remainder were to seek employment by free contract.

The general attitude of the Crown towards the whole question of labour and tribute is well illustrated in the instructions issued to the second viceroy of New Spain, Luis de Velasco, 'the liberator', who succeeded Mendoza in 1550:

> The Indians must be made to work for wages in the fields or in the cities, so that they have no excuse for idleness.... This order must be enforced by our justices; private Spaniards must not be allowed to bring pressure upon the Indians, even within their own *encomiendas*. You are to give orders for proper daily wages to be paid to the Indians themselves, and not to their chiefs, or to any other intermediaries. They are not to be overworked; and it must be made clear that Spaniards who disregard these orders will be severely punished.[2]

In the matter of tributes:

> Since in many Indian *pueblos* the scale of tributes is uncertain, and no one knows exactly how much they ought to pay, with the result that they are often overtaxed: you are to issue orders for definite assessments to be made and declared, so that the Indians know what they are to pay....[3]

In general:

> You are to do justice, and to see to it that the grievances of the Indians are removed, and their tributes lightened; observing and enforcing in all things the provisions made by the New Laws for the good government of the Indies. You are to study a royal decree which

orders. Corresponding documents for New Galicia in the sixteenth century have unfortunately not survived, though there is no doubt that the audiencia issued them.
[1] *Recopilación de Leyes de Indias*, vi. xii. 22, 23.
[2] Excerpts from 'Instrucciones de la Corona para Luis de Velasco'. Published in S. Zavala, *La Encomienda Indiana*, p. 125 (Madrid, 1935).
[3] Ibid. See also *D.I.I.* vol. xviii, p. 476. 8 de Junio 1551: 'Provisión general para todas las audiencias, confirmando el capítulo de las Leyes nuevas, disponiendo la manera de efectuar la tasación de los tributos de los Indios...."Para que sea menos que lo que solían pagar en tiempo de los Caciques y Señores que los tenían antes de venir a nuestra obediencia".'

we have issued concerning the services of the Indians, and are to observe and enforce it.[1]

Velasco himself regarded the revised labour laws and the pension-*encomienda* as indispensable, if peace was to be maintained in the colonies. He even succeeded in extending titles to *encomiendas* to cover a third life, by way of a legal fiction.[2] In other respects, however, he was altogether upon the side of reform, and strove continually to achieve the abolition of personal servitude and the reasonable assessment of Indian tributes based upon the scale of payment existing before the conquest.[3] His chief difficulty was to find suitable agents to carry out the work—men of known reliability, and of sufficient standing to be above bribes and threats, for the *encomenderos* might well resort to such methods to prevent decisions being given against their interests.[4] The *oidores* of the audiencia of Mexico was already fully occupied. The solution came in a decree[5] empowering Velasco to employ two of the *oidores alcaldes mayores* of New Galicia in *visitas* in any part of New Spain, at his own discretion. Incessant correspondence on the subject had evidently convinced the Council of the Indies that four justices of appeal were not needed in Compostela, for supplementary decrees added that when reporting to Mexico City, the *oidores visitadores* were to assist in the work of the viceregal audiencia,[6] and that in New Galicia, suits involving less than the statutory 500 *pesos* might be settled by one *oidor* sitting alone; or, in the case of a retrial, by two.[7] In 1551, accordingly, viceregal commissions were issued to the licentiates Contreras and Lebrón de Quiñones to set out upon extended *visitas* in the Pacific provinces of New Spain. De la Marcha and Oseguera (the new *oidor* who replaced Sepúlveda) were to remain at Compostela to continue the work of the audiencia.

Few records survive of the activities of de la Marcha and

---

[1] S. Zavala, *Encomienda*, p. 125.

[2] 'Se mandó disimular en la tercera.' *Recopilación de Leyes de Indias*, VI. xi. 14.

[3] Investigations were made with this object; cf. S. Zavala, *Encomienda*, p. 139; Puga, *Cedulario*, vol. II, p. 229: 'Serie de preguntas, con intento de basar los tributos de los Indios en los de la época gentil, 1553'; M. Cuevas, *Colección de documentos*, p. 235: 'Fray Domingo de la Anunciación, respondiendo desde Chimalhuacán.'

[4] See H. Ternaux-Compans (ed.): 'Rapport sur les chefs de la Nouvelle Espagne' (report of Alonso de Zorita, 1558), p. 307 (in the series *Voyages, Relations et Mémoires*).

[5] *A.G.I.* Auda. de México, 18, lib. v, fol. 201. Abril 1550.

[6] Ibid. lib. x, fol. 132. Agosto 1552.

[7] *A.G.I.* Auda. de Guadalajara, 230, Z 1, fol. 212. Diciembre 1550.

Oseguera during the four years' absence of their colleagues. Their work cannot have been heavy, and seems to have consisted mainly of local Indian suits and the issue of writs of course at the petition of Spaniards living in Compostela; the town was remote from the principal Spanish centres, and occasional important suits concerning land and Indians in New Galicia tended to go to Mexico without the formality of a first appeal to Compostela.[1] The construction of the royal house at Compostela was proceeding slowly; a letter from the audiencia in July 1551[2] announced that the work was half finished, but that 1500 *pesos* had already been spent and the treasury officials refused to release more money without express order. Presumably the *oidores* were still billeted upon the inhabitants.

The same letter urgently requested that a *fiscal* be appointed: 'There are no lawyers in this audiencia, for no one will come to such a forsaken place.' The demand for a *fiscal* was echoed, for rather different reasons, by the Franciscan missionaries: 'It is very necessary that Your Majesty appoint a protector and defender of the Indians in New Galicia...and allow him a sufficient salary...; if he were qualified, he could also exercise the office of *fiscal* in the audiencia; at present the *oidores* have to act as public prosecutors, and justice suffers in consequence.'[3]

The diocesan authorities in Guadalajara continued to denounce the audiencia as expensive and unnecessary, and to demand that the government of the kingdom be entrusted to the viceroy.[4] The colonists in general, however, soon ceased their attacks upon the *oidores*. De la Marcha was their supporter,[5] Oseguera an industrious nonentity. The general decrees concerning the assessment of tributes and the abolition of forced labour were not being enforced with any great vigour.[6] Those who were opposed to reform reserved their venom for Lebrón de Quiñones when he should

[1] See ch. VI, p. 125.
[2] *A.G.I.* Auda. de Guadalajara 51, 'Audiencia al Rey. 7 de Julio 1552.'
[3] Orozco y Jiménez, *Colección*, vol. V, p. 140.
[4] *A.G.I.* Auda. de Guadalajara 51: 'Deán de la Galicia al Rey. 10 de Feb. 1552.'
[5] 'Si algún oidor de sus compañeros viendo los agravios tan manifiestos quieren hacer justicia, muchas veces es impedido de este Licenciado de la Marcha, ý es tan parcial y favorece tanto a los Españoles que para pedir cosas que son en agravio y vejación de los Indios aguardan a que el Licenciado de la Marcha tenga la semana de proveer.' Orozco y Jiménez, *Colección*, vol. V, p. 135: 'Carta de los frailes definidores de la Orden de San Francisco a S.M. 8 de Mayo 1552.'
[6] Ibid. p. 132.

return, and the missionary friends of the Indians prayed that his return would be soon:

The *oidores* who are now here [wrote one such friar] are very bitter against the Indians.... If a poor friar speaks, they accuse him of wishing to make himself governor.... I have seen four hundred slaves in a single mining camp beg for their liberty, and receive lashes instead; and many of those who are not slaves, but are called *naborias*...wished to return to their lands; but none were given permission. But the licentiate Lebrón, during the short time that he was here alone, did much to help the Indians, for which he earned the hatred of many (Spaniards). He is a man whom your Majesty may trust and who will carry out whatever orders he receives. The Indians recognise no other *oidor* but he, and call him among themselves 'vey tlatouani', which means 'great lord'; and truly they have no father but he.[1]

Lebrón's commission[2] entrusted to him a general *visita* of the provinces of Colima and Zacatula, including Zapotlán, Tuspa, Tamazula 'and all other villages, whether held by the Crown or in *encomienda*'. The *visita* completed, he was to inspect the villages on his way to Mexico City. He was to enforce the New Laws, and all other decrees and ordinances; to inquire whether adequate provision was made for religious instruction; to punish *encomenderos* who placed obstacles in the way of the missionaries; and to see that proper provision was made for the bodily and spiritual welfare of Indians working in the mines. Indians illegally enslaved were to be freed, and *encomiendas* held without proper title to be annulled. Tributes were to be assessed at reasonable amounts,[3] and penalties placed upon *encomenderos* who demanded illegal service, or overtaxed their Indians, and upon native *caciques* who embezzled tribute money. Idle Indians were to be set to work—the clergy if necessary using their powers of persuasion—and proper wages paid: 12 *maravedíses* a day to labourers, 24 to native officials. The mountain Indians were to be induced to settle in villages and till the land 'like reasonable people'; Spanish stock farms were to be kept away from the cultivated land of the Indians, undesirable Spaniards expelled from the villages, and roads and bridges built

[1] M. Cuevas, *Colección de documentos*, p. 156: 'Carta de Fray Rodrigo de la Cruz al Emperador Carlos V. 4 de Mayo 1554.'

[2] *A.G.I.* Patronato 181, Rº. 22: Contreras received a similar commission for the *Pueblos* of Avalos and western Michoacán.

[3] The exact procedure for carrying out this task was prescribed by law. *Recopilación de Leyes de Indias*, VI. v. 21.

to accommodate pack animals, in order to remove all excuse for employing Indian carriers. Finally, Lebrón was to investigate the records of all *corregidores*, *alcaldes mayores*, *tenientes* and *alguaciles* and to take *residencia* of those retiring. With this formidable assignment he left Compostela in the spring of 1551, accompanied by his personal servant, a notary, a constable, and a native interpreter.

Lebrón spent the next four years incessantly travelling through a rough, wild country, in a climate which at some seasons was (and is) desperately unhealthy. He was seriously ill, and heavily in debt, when he reached Mexico City. The viceroy himself, in recommending him for a special grant to cover his expenses,[1] testified to the zeal and competence which he had displayed.[1] Lebrón's own report—a lengthy but lucid and extremely frank document—revealed a state of affairs very different from that contemplated by the royal legislation;[2] his findings fell under four headings: a description of all the villages visited, with the names of the *encomenderos*, and the titles, where titles existed; a survey of the town of Colima, the municipal administration, judicial arrangements, administration of *Real Hacienda*; administrative orders made by the *visitador*; and law-suits arising from the *visita*—chiefly against Spaniards holding Indians without title, or ill-treating the Indians. A diatribe against the idleness or indifference shown by the *oidores* of Mexico in these matters, completed the *visitador's* findings.

The province of Colima had been populous and rich; but now, wrote Lebrón, 'of valleys filled with thriving settlements, only the names are left'.[3] Of the two hundred independent *pueblos* of the district, no fewer than seventy-seven were held without lawful title by seventeen *encomenderos*, of whom seven were permanently absent from the province without the viceroy's licence and made no attempt to fulfil their obligations of defence. Some *encomenderos* were also accused of forging deeds of sale in order to conceal their seizures of Indian land. Lebrón instituted proceedings against all those accused, to have their Indians released and their grants formally annulled.

[1] M. Cuevas, *Colección de documentos*, p. 205: 'Carta de don Luis de Velasco, el primero, a Felipe II. 7 de Febrero 1554.'
[2] *A.G.I.* Patronato 20, no. 5, R°. 14: 'Visita que hizo en Nueva España (provincia de Colima) el Lic. Lebrón de Quiñones a doscientos pueblos. 10 de Sept. 1554.'
[3] Ibid. fol. 2.

The town of Colima had no town council, nor even a legal title to be regarded as a corporate town. The judicial and other offices of the place were shared among the self-styled *cabildo*, a small clique, who used their powers to grant plots of land, often seized from Indian owners, to their friends, but who made no effort to hold court or to perform the duties of their station. Lebrón drew up a series of ordinances based on those of Mexico, gave orders for a court-room to be built and proper courts to be held, and threatened the *alcaldes* with penalties should they neglect their duties in future. He insisted that all Indians constrained to personal servitude should be sent back to their homes, and organised a *repartimiento* in accordance with the decrees of 1549, by which each of the *pueblos* within a radius of eight leagues should in turn provide fifty Indians each week, to be employed by the *vecinos* at proper wages and under reasonable conditions.

Most of the orders issued by Lebrón concerned the treatment of Indians. He liberated during his *visita* more than six hundred slaves, and an even greater number of *naborias*, 'who although they had neither deed nor brand of slavery, were treated as slaves... orders were given for them to receive compensation for the injustice they had suffered...the Spaniards took this very ill'.[1] Lebrón interpreted literally the royal decrees upon the subject of slavery[2] which threw upon the slave-owner the burden of proof that every male slave had been taken in the act of rebellion, and was held by lawful title. In the absence of such title, the slave was released. The enslavement of women, or of children under fourteen years of age, was in all cases forbidden. The *visitador* also strictly forbade the practice whereby Indians paying tribute in kind were required to carry their produce to central depôts without pay: 'for many of them come ten, twenty and thirty leagues, once every month, carrying produce over high mountains and swift rivers...'; in future, tributes were to be paid and assessed in the village of their origin, and reckoned at local prices.[3] In every village, Lebrón published what he considered a reasonable assessment of tribute, and distributed copies of the assessment both in Spanish and in Aztec characters.[4]

[1] *A.G.I.* Patronato 20, no. 5, fol. 69.
[2] Puga, *Cedulario*, vol. II, p. 117.
[3] *A.G.I.* Patronato 20, no. 5, R°. 14: 'Visita...', fol. 70.
[4] The current idea of a reasonable assessment in New Galicia was 'for every married

Like most Spanish officials, Lebrón distrusted the Indian *caciques*. In many Indian *pueblos*, these headmen were—and are—shamans and custodians of sacred ritual rather than political leaders; sometimes their very identity was secret. The Spaniards—despite the official policy of supporting and employing the *caciques*—found it difficult to make use of dignitaries of this type—impractical, unadaptable, and naturally hostile to Christianity. The village councils, in whom was vested such political authority as existed, usually allowed themselves to be guided in everything by the *caciques*. Lebrón's solution of the problem was to appoint or induce the village councils to elect Indian governors, judges and constables, who should be responsible to the local Spanish governors for collection of tribute and maintenance of the peace. The Spanish officials were thus able to side-track the power of the *caciques*, while observing the letter of royal decrees, which upheld the authority of the Indian rulers. Lebrón's procedure was followed widely throughout New Spain. In some villages, European forms of government were adopted willingly, even enthusiastically; but in many places the village councils to this day elect 'governors' upon the advice of the *caciques*. The officials so elected may be quite negligible persons, while the *caciques* really rule.[1]

In the economic as in the political life of the Indian villages, Lebrón was ready with constructive reforms. He established ferries over the deeper rivers, permitting Indian ferrymen to levy reasonable charges; he gave orders for inns to be maintained in villages along the principal routes, at which Spanish travellers were to stay, and pay for what they consumed, instead of 'living upon the country' in the manner of the *conquistadores*; he persuaded the village Indians to experiment with European crops, and offered grants of land and seed to mountain Indians who would build permanent settlements in the valleys.

The opposition with which both Lebrón and Contreras had to contend received no mention in their official reports. The covering

Indian householder, six *reales*, one *fanega* of corn, and a fowl, every year.' See *A.G.I.* Auda. de Guadalajara 6 *passim*. In New Spain, the official assessment enforced by the *visitador* Valderrama in 1564 was two *pesos*, or one *peso* and half a *fanega* of corn. H. H. Bancroft, *Pacific States*, vol. v, p. 587. The *fanega* contained slightly more than an English bushel. 1 *real* = 34 *mrs.* or one-eighth of a silver *peso*.

[1] For a detailed study of the process whereby *gobernación* replaced *cacicazgo* in the Indian villages of New Spain, see L. Chávez Orozco, 'Las instituciones democráticas de los indígenas mexicanos en la época colonial', *América indígena*, vol. III (1943).

letter[1] which accompanied Lebrón's report, however, gave an account of the threats and beatings with which some of the *encomenderos* sought to prevent their Indians from giving evidence; of the suborning of *corregidores* and *alcaldes*; of attempts to intimidate the *visitadores* themselves, and of lampoons and public insults levelled against them. Lebrón, with his simple directness of purpose, never fully understood the power of the interests which opposed him; his denunciations contained always a note of surprise, especially when they concerned the attitude of the audiencia of Mexico. The *oidores* of that audiencia, bitterly jealous of interference in their province by justices from the subordinate court, and fearful, as always, of any policy which might lead to disaffection among the colonists, had reversed Lebrón's judgements and dismissed his charges wherever possible. A single illustration will suffice:

One Pedro de Figueroa, *vecino* of Colima, beat and half killed an Indian governor of the province of Tuxpa, a great man according to Indian notions, to whom I had entrusted a rod of justice and a commission to investigate some disputes among the natives there. The Indian was an able and trustworthy fellow, who had previously conducted similar inquiries for the viceroy.... The charge of assault was not denied, and I duly gave sentence of two years of exile and a hundred *pesos* damages; thinking myself very lenient, in not sentencing the culprit to lose his hand.... The *oidores* of Your Majesty's royal audiencia laughed at the severity of the sentence, reversed my judgement, and remitted the case for settlement to the *alcalde* at Colima.[2]

Lebrón suggested (though without giving specific examples) that the *oidores* had friendships and economic interests throughout the provinces, which made them reluctant to administer justice impartially. Even the viceroy, though a loyal servant of the king and a good friend of the Indians, was unable to enforce the laws against *oidores* owning property and engaging in business.[3]

Though Lebrón's *visita* had been in the area of the audiencia of Mexico, New Galicia did not escape the lash of his condemnation.

[1] *A.G.I.* Auda. de Guadalajara 51: 'Lic. Lebrón de Quiñones al Rey, de Tlaximoroa en Michoacán. 10 de Sept. 1554.'
[2] Ibid.
[3] Velasco himself did not escape accusation of nepotism. See García-Icazbalceta, *Documentos*, vol. II, p. 484: 'Informe al Rey por el cabildo eclesiástico de Guadalajara. 20 de Enero 1570.' The charges were never substantiated.

He scouted the notion that an audiencia was superfluous in New Galicia. The *oidores* of Mexico, he asserted, had originally advocated the foundation of the subordinate audiencia, realising that their district had grown too large for effective administration; but now, inspired by jealousy of a new jurisdiction, they had changed their minds. Actually, they knew nothing of the facts. The recent growth of population in New Galicia had created more work than ever for the judges there. The *oidores* at Compostela, however, could never agree among themselves, and were as remiss as those of Mexico in enforcing the law, especially in cases concerning Indians. 'One of the answers regularly made to me in dealing with Indian affairs is that the orders laid down in twenty or more royal decrees must not be obeyed, because some of the other *oidores* do not wish it.'[1] A possible remedy, Lebrón thought, lay in the appointment of a president, who should act as governor and supervise the *oidores* in the discharge of their administrative duties.

This letter, written with the peculiar mixture of formal deference and confiding familiarity which the paternal government of Spain encouraged, contained personal requests as well as political suggestions. Lebrón sought royal licence to marry a woman who held an *encomienda*, not in New Galicia, but in New Spain, and asked that if his bride were compelled to give up her Indians upon marriage to an *oidor*, she should receive some compensation, since the salary of an *oidor* was inadequate to support a married household, and a virtuous single life difficult for a man of Lebrón's age. He declared himself willing to resign his judicial office at Compostela, if that were held an insuperable obstacle to his marriage. Finally he reminded the king of an old promise, that the first promotion from the subordinate audiencia should be offered to him; in support of his application he recited the services of his father and brother, and begged to be removed from New Galicia—'that inferno'. He was beginning to realise how thoroughly he was hated, for his fearless prosecution of influential law-breakers in all the provinces of his jurisdiction. For three years the *oidores* of Mexico, the treasury officials, the *encomenderos*, and even their own colleagues at Compostela had vied with one another in abusing Lebrón and Contreras in letters to the authorities in Spain. Soon the campaign against them was to take effect.

[1] *A.G.I.* Auda. de Guadalajara 51: 'Lic. Lebrón de Quiñones al Rey, de Tlaximoroa en Michoacán. 10 de Sept. 1554.'

The laws of the Indies provided a means by which aggrieved persons might bring charges against officials, in the *residencia*, the inquiry to which every servant of the Crown was required to submit, upon relinquishing any office. Often the *residencia* was purely formal, being conducted by a successor who proposed to practise the same abuses as the outgoing official; often, again, the only result might be a fine, which the offender could pay out of the more or less legitimate perquisites of his office. A special judge, however, might be appointed to hold a *residencia*, and if the outgoing official had been marked down by the authorities in Spain for severe treatment, or if he had offended powerful interests in his district, his *residencia* might become a terrible ordeal. Some of the most famous conquerors—Nuño de Guzmán, for instance, and the gallant Montejo in Yucatán—had been utterly broken by their *residencias*. Lebrón and Contreras had offended powerful interests, and complaints about the whole conduct of the audiencia had been pouring into Spain since its foundation. Accordingly in February 1556, upon receiving a request from de la Marcha, for permission to retire from office and return to Spain, the Council of the Indies issued a commission to the Licentiate Pedro Morones to take de la Marcha's place as *oidor alcalde mayor* at Compostela, to conduct de la Marcha's *residencia*, and to hold an inquiry (*pesquisa secreta*) into the conduct of all the *oidores alcaldes mayores* since their appointment.[1] Ninety days were allotted for the collection of evidence and the hearing of complaints. The justices were to be suspended from office until their cases had been considered by the council, unless Morones saw fit to recommend any of them for reinstatement. During the period of suspension, Morones was to carry out their duties, allowing those dissatisfied with his decisions to appeal to Mexico.

Morones represented a common type of swashbuckling, hard-swearing colonial lawyer, an Indian-baiter and a would-be *conquistador*. His principal object in going to New Galicia was to organise an expedition to Chiametla and the north for, like so many of his contemporaries, he was attracted by tales of fabulous cities to the north of the settled regions of New Galicia. He had been *fiscal* to the audiencia of Mexico, until promoted to the rank of *oidor* in 1555, the year before his appointment to New Galicia.

---

[1] *A.G.I.* Auda. de Guadalajara 230, Z 1, fol. 14 verso. Morones described himself as a 'Doctor', but in the official decrees he is 'Licentiate'.

On his new commission, no doubt after consultation with his colleagues in Mexico, he placed two interpretations for which his instructions contained no warrant: the first, that his jurisdiction included the *visitas* conducted in New Spain under the viceroy's mandate; the second, that his real duty was to break Contreras and Lebrón de Quiñones. De la Marcha and Oseguera received scant attention. Of de la Marcha, Morones later reported that, as he had already retired, no case had been brought against him— an extremely frank confession of neglect of his duties by a *juez de residencia*. Oseguera, suspended from office with the others upon Morones's arrival in Compostela towards the end of 1556, was convicted of receiving gifts from litigants, fined, and after due recommendation, reinstated in his post.[1]

In the case of Lebrón, investigations were delayed by a dispute over procedure. Morones appointed a *vecino* of Guadalajara, Sancho de Cañego, to conduct an inquiry in Colima, concerning Lebrón's conduct there; Lebrón protested that Cañego was a personal enemy and that if the evidence of the inhabitants of Colima were relevant to the *pesquisa*, it should be demanded from the justices there by the ordinary writ *receptoria*, issued by authority of the audiencia. Morones refused to adopt this procedure, but offered to send, instead of Cañego, one of the members of the town council of Compostela—a body which entertained no friendly feelings towards Lebrón;[2] this offer was naturally refused, and Cañego departed for Colima, with a commission from Morones. Arrived there, however, he was arrested by the viceroy's agents, upon the charge of attempting to set up an illegal jurisdiction in New Spain. Morones, later, experienced some difficulty in securing his release; meanwhile, the prosecution was compelled to rely upon the evidence of inhabitants of New Galicia, and though many colonists testified readily enough against Lebrón and Contreras, the Indians showed great reluctance to do so. The reluctance was attributed to fear of Lebrón's vengeance; Morones himself stated that he had ordered repeated floggings as a means of extracting

[1] *A.G.I.* Auda. de Guadalajara 51: 'Dr Morones al Rey, sobre la visita de la Nueva Galicia. 17 de Agosto 1557.'

[2] Cf. *A.G.I.* Auda. de Guadalajara 51: 'Regimiento de Compostela al Rey. 28 de Julio 1557.' A hearty endorsement of Morones's actions, with fulsome reference to the deserving colonists who had been oppressed by the *oidores alcaldes mayores*. A plea for the abolition of the audiencia, the appointment of a governor from among the colonists, and the restoration of personal forced labour in the *encomienda*.

evidence from Indian witnesses, but that even this failed to overcome their fear of Lebrón; the Indians so beaten contradicted themselves each time they spoke.[1] Despite the loyalty shown to them by 'persons of little credit', the *juez pesquisidor* succeeded in drawing up a case against the two *oidores* within the allotted ninety days and, as a result of his findings, sentenced them both to deprivation of office and payment of very heavy fines. Contreras paid his fine; Lebrón failed to do so, having (it was alleged) placed the proceeds of eight years of extortion under the protection of the monasteries. He was duly imprisoned, and a fraction of his supposed debt to the king paid off by the forced sale of his clothes and other personal effects and of his small but treasured library. Both sentences were endorsed by the audiencia of Mexico, and both victims appealed to the Council of the Indies.

The charges brought against Lebrón by Morones were as vague as they were venomous. He was 'a bad Christian...a slanderer of honest men...vicious and revengeful...totally devoid of education and knowledge of law...unfitted for judicial office'. Of his moral character, Morones wrote: 'The notorious looseness of his life, and his disgraceful relations with married women, made so unpleasant a story that I forbade the witnesses to make specific statements, for fear of scandal.' Some definite charges were made, however. Lebrón was alleged to have seduced the wife of one Alonso López, *vecino* of Compostela; and Contreras to have ravished the same López's daughter; both were suspected of complicity in poisoning the licentiate Villagar, *alcalde ordinario* of Compostela. The evidence cited in support of these charges was so flimsy that the judges of the Council of the Indies, when the case came before them, dismissed the charges summarily. The remaining counts consisted of unsupported accusations of cruelty practised against the Indians, and seduction of Indian women; assertions of favouritism in dealing with *encomiendas*; a supremely ridiculous statement that Lebrón, during his *visita*, had spent most of his time at fiestas and bullfights; and the charge of converting to their own use the fines imposed by both *oidores* in cases tried on *visita*.

It may have been true that the treasury ledgers of New Galicia contained no entries of money paid in by the *visitadores*; but as the accounts had not been audited for twelve years, and as the treasurer of the time was convicted shortly afterwards of embezzling

---

[1] *A.G.I.* Auda. de Guadalajara 51: 'Morones al Rey. 17 de Agosto 1557.'

large sums from the royal revenue,[1] no satisfactory evidence could be produced against Lebrón and Contreras on that score. The charge resulted only in a decree forbidding any official of the audiencia to act as 'depositario de penas de cámara'.[2]

The charges against Lebrón were amply refuted by the detailed clarity of his own reports and by the testimony of Velasco and of the missionaries. The Franciscans of Guadalajara supported Lebrón as far as they could, and wrote an emphatic joint letter to the king, in which they proclaimed that

> the remedy for all these troubles...is clear and will cost your Majesty very little: the licentiate Lebrón de Quiñones...has been like a lily among thorns (*como lirio entre espinas*), a thoughtful man, devout, honest, stern and zealous for justice; he punished the injuries committed against the poor and against the helpless Indians...and all who knew him well were inspired by his noble example;...for these reasons we beseech your Majesty to appoint him governor of this kingdom of Galicia, because the present audiencia is useless.[3]

Opinions about Contreras were more conflicting. He had been severely criticised by the friars for his hasty temper and his disorderly life, and his learning and legal attainments were often questioned. The general nature of the evidence indicates, however, that he too had been arrested principally because he had offended powerful interests, though he was less uncompromising than his colleague, and succeeded eventually in making his peace.

Audiencia rule had indeed broken down. Lebrón, despairing of justice in Compostela, took the law into his own hands in the summer of 1557, broke prison, and fled to Mexico, where he was hospitably entertained in his distress by the Franciscans, and protected from molestation by the favour of the viceroy. Velasco still befriended Lebrón, and though he had no power to reverse Morones's decisions, he offered the suspended *oidor* another commission, for a *visita* in Oaxaca, to occupy the time during which his case was awaiting review;[4] but Lebrón refused to undertake further judicial work until he had been cleared and reinstated in office. In January 1558 he wrote a letter to the king, begging

---

[1] *A.G.I.* Auda. de Guadalajara 230, Z 1, fol. 75 verso: 'Carta dirigida a la real audiencia, acerca de la cuenta que acabóse de tomar. 18 de Enero, 1562.'

[2] Ibid. fol. 102. 23 de Marzo 1562.

[3] Orozco y Jiménez, *Colección*, vol. v, p. 123: 'Los frailes definidores de la orden de S. Francisco a S.M. 20 de Mayo 1557.'

[4] *A.G.I.* Patronato 181, R⁰. 33.

permission to return to Spain to answer in person for his conduct, and complaining of the personal animus displayed against him, the refusal of the judge to furnish him with a list of the charges, and the general conduct of the trial.

> Dr. Morones has sought to prove my guilt by bribing or intimidating reluctant witnesses, by torturing my servants until they testified according to his instructions, and by allying himself with those who were my confessed enemies, because I had formerly executed your Majesty's justice upon them. . . . It is not right that a man of quality, the son of a faithful servant of your Majesty, and one who has himself sought with all his power to serve, should be treated worse than a common malefactor, and slandered and dishonoured by a partial judge.[1]

Lebrón followed up this letter by soliciting the help and influence of the one man in all Spain who had least love for colonial officialdom—the veteran 'apostle of the Indians', Fray Bartolomé de las Casas.[2] Fray Bartolomé had taken a prominent part in framing the New Laws, as Lebrón had in enforcing them, and his voice still carried great weight in Indian affairs. Whether by his influence or not, Lebrón obtained his licence to return to Spain, and a writ issued by the Council of the Indies of 1560 ordered the audiencia of Mexico to forward all papers relating to the case, without informing or consulting Morones.[3]

Lebrón's presence, and possibly Fray Bartolomé's influence, secured a quicker trial than was usual in such cases. In November 1561 he was acquitted of all the charges brought against him, and reinstated in the audiencia of New Galicia as senior *oidor*.[4] He was to receive his salary for the period of his suspension, and an advance of 300 ducats to cover the cost of his journey. The following January, he received the necessary licences—licence to take money out of Spain; licence for the weapons needed by his household; licence for his four servants (one a negro brought from New Galicia); and licence for his nephew, aged sixteen, to accompany him.[5] He set sail soon afterwards, but death overtook him

[1] *A.G.I.* Auda. de Guadalajara 51: Lic. Lebrón de Quiñones al Rey. 22 de Enero 1558.'
[2] *D.I.I.* vol. vii, p. 250: 'Carta del Lic. Lebrón de Quiñones a Fray Bartolomé de las Casas. 16 de Junio 1558' (the date is given erroneously in the published collection as 1568).
[3] *A.G.I.* Auda. de Guadalajara 230, Z 1, fol. 49. 8 de Julio 1560.
[4] Ibid. fol. 71. 23 de Nov. 1561.
[5] Ibid. fol. 73 verso. 10 de Enero 1562.

before he reached his post—no doubt to the relief of many in New Galicia. He was thus spared the ordeal of working with Morones as his colleague; his reinstatement in the same audiencia as his late judge was altogether characteristic of the slow, well-intentioned, utterly impersonal working of Spanish justice—that justice which he had served so well.[1]

Contreras had been living in Mexico all this time, and his case came up for review later than Lebrón's. In 1562 he too was acquitted, except upon one charge, that of accepting gifts from litigants; the treasury officials of New Galicia were ordered to refund the fines which he had paid.[2] Four years later he was again appointed to New Galicia as senior *oidor*, with three colleagues— the licentiates Alarcón (appointed in 1560), Mendiola (in 1564) and Orozco (in 1565). Under their joint rule the audiencia re-established its authority and reverted to a modified form of the Indian policy of Lebrón de Quiñones. Prosecutions under the Indian laws again figured in the proceedings of the court[3] and the slow process of incorporating *encomiendas* in the Crown was resumed, softened by arrangements for the paying of a compensatory pension over a term of years to the heirs of the *encomendero*.[4]

A minor mystery arose from the *residencia* in 1559, in the issue of a decree granting permission to de la Marcha to return to New Galicia, if he so desired, as the colleague of Morones and Oseguera.[5] The ground for this reinstatement was said to be a petition from de la Marcha, complaining that his original letter of resignation had been a forgery compiled by an enemy who wished to be rid of him. The petition itself was more likely to have been a forgery; it was improbable that a judge retired from the New Galicia service would wish to return there—Alarcón, appointed to succeed de la Marcha, so much disliked the prospect that he allowed three years to elapse before taking up his duties. The mystery was never

[1] The space devoted to this attempt to justify Lebrón de Quiñones might seem excessive, were it not for the fact that the historians of that part of Mexico, following Tello, have all accepted the charges brought by Morones at their face value. Tello, *Crónica miscelánea*, cap. CLXXXII; H. H. Bancroft, *History of the Pacific States*, vol. v, p. 548; J. Ll. Mecham, *Francisco de Ibarra*, p. 93.

[2] *A.G.I.* Auda. de Guadalajara 230, Z 1, fol. 120. Diciembre 1562.

[3] See ch. VI, below.

[4] See, for example, the royal order for incorporating in the Crown the *encomienda* of Gonzalo López, printed in A. F. A. and F. R. Bandelier, *Historical Documents relating to New Mexico, New Vizcaya, and approaches thereto* (Washington, D.C.), vol. I, p. 94.

[5] *A.G.I.* Auda. de Guadalajara 230, Z 1, fol. 33. 5 de Junio 1559.

solved; neither resignation nor petition have come to light, and de la Marcha died before his decree for reinstatement could take effect. Three years later the fisc was still trying to recover from his heirs an advance of salary paid to him before his death.[1] He was long remembered by the colonists as a model judge. In a law-suit concerning the property of his daughter, who married an *enco- mendero* in New Spain, he is constantly described by witnesses as 'a grave judge, who served the king ten or twelve years in New Galicia and more than thirty in Spain, and was moreover a leading personage in New Spain, a gentleman well connected and greatly respected by all'.[2]

Even without de la Marcha, the cause of the Indians had received a serious setback in the interval between 1557 and 1563. Throughout the whole viceroyalty, indeed, the policy of Velasco was weakened at this time through the growth of the faction of Martín Cortés, supported in the viceroy's last years by the over-weaning *visitador* Valderrama, whom Torquemada was to brand as the 'Afligidor de los Indios'. In New Galicia Morones, the unofficial president of the audiencia, obstructed the viceroy's policy, while occupying himself mainly with the proposed conquest of Chiametla, and with attempts to secure a grant for that purpose from the royal chest. It was a rule of fiscal policy that intending *conquistadores* should finance their expeditions themselves. Morones endeavoured to soften this unpopular request by suggesting ways of increasing the royal revenue, such as raising the scale of Indian tributes, taxing each dependent village separately instead of each group of villages under a *cabecera*, and adding to the number of saleable offices.[3] He secured as a result a decree permitting him to 'adjust' tributes, provided that no injustice were done;[4] a few extra notaries' practices (*escribanías*), were created and offered for sale, but found no purchasers—fortunately for the Indians; for the tag-rag and bob-tail of the legal profession lived largely by inciting Indians to expensive litigation.[5] No grant was forthcoming for Morones's conquest, nor did a policy of nepotism enable him to plunder the royal chest, for the Council of the Indies refused to

[1] *A.G.I.* Auda. de Guadalajara 230, Z 1, fol. 89 verso. 11 de Feb. 1562.
[2] Archivo General de la Nación, Mexico, D.F.: 'Ramo de Civil, tit.430,fol. 1(1580).'
[3] *A.G.I.* Auda. de Guadalajara 51: 'Morones al Rey, 28 de Septiembre 1557. 4 de Enero 1561,' etc.
[4] *A.G.I.* Auda. de Guadalajara 230, Z 1, fol. 101. 23 de Marzo 1562.
[5] See ch. VIII, below.

confirm his action in appointing his brother to the post of auditor (*contador*) and rebuked him for creating unnecessary offices with excessive salaries[1] and for conniving at carelessness in remitting *bienes de difuntos*—the property of men who died in the colonies—to their heirs in Spain.[2] The *oidores*, in future, were to appoint deserving 'old conquerors' and settlers, not their own friends and relatives, to lucrative offices.[3]

Oseguera, during the first three years of Morones's administration, was fully occupied with the *cuenta* of the royal treasury officials, which had not been taken since the *visita* of Tejada in 1544, and which presented an almost impossible task. Pedro Gómez de Contreras, the treasurer, failed to account for 14,000 *pesos* out of a total of 34,000.[4] He asked, and received (much to the disgust of the Council of the Indies) two years' grace in which to produce that sum, but died before he could do so, leaving to his colleagues, under Oseguera's supervision, the task of recovering numerous unauthorised payments which he had made to individuals.[5] Many of the treasurer's friends had been living almost entirely upon the tributes in kind brought in by the Indians of the Crown *pueblos*. Oseguera succeeded eventually in reducing the accounts to order; his report elicited a series of instructions to the *oidores*, to exercise more careful supervision, to take the *cuenta* fully every year, and to attend in person at the sale of tribute produce from the Crown *pueblos*.[6]

The one constructive act of the Morones-Oseguera régime was to induce the king at last to authorise the removal of the audiencia from Compostela to Guadalajara.[7] This was a period of great building activity in Guadalajara. In 1560, for instance, at the petition of the city council, the audiencia was ordered to arrange for the building of a bridge over the Río Grande.[8] The necessary labourers were to be supplied by a *repartimiento* in the neighbouring

[1] *A.G.I.* Auda. de Guadalajara 230, Z 1, fol. 76.
[2] Ibid. fol. 102.
[3] Ibid. fols. 94, 96. Morones was accused of appointing his servants as *tenientes de corregidores*, instead of paying them wages.
[4] Ibid. fol. 75 verso. 18 de Enero 1562. Guadalajara 51 : 'Morones al Rey. 8 de Oct. 1559.'
[5] Ibid. fols. 77, 104—a series of royal orders for the recovery of such unauthorised payments (1562).
[6] Ibid. fol. 77. 18 de Enero 1562.
[7] Orozco y Jiménez, *Colección*, vol. 1, p. 261.
[8] *A.G.I.* Auda. de Guadalajara 230, Z 1, fol. 35 verso. 7 de Febrero 1560.

Indian villages at the direction of the audiencia; a quarter of the cost would be borne by the royal chest, provided that the grant made did not exceed 400 *pesos*; the rest of the cost was to be divided by the audiencia among those who would benefit by the bridge, with the proviso that no Indian village should contribute both money and labour. Similar orders were issued in 1561, concerning work on the new cathedral, which was not completed, however, until after 1600.[1] A vexatious lawsuit between the audiencia and the landlord of the temporary premises which it occupied upon its arrival at Guadalajara, led to a hurried appropriation for the building or purchase of a suitable 'royal house', as the alternative to a constitutional conflict with the audiencia of Mexico, to whom the landlord appealed.[2] The viceregal audiencia received a sharp rebuke from Spain, and an order not to meddle in the internal affairs of New Galicia, while the subordinate court eventually secured a home worthy of its dignity.

The removal of the audiencia from Compostela not only stimulated activity in Guadalajara, but produced a considerable increase of litigation.[3] The inhabitants of the mining settlements now found it convenient to appeal to the local audiencia, instead of to Mexico, especially since Morones proved more accommodating than the former *oidores* in matters involving Indian labour. The first-instance jurisdiction of the audiencia, within a radius of twelve leagues from Guadalajara, also produced much more work for the court, than it had done in the neighbourhood of Compostela. Disputes concerning gardens and building sites in the neighbourhood of the city were especially frequent at this time, and a tendency of the audiencia to interfere in matters of civic government had to be checked by royal decrees.[4]

The establishment of the court in the natural administrative centre of its district produced a fresh desire on the part of the *oidores* to extend the boundaries of their jurisdiction. Morones's interest in conquest and expansion, and the licences which he had secured, proved an uncomfortable legacy, which brought the

[1] J. Iguíniz, *Biblioteca Histórica Jalisciense*. The existing Baroque structure replaced an adobe building with a thatch roof, described in 1560 as 'beyond repair'.

[2] *A.G.I.* Auda. de Guadalajara 51: 'Audiencia al Rey 2 de Feb. 1562.' (Marginal notes indicate approval of *oidores*' actions in the matter of the royal house.)

[3] Ibid.

[4] *A.G.I.* Auda. de Guadalajara 230, Z 1, fol. 38. 7 de Feb. 1560; fol. 143 verso. 2 de Jun. 1563.

audiencia into conflict with the most energetic of the later *conquistadores*—Francisco de Ibarra. The lawyer turned *conquistador*, after the example set by Nuño de Guzmán, was still a familiar and a highly unpopular figure upon the northern frontier. With such men upon the Bench, justice inevitably suffered. The events of the decade from 1562 to 1572 were to draw a new and much needed distinction between the functions of the conqueror and those of the judge.

CHAPTER IV

THE AUDIENCIA AND THE CONQUISTADORES

The dream of the golden cities of Cíbola was never far from the minds of Spaniards in sixteenth-century New Spain. The failure of the Coronado expedition and the distraction of the Mixton war for a time damped the ardour of intending explorers, but exaggerated descriptions of the *pueblos* of the Río Grande del Norte continued to filter through to the Spanish settlements, and every viceroy of New Spain held as his dearest ambition the conquest of New Mexico by Spanish arms. Adventurers, knowing little of the wide deserts of northern Mexico, clung to their belief in prosperous kingdoms beyond; missionaries, though they frequently opposed the dispatch of secular expeditions, themselves longed for opportunities to preach to the inhabitants of the cities of the north.

The settlements of New Galicia—Guadalajara, Culiacán, Zacatecas—were the natural starting-points for such projects. The *oidores alcaldes mayores* appointed in 1548 quickly fell under the spell of popular rumour, and one of their first official undertakings was the organisation of an exploring expedition under the leadership of Ginés Vázquez Mercado, a *vecino* of Guadalajara, to search for a silver mountain which Indian legend placed to the north of the settled areas. Mercado's report,[1] addressed to de la Marcha as 'president', told the story of a fruitless expedition. He marched north from Guadalajara, meeting little resistance, but pausing from time to time to give military aid to settled villages against incursions from the mountain Indians; passed the future sites of Jacotlán, Chalchihuites, San Martín, and Sombrerete—all destined to become mining towns in later years—and finally reached the valley in which the city of Durango now stands. Here he found, indeed, a wonderful shining mountain; which proved to be, not silver, but solid iron ore. This hill, which rises to a height of 600 feet above the surrounding level, is called the Cerro de Mercado to this day; it marks the limit of Mercado's exploration. He returned to Guadalajara in utter dejection, his army mutinous and disorganised. The most noteworthy fact about his expedition was that, in accordance with the strict orders of the audiencia, he took

[1] *A.G.I.* Patronato 181, R⁰. 14 (1552).

with him an abundance of livestock for the support of his forces. Being relieved of the necessity of extorting supplies from the Indians, he was able to maintain comparatively friendly relations with the peoples through whose territory he passed. He failed, however, to make any permanent settlement.

The audiencia learned its lesson from Mercado's failure, and for a time abandoned its direct interest in exploration and conquest, more especially since royal orders, inspired by agitation of the Franciscan Order at Court, forbade future expeditions to be undertaken without express royal licence.[1] Private exploration continued, however, and during the 1550's expeditions radiating from Zacatecas established numerous settlements along the northern frontier—San Martín, Aviño, Sombrerete, Ranchos, Chalchihuites, and others—which came to be included in the kingdom of New Galicia, since the audiencia lost no time in appointing *alcaldes mayores*, to represent its authority in the newly conquered districts. The existence of these frontier camps was extremely precarious. Each new find drew population away from previous settlements, and camps so weakened fell an easy prey to Indian raids. The natives of the Zacatecas mountains lacked all but the most rudimentary culture; the Zacatecos built rude huts of wood or adobe similar to the hogans of the modern Navajo, but had no agriculture; the cannibal Guachichiles lacked even a fixed dwelling, lived upon wild plants, and ate the flesh of captives taken in their raiding expeditions to the valleys. All the mountain peoples were strong and made good porters, but they never reconciled themselves to Spanish rule, as the settled village-dwellers did, and their savage hostility made them extremely dangerous neighbours. In the mines of Mazapil—to take one instance among many—the population increased to a hundred and fifty householders within a year of the discovery of silver deposits; three years later, the superior attraction of other sites drew away all but forty, and these were almost wiped out in a Zacateco raid. Even the main route between Zacatecas and Guadalajara, along which provisions for the mines and silver for the treasure fleets had to travel, was never safe. The establishment of a unified command for the pacification of the northern

[1] Cf. *Cartas de Indias*, pp. 103–18. P. Valencia and others to the Emperor, 8 May 1552, cited by H. H. Bancroft, *Pacific States*, vol. v, p. 550. The heads of the Order complained of the cruelties inflicted upon the natives by unauthorised military explorers, and added that it would be better to abandon all further attempts at conversion, than to make the spreading of the Gospel a pretext for local tyranny.

frontier became a matter of vital interest for the whole of New Spain.

The audiencia of New Galicia never effectively assumed such a command. For ten years after the failure of Mercado, the *oidores* took no direct interest in exploration, and when Pedro Morones came to revive the exploring spirit, he turned his attention to the coastal provinces rather than the mountains of Zacatecas. Morones was convinced—upon rather flimsy grounds—that the province of Chiametla contained gold mines, and that through it lay the route to the fabulous kingdom of Cíbola. In addition, Chiametla had a strategic importance of its own. Nuño de Guzmán had granted *encomiendas* there, and had founded the town of San Miguel de Culiacán farther north; Culiacán (central Sinaloa) had enjoyed a modest prosperity, but Chiametla, for a variety of reasons—the unhealthy climate, the poverty of the *encomiendas*, the sullen hostility of the natives and the reports of gold mines in Peru—had been deserted by its Spanish settlers shortly after Nuño's return south. Culiacán, therefore, was cut off from the rest of New Galicia; neither the report of the *visitador* de la Marcha, nor the *cuenta* of 1558, made any mention of the province; no tributes found their way to the royal chest, and no succour, in case of danger, could reach Culiacán in time. The interests of the Crown and the audiencia alike demanded that Culiacán should be connected with Compostela by a permanent chain of settlements. Morones accordingly received in 1560 a commission[1] to undertake the conquest of Chiametla, at his own expense, and with the wise proviso that not more than one-fifth of the *vecinos* of any Spanish settlement might join the expedition.

The moment was most inopportune for such a project. The audiencia was busy settling into new quarters in Guadalajara, and handling the increased litigation which followed the move. The court was short-handed, and its governmental authority had been greatly weakened by recent events. Morones, having served the turn of the *encomenderos* and mine-owners in ridding them of Lebrón de Quiñones, proved himself quite unable to maintain order among them. His popularity lasted so long as he was their tool; it was clear that the province would not support him in a career of conquest. An armed visit which he paid to Xocotlán with the intention of enforcing his authority there, resulted merely in driving the wilder

[1] *A.G.I.* Auda. de Guadalajara 230, Z 1, fol. 38. 11 de Feb. 1560.

spirits out to Zacatecas to join the following of Francisco de Ibarra.[1]

The support of the viceroy, which was essential for any extensive and permanent conquest, had been thoroughly alienated by the conduct of the *residencia*, by Morones's disregard of the official Indian policy, and by his incompetence. In the summer of 1561, after repeated complaints of the failure of the audiencia to maintain order in the mines and frontier posts of New Galicia, Velasco himself dispatched a judicial commission to Guanajuato—one of the most important and most disorderly settlements—and removed from office Rodrigo de Frías, the incompetent and corrupt *alcalde mayor* of Comanja, near-by. Frías was a *vecino* of Guadalajara, and the *cabildo* of that city promptly took up his cause, urging the audiencia to protest to the king against the illegal extension of the viceregal authority. A case was prepared accordingly[2] which established that the boundary of New Galicia ran from Querétaro (granted in *encomienda* by Nuño de Guzmán) to the river fork at the 'paso de Nuestra Señora' (where Nuño had first crossed the Lerma) and thence downstream to Lake Chapala. Guanajuato and Comanja were both well to the north of this line, and undoubtedly belonged to the jurisdiction and government of New Galicia. The viceroy did not press his case; he was old and ailing, was preoccupied with the faction of Martín Cortés and his *encomendero* associates, and was awaiting the arrival of a more than usually inopportune royal *visitador* (Valderrama). The question of Guanajuato was allowed to drop, therefore, until taken up thirteen years later by the audiencia of New Spain.[3] The quarrel indicated that Velasco, if he could avoid doing so, would not entrust any extension of territory to Morones.

About the same time a much more serious problem arose, in the form of a widespread Indian outbreak which had been brewing ever since the departure of Lebrón de Quiñones. The Guachichiles and Zacatecos, contrary to their casual custom of guerrilla warfare, succeeded in forming a powerful, though short-lived, league against

[1] A. Tello, *Crónica Miscelánea*, cap. clxxxii.

[2] *A.G.I.* Patronato 182, R⁰. 3, 1561: 'Información recibida de la ciudad de Guadalajara del Nuevo Reino de Galicia...por la que se acredita que aquel Nuevo Reino tiene por límites con la Nueva España el Río Grande...hasta el pueblo de Querétaro... cuyos límites no sean desmembrados y agregados al virreinato de México.' Part of this *expediente* is printed in Orozco y Jiménez, *Colección*, vol. v, p. 27.

[3] *A.G.I.* Patronato 182, R⁰. 45: 'Expediente...sobre la observancia de límites entre las dos audiencias de Nueva España y Nueva Galicia, y sobre que las minas de Guanajuato y Comanja estén sujetos a la N. España. 1574.'

the Spaniards;[1] some of the settled Caxcane *pueblos*, exasperated by the increase of slave-raiding and other abuses since the *residencia*, joined the league, and hostilities spread westward to the coast until the whole northern frontier was in an uproar and even in Chiametla the Indians took up arms. Zacatecas and San Martín were cut off for some weeks from supplies and from all communication with other Spanish settlements. The audiencia commissioned one Pedro de Ahumada to raise a force against the Indians; for eight months Ahumada patrolled the mountains west and north of Zacatecas, without ever coming to grips with his elusive foe. Apart from burning a number of 'Chichimeca' villages, his expedition achieved no lasting result, and proved a source of financial embarrassment to the audiencia, since the local treasury officials refused to release funds to pay Ahumada and his men, without express order. Ahumada had to apply to Spain for a royal decree commanding the viceroy to investigate his claim and to arrange for his expenses to be paid.[2] These and similar episodes made it clear that more thorough and permanent measures were needed to restore order on the frontier, and that responsibility would rest ultimately with the viceroy.

Morones, meanwhile, still cherished his design upon Chiametla in spite of all difficulties. In 1561 he complained to the king that his means were insufficient to cover the cost of the expedition, and demanded a grant from the royal chest, a licence to allot *encomiendas*, and permission to recruit Indians for forced labour in the mines, or to import negroes.[3] None of these requests was granted, and towards the end of 1563 Morones died. His colleagues, Oseguera and Alarcón, at once arrogated to themselves the rights which Morones had held but never exercised. At this point the audiencia for the first time came into serious conflict with the 'phoenix of the *conquistadores*', then at the height of his power.[4]

---

[1] *A.G.I.* Patronato 182, R⁰. 4: 'Relación hecha por Pedro de Ahumada, por orden del virrey de Nueva España, Don Luis de Velasco, sobre la rebelión de los Indios Zacatecos y Guachichiles, y providencias tomadas para su sosiego, 1563.' Part of this report is printed in Orozco y Jiménez, *Colección*, vol. v, p. 102.

[2] A. F. A. and F. R. Bandelier, *Historical Documents relating to New Mexico, Nueva Vizcaya, and approaches thereto* (Washington, D.C., 1923), vol. i, p. 90: 'Real Cédula... relativa a los gastos de Pedro de Ahumada Samano en la jornada contra los Indios Zacatecos y Guachichiles. 17 de Oct. 1562.'

[3] *A.G.I.* Auda. de Guadalajara 51: 'Morones al Rey. 2 de Enero 1561.'

[4] For a detailed study of Ibarra's career, cf. J. Ll. Mecham, *Francisco de Ibarra and the founding of Nueva Vizcaya* (Duke Univ. Press, 1928).

Francisco de Ibarra was the nephew of Diego de Ibarra, son-in-law of Luis de Velasco and one of the four discoverers of Zacatecas. Since coming to Zacatecas, Diego had been crippled in an accident and so debarred from further active exploration, but his fortune and his influence with the viceroy were from the first at the service of his adventurous nephew. In 1550 Francisco entered the vice-regal court as a page. Four years later he secured a viceregal commission to explore the northern frontier region, and moved to Zacatecas, where he became the leader of a wild crew of frontiersmen, mostly of Basque origin, whose turbulence was even then troubling the authority of the audiencia. Francisco's fame as an explorer soon eclipsed that of Cristóbal de Oñate himself; he claimed in his 'información de méritos y servicios'[1] to have been the original founder of San Martín, Fresnillo, Sombrerete, Nieves, and many other settlements, all of which were duly included in the jurisdiction of the audiencia and placed under an *alcalde mayor* stationed at San Martín.[2] These exploits received public recognition in 1562 at the height of the Indian crisis, when the viceroy, seeking a suitable man to take military command of the whole frontier region, selected Ibarra, and conferred upon him the title of Governor of New Vizcaya, including 'Copalá' and all uninhabited provinces which he might discover 'beyond Aviño and San Martín'.[3] His conquests were to be at his own expense—the governorship of New Vizcaya did not become a salaried office until 1574—and he was to observe an elaborate set of instructions for maintaining friendly relations with those natives who might receive him in peace.

The authority of the audiencia had already extended beyond San Martín. Early in the year of Ibarra's commission, the *alcalde mayor* of San Martín, Diego García de Colio, had appointed officials in the advanced mission settlement of Nombre de Dios, founded by wandering friars four years before. Colio was a tough old *conquistador*, who had been at the taking of Mexico and had served subsequently in Guatemala, and under Francisco Cortés in Chimalhuacán.[4] He was a *vecino* of Guadalajara, a person of

[1] *D.I.I.* vol. xiv, p. 463: 'Información...de Francisco de Ibarra.'
[2] H. H. Bancroft, *Pacific States*, vol. v, p. 597.
[3] *A.G.I.* Auda. de Guadalajara 103-3-1: 'Reales órdenes dirigidas a las autoridades del distrito. Francisco de Ibarra—título, 1562.'
[4] *A.G.I.* Patronato 1-3-10: 'Información de los méritos y servicios de Diego de Colio 1560.'

89

considerable social influence in New Galicia, and according to Tello one of the few Spaniards who endeavoured to secure a fair hearing for Lebrón de Quiñones and his colleagues in 1556.[1] His worth had not passed unnoticed; in 1562 a royal letter of favour addressed to the audiencia had recommended him for further office and authorised the enlargement of his *encomienda*.[2] Throughout his life he remained staunchly loyal to the king and the king's representatives in the audiencia; accordingly, when Ibarra, passing through San Martín, demanded recognition of his authority over Nombre de Dios as part of New Vizcaya, Colio refused. An angry scene ensued, in which Colio was injured. Ibarra went on to Nombre de Dios with his men, expelled Colio's officials, and formally 'founded' the place a second time.[3] After his departure, Colio re-established the jurisdiction of the audiencia in the disputed village, and sent an angry letter of complaint to the king—the first broadside in a long wordy battle.[4]

Meanwhile, Ibarra's kingdom was taking shape. By the end of 1563 he had set up his capital at Guadiana (modern Durango), to-day a flourishing city and a State capital; encouraged by the death of Pedro Morones in Guadalajara, he then embarked upon the most ambitious of all his plans—the extension of his territory to the sea. Operating from the lonely settlement of San Miguel de Culiacán, where he was enthusiastically welcomed by the *alcalde mayor* and the *vecinos*, he quickly brought under his sway the deserted area of Chiametla, between the Cañas and Mazatlán rivers, founded the town of San Sebastián and granted the Indians of that region in *encomienda* to his followers. The *oidores* of Guadalajara at once protested; but the *jueces de comisión* whom they dispatched to the spot were powerless to dislodge Ibarra; the viceregal throne was vacant, owing to the death of Luis de Velasco in 1564; no favourable decision could be expected from the audiencia of Mexico. The *oidores* could only forward their complaints to the

[1] Tello, *Crónica miscelánea*, cap. clxxxii.

[2] *A.G.I.* Auda. de Guadalajara 230, Z 1, fol. 74. 10 de Enero 1562. Colio's *encomienda* of Yscatlán yielded an annual tribute of 100 silver *pesos*, 50 *fanegas* of maize, and 80 chickens, which was deemed insufficient for the support of his household.

[3] Tello, *Crónica miscelánea*, caps. clxxxviii, cxci. Tello is unreliable over dates. Characteristically, he explains everything by saying that Ibarra 'era Vizcaino, en quien no hay más razón que quiero o no quiero, porque sí o porque no!'

[4] *A.G.I.* Auda. de Guadalajara 51: 'Diego de Colio al Rey 1563.'

king[1] and hope that the new viceroy, when he arrived, would support their case.

The audiencia made three distinct claims; the first that Nombre de Dios had been effectively occupied by its agents before the issue of Ibarra's commission; the second, that both Culiacán and Chiametla belonged to New Galicia, having been discovered by Nuño de Guzmán and subsequently granted by royal licence to Pedro Morones; the third that although the administration of New Vizcaya lay in the hands of the new governor, judicial appeals from the whole area should be heard in the audiencia of Guadala-jara, not in that of Mexico.

This third contention represented fairly the normal practice in assigning jurisdiction over newly conquered territory. The principle implied in the *oidores'* argument received legislative recognition ten years later in the *Ordenanzas sobre descubrimientos* of 1573.[2] This celebrated and remarkably humane code, which was to regulate the terms of all future Spanish conquests, was itself a compilation of earlier customs and decrees. The sixty-ninth ordinance of the code laid down that conquerors holding the title of *adelantado* should be free of all control except that of the Council of the Indies; the eighty-eighth, that all other conquerors must allow appeals from their decisions to be carried to the nearest audiencia.[3] Ibarra was not an *adelantado*; but he affected to recognise only one jurisdiction, that of the viceroy and the audiencia of Mexico. New Vizcaya, under such conditions, afforded a convenient asylum for fugitives from justice in New Galicia; and the privilege secured by Ibarra in his commission, that silver mines in New Vizcaya should for a time pay only one-twentieth of their gains to the royal chest,

---

[1] *A.G.I.* Auda. de Guadalajara 51 : 'Audiencia de la Galicia al Rey, 18 de Abril 1563; 31 de Enero 1564; 16 de Febrero 1566.'

[2] *D.I.I.* vol. XVI, p. 142. Complete text of 'Ordenanzas sobre descubrimientos, 1573'. The key to the spirit of the code is in clause XX: 'Los descubridores por mar o tierra no se empachen en guerra no conquista en ninguna manera, ni ayudar a unos Indios contra otros, ni se revuelvan en cuestiones ni contiendas con los de la tierra, por ninguna causa ni razón que sea, ni les hagan dano ni mal alguno; ni les tomen contra su voluntad cosa alguna suya, sino fuere por rescate, o dándose ellos de su voluntad.' The exploits of Legaspi in the Philippines and of Urdiñola in Chihuahua, both almost bloodless conquests, represented most closely the Spanish notion of 'ideal' imperial expansion.

[3] Cf. also Clause LXXXVII: 'Descubrimiento, población y pacificación con título de adelantado solamente se dé y conceda de las provincias que no confinan con distrito de provincia de virrey o audiencia...para donde se pueda tener recurso por vía de apelación y agravio.'

was a standing inducement for inhabitants of New Galicia to leave their homes and travel north.[1]

In support of Ibarra it might be claimed—and was, indeed, emphatically claimed by the chronicler of his expeditions[2]—that he had performed a signal service to all the Spanish settlements of New Spain by pacifying the northern frontier; and that the *oidores* were inspired merely by jealousy of exploits which they could not hope to emulate. The practical claims of Ibarra were likely to appeal far more strongly to a military viceroy than were the legalistic arguments of the audiencia. The third viceroy, the Marquis of Falces, shortly after his arrival, confirmed Ibarra's commission, approved the seizure of Culiacán and Chiametla, and decreed that appeals from Ibarra's decisions, or the decisions of justices appointed by him, should be heard in Mexico.[3] The *oidores alcaldes mayores* continued to protest, and towards the end of 1567 Falces was induced to compromise, to the extent of allowing the subordinate audiencia an appellate jurisdiction in Chiametla.[4] With that the *oidores alcaldes mayores* had to content themselves until the arrival of a new viceroy.

The audiencia meanwhile had continued to exercise full authority in Nombre de Dios, including appeals and confirmation of elections, since 1563. In 1569, however, Ibarra followed up his legal victories by a second *coup d'état* in Nombre de Dios, which so enraged the *oidores* that they immediately dispatched one of their number, the licentiate Orozco, at the head of three hundred men, to expel Ibarra and his followers by force.[5] An ugly conflict was averted by the intervention of the uncle, Diego de Ibarra, at that time *alcalde mayor* of Zacatecas, who persuaded both parties to hand over the village to the direct control of the viceroy; neutral *alcaldes* were accordingly installed in Nombre de Dios. This compromise lasted until 1576, when the king appointed Juan de Ibarra to succeed his brother as governor (against the advice of the audiencia of Guadalajara) and took the occasion to include Nombre de Dios

---

[1] *A.G.I.* Auda. de Guadalajara 51: 'Audiencia de la Galicia al Rey. 18 de Abril 1563.'
[2] Baltazar de Obregón, *Historia de los Descubrimientos* (M. Cuevas, ed. Mexico, D.F., 1924), cap. XVII.
[3] *A.G.I.* Auda. de México 19: 'Falces al Rey 1567.'
[4] *A.G.I.* Patronato 17, Rº. 22. 10 de Sept. 1567.
[5] *A.G.I.* Auda. de Guadalajara 51: 'Lic. Alarcón al Rey. 10 de Abril 1570.' A spirited account of the quarrel.

in the kingdom of New Vizcaya.[1] The *oidores* were then severely blamed for allowing the intervention of Orozco seven years before. After many petitions and counter-petitions, the much disputed and quite insignificant settlement fell finally under the rule of the governor of New Vizcaya in 1611.

The great bitterness with which these disputes were conducted can only be understood in connection with contemporary events in Mexico.[2] The old viceroy Velasco died in 1564. His last years had been troubled by quarrels with Martín Cortés, Marquis of the Valley of Oajaca, the son of Hernán Cortés and heir to the conqueror's immense estates. The extent of the influence exercised by the Cortés family had long been a source of anxiety to the Crown, and in 1562 attempts were made to count the Indians of the Cortés grant, and to reduce them to the number of 23,000 allotted by Charles V. The Marquis in retaliation placed himself at the head of a faction of *encomenderos* who clamoured for changes in the Indian laws, especially for legislation permitting the entailment of *encomiendas*, and for a greater degree of local autonomy. The royal *visitador* Valderrama, who arrived in 1563, sympathised publicly with the Marquis, dismissed two of the *oidores* who were opposed to the Cortés interest, and in general treated both viceroy and audiencia with scant consideration. Upon the death of Velasco, the *encomenderos* endeavoured to prevent the audiencia assuming interregnal authority, by urging Valderrama to stay in Mexico and perform the functions of a governor. Valderrama, however, sailed for Spain in 1565. The Council of the Indies and the audiencia both remained firmly opposed to any legislative change of the type which the *encomenderos* desired, and exasperated faction began to show signs of developing into revolt. Plots and rumours of plots filled the capital. In 1566 the audiencia arrested and condemned to death the brothers Avila, for treason and conspiracy; Cortés was implicated, and stories became current of plans to make him independent sovereign of New Spain. The new viceroy, the easy-going Marquis of Falces, when he arrived in the autumn of 1566, declined to take these stories seriously and showed a tendency to exculpate the disaffected *encomenderos*. The audiencia thereupon denounced

---

[1] *A.G.I.* Indiferente General 139. 1. 2. 20 de Feb. 1576. The audiencia had recommended Hernando de Trejo, Francisco de Ibarra's lieutenant, as his successor. *A.G.I.* Auda. de Guadalajara 5: 'Audiencia al Rey. 16 de Sept. 1575.'

[2] See H. H. Bancroft, *Pacific States*, vol. v, ch. xxix.

the viceroy to the king as an accomplice in the various conspiracies, real or imaginary, to detach New Spain from the Spanish Crown, and actually persuaded the suspicious Philip II to suspend him from office. Two judicial commissioners, Muñoz and Carrillo, arrived with full powers to supersede him in October 1567. These two men were chiefly notorious for their unflagging zeal in torture and for their noisome extensions to the public gaols, necessitated by the increase in the number of political prisoners. Their reign of terror lasted only six months, during which time they tortured and banished the Marquis's half-brother[1] and executed many others. In April 1568 they were in their turn superseded by Puga and Villanueva, the two *oidores* whom Valderrama had dismissed, now acquitted and reinstated in office. Thereafter the audiencia governed in peace until the arrival of a new viceroy, political passion having apparently burned itself out. There remained in the minds of many Spaniards, however, a sullen hatred of lawyers' government. Muñoz and Carrillo had subjected distinguished colonists to treatment as cruel and arbitrary as any which the Indians had suffered at the hands of the *conquistadores*, and this contrary to law; for *hidalgos* might not lawfully be put to torture.[2] The regular audiencia had indeed governed more mildly than the special commissioners, and with more respect for legal procedure; but it had driven out a popular viceroy and had executed Spaniards of high rank whose deaths, whether deserved or not, were not forgotten or forgiven by their contemporaries.

An extravagant assertion of the arbitrary powers of the professional judges was common, therefore, to both New Spain and New Galicia in the 1560's. In New Galicia the subordinate audiencia, operating on a smaller scale, had recovered strength and assertiveness during the absence of effective viceregal authority. Though legally without any military powers, it had been forced by the emergencies of the frontier situation to supervise military activities. These undertakings, from the very nature and limitations of the court, were rarely effective; but the acquired taste for military authority had grown and had led the *oidores* to interfere factiously with the viceroy's dispositions on the frontier, to obstruct his accredited agents and even to resort to arms against a recognised military governor over a minor boundary dispute. Questions of

[1] This Cortés, also christened Martín, was the illegitimate son of Hernán Cortés and Marina.
[2] See ch. VIII, p. 161.

boundaries and conflicts of authority also continually disturbed the relations between the subordinate audiencia and the superior court. The time was ripe for the arrival of a powerful viceroy who, while recognising the valuable work of the courts, should define their powers and duties, fix geographic and constitutional boundaries between them, and put an end to military and administrative chaos in the new frontier districts.

Martín Enríquez de Almansa (a sound administrator though a treacherous enemy—it was he who trapped John Hawkins in Vera Cruz harbour) entered upon his duties as viceroy at the end of 1568. His policy, from the first, was to concentrate all administrative and military authority throughout New Spain in the hands of the viceroy or of governors acting under his orders; and to divide judicial authority into districts according to geographical convenience, irrespective of legal precedent. His reign saw several rectifications of administrative and judicial boundaries, and he quickly perceived the legal anomaly which compelled litigants from New Vizcaya to pass through Guadalajara, in order to lodge appeals in Mexico. In a report to the king early in 1573 he recommended that appeals from the whole of Francisco de Ibarra's conquests should be heard by the audiencia of Guadalajara.[1] Later in the same year, accordingly, a royal decree extended the appellate jurisdiction of New Galicia to cover the whole of New Vizcaya—an arrangement which lasted until the War of Independence.[2]

The vexed question of which audiencia should exercise jurisdiction in the coastal provinces originally conquered by Avalos, Alvárez Chico, and Francisco Cortés, also received the royal attention during the reign of Enríquez de Almansa. In 1568 the *oidores alcaldes mayores* were invited to prepare a properly attested case for the transfer of the disputed provinces; their evidence,[3] collected from a variety of sources, revealed the fact that many Spaniards and Indians living within ten or twelve leagues of the capital of New Galicia were required to travel the hundred leagues or more to Mexico when they wished to go to law. An old demand, first made by Lebrón de Quiñones, was revived—that Jacona in

[1] *A.G.I.* Auda. de México 69: 'Enríquez al Rey. 19 de Marzo 1573.'
[2] *A.G.I.* Auda. de Guadalajara 230, lib. Z 2, fol. 3 verso. 26 de Mayo 1573.
[3] *A.G.I.* Patronato 182, R°. 29: 'Información y otras diligencias hechas en México y Guadalajara sobre si convendría o no separar unos pueblos unidos a la jurisdicción de la audiencia de México y agregarlos a la de Guadalajara, por estar más inmediatos a esta. 1568.'

Michoacán be made the boundary of the audiencia of New Galicia, as it was already the boundary of the diocese. A decree of 1571[1] shelved the problem of transfer, but in 1574-5, probably through the influence of Enríquez, the provinces of Colima, Zacatula and Avalos were finally placed beneath the jurisdiction— though not the administration—of the audiencia of New Galicia.[2] The *oidores* of Mexico, after the event, protested against the transfer, and suggested the removal of the audiencia of New Galicia away from the coastal provinces, to Zacatecas or Durango, or alternatively the establishment of a second audiencia in New Vizcaya;[3] but nothing came of these proposals.

Enríquez, though prepared to allow the *oidores alcaldes mayores* what he held to be their due, refused to tolerate the interference of lawyers in matters concerning his military authority. He visited New Galicia several times, took the field personally in the Chichimec campaigns of 1568-70, and supervised the erection of blockhouses along the road leading from Guadalajara to Zacatecas and the north—work that should have been done long before, had there been an appropriate authority on the spot.[4] A decree of 1568[5] expressly warned the *oidores* against obstructing the work of the viceroy as captain-general, and against undertaking military expeditions, except in cases of serious emergency. Enríquez regarded the audiencia simply as a court of appeal; he was partly responsible, indeed, for depriving it for a time of all its administrative authority. The president soon recovered the ground which the *oidores* had lost; but the reign of Enríquez set definite limits to the powers of the audiencia as far as frontier administration was concerned and achieved at least a temporary concentration of administrative authority in the hands of the viceroy. Francisco de Toledo was pursuing a similar policy in Peru. Throughout the Indies the lawyer-*conquistador*, of the type of Nuño de Guzmán and Pedro Morones, was disappearing from the frontiers; the soldier-administrator was taking his place, as the audiencias were left further behind the lines and were recalled to their true duties, those of advisory councils and high courts of justice.

---

[1] *A.G.I.* Auda. de Guadalajara 230, lib. Z 1, fol. 233 verso. 1 de Julio 1571.

[2] Ibid. lib. Z 2, fol. 6. 18 de Febrero 1574 (Colima and Zacatula), fol. 29. 3 de Mayo 1575 (Avalos). *Recopilación de Leyes de Indias*, II. xv. 7.

[3] *A.G.I.* Auda. de México 69: 'Audiencia [de México] al Rey. 31 de octubre 1576.'

[4] Cf. H. H. Bancroft, *Pacific States*, vol. v, p. 656.

[5] *A.G.I.* Auda. de Guadalajara 230, fol. 200 verso. 31 de Dic. 1568.

CHAPTER V

THE AUDIENCIA AND THE CHURCH

The immense power and social influence wielded by the clergy was one of the most striking features of Spanish history during the colonial period. Religious enthusiasm among all classes had been maintained at a high pitch by the long wars against the Moors, by the great movement for religious unity and reform under the Catholic monarchs, and by the appearance of the Lutheran menace under Charles V. There were few families in sixteenth-century Spain which could not count a cleric among their members, and the power of the Church affected the whole economic life of the nation, through the vast area of land held in mortmain—a situation against which the Cortes protested in vain, since to the mass of the people the riches of the Church were a source of genuine pride.

If the Church was powerful, however, it was by no means independent. Its peculiar strength lay largely in its close alliance with the Crown. In 1523 Charles V secured from his old tutor, Adrian VI, a perpetual grant of the right to present to bishoprics and abbacies in Spain, which right was used under pressure from the Cortes to confine ecclesiastical preferment in Spain to Spanish subjects. This royal patronage was at all times jealously guarded, and as a corollary the wide judicial powers of both episcopal courts and Inquisition in Spain were exercised under strict royal control and supervision.[1]

In the Indies the royal control was in theory even more absolute. As early as 1501, a bull of Alexander VI conceded to the Catholic monarchs the right to collect the tithes and other dues by which the ecclesiastical organisation in America was to be supported.[2] In 1508 Julius II at the instances of Ferdinand the Catholic recognised the royal patronage in all ranks of the Church in the Indies.[3] The colonial clergy, therefore, became salaried servants of the Crown at an early date. Legislation completed the theoretical royal control by requiring that all bulls and briefs destined for

---

[1] R. Altamira, *Historia de España*, vol. II, § 590; vol. III, §§ 717-19.

[2] F. J. Hernáez, S.J., *Colección de Bulas, Breves y otros Documentos relativos a la Iglesia de América y Filipinas* (Brussels, 1879), vol. I, p. 20.

[3] Ibid. p. 24.

America should first receive the assent of the Council of the Indies.[1] In spite of these comprehensive enactments, however, the clergy in America enjoyed in practice a much greater degree of independence than in Spain. Royal control was naturally difficult to enforce at a distance, and though the bishops might be kept under supervision, missionary friars easily eluded authority. The Crown and the royal courts, indeed, not wishing to hamper the friars in their work of conversion, often connived at their independence both of royal and episcopal control.

The astonishing results of missionary work in New Spain sprang mainly from the activity of the regular preaching Orders, though the secular clergy also emigrated in considerable numbers, despite royal discouragement, and found livings in the *encomiendas*. *Encomenderos*, bound by law to provide clergy for the villages within their grants, preferred to appoint men in minor secular orders, who were more subservient and worked for smaller salaries than the 'regulars'. These secular clergy acquired an unenviable reputation for ignorance and immorality.[2] The records of the episcopal courts—later, of the Inquisition—are full of cases of minor clergy, not in priest's orders, prosecuted for administering the sacraments illegally, for neglecting their work, and for cheating and seducing their charges.

In the missions of the regular Orders a more austere way of life prevailed. Indians, often left spiritually stranded by the success of Spanish policy in destroying the influence of their noble and priestly castes, saw frequent examples of the courage and kindliness of the friars—their willingness to share the hard life of the mountain tribes; their indifference to exile and suffering; their not infrequent stoical acceptance of martyrdom. Not only did the Orders support an Indian policy radically opposed to the *encomienda*; they competed with the colonists by establishing mission communities in which the preaching of the Faith went hand in hand with the practice of improved cultivation on communal lines. The movement in New Spain and New Galicia never achieved the completeness of the benevolent autocracy evolved by the Franciscans in California and by the Jesuits in Paraguay; but everywhere it was a powerful

---

[1] *Recopilación de Leyes de Indias*, I. ix. 2, 3; I. vii. 55. On the general question of royal control of the Church in America, see L. Ayarragaray, *La Iglesia en América y la Dominación Española* (Buenos Aires, 1920); P. Leturia, 'El orígen histórico del Patronato de Indias', *Razón y Fe*, vol. LXXVIII.

[2] See Torquemada, *Monarquía Indiana*, lib. xv, cap. i.

ally of the royal authority, in persuading the wilder tribes to settle under Spanish rule. Not all the mission fathers were kindly and wise; many proved idle, immoral and tyrannical in their dealings with the natives. In general, however, there could be no doubt as to the choice which a free Indian would make, between the Christianity of the missionary friars and that of the secular clergy; between working in a mission community, and labouring to produce tribute for an *encomendero*.

Under Charles V, the practice grew of elevating friars to colonial bishoprics, in the hope that the bishops would co-operate with the missionaries, both in converting the natives and in enforcing legislation concerning their treatment. This policy was not entirely successful. It is true that the Orders contributed a number of great names to the colonial episcopate. Vasco de Quiroga, *oidor* in the second audiencia of New Spain and bishop of Michoacán, acquired a lasting reputation for sanctity and kindliness;[1] even to-day in remote parts of that State illiterate *peones* uncover their heads when passing certain stones at the roadside, giving as their reason that 'Tete Don Vasco once rested there'. Juan de Zumárraga, first bishop and archbishop of Mexico, and Diego de Landa, bishop of Yucatán, both strove continually to protect the mass of the Indians from exploitation, though they are condemned from a modern humanitarian point of view for their ruthless inquisitorial proceedings against native priests and nobles in cases of idolatry and apostasy, and for their destruction of Indian pictogrammic writings. Both met with violent opposition and some ill-treatment at the hands of Spaniards for their support of the Indian cause. Bartolomé de las Casas, the most famous of the friends of the Indians, was compelled by the hatred of the colonists to resign the see of Chiapas, and to return to Spain.

These men were exceptional. Many friars refused bishoprics, and of those who accepted the greater number gradually came to accept also the point of view of the classes with whom they were most in contact—the *encomenderos* and the secular clergy. Mendieta records as a rare and peculiar virtue in Zumárraga, that after his elevation he continued to observe the rule of his Order and to maintain personal contact with the Indians.[2] Most bishops directed such activity as they undertook outside the bounds of the

---

[1] See S. Zavala, *Ideario de Vasco de Quiroga* (Mexico, 1941).
[2] G. de Mendieta, *Historia Eclesiástica Indiana* (Mexico, 1870), cap. xxviii.

Spanish settlements, to asserting episcopal authority over the missions and convents, and to curbing the dangerous reforming zeal of the missionary brethren.

The friars, defending their independence, often appealed to the audiencias, which were not unwilling to receive such appeals. The audiencias could harass the bishops in many ways by using the general supervisory powers entrusted to them, and could moreover compel bishops to perform uncongenial duties such as visitations in remote districts and attendance at councils in places far distant from their sees.[1] The bishops, for their part, might denounce and excommunicate the judges as sacrilegious innovators and disturbers of the peace. Battles of writs between audiencias and prelates over the related problems of Indian policy and the independence of the missions were common throughout the sixteenth century.

The ecclesiastical authorities had, of course, their own courts and their own well-established and elaborated rules of Canon Law.[2] The Inquisition dealt with heresy and its allied crimes, idolatry and blasphemy, and under Philip II with solicitation—the crime of a priest seducing women in the confessional.[3] The episcopal courts heard all other charges against clerics; matrimonial causes; cases of usury and perjury, and in general all cases involving the sanctity of oaths. Such a jurisdiction might be stretched indefinitely by an aggressive prelate. Any slight neglect of duty by an official might be treated as a breach of his oath of office and so a spiritual offence. Solórzano later found it necessary to devote a lengthy paragraph to refuting the claims of the churchmen in this particular.[4] Moreover, during a great part of the sixteenth century the bishops acted as inquisitors; from the first creation of dioceses in New Spain in 1527 to the establishment of a regular tribunal of the Holy Office there in 1571, full powers were delegated to the bishops by the Inquisitor-General, except when special inquisitorial commissioners visited the country.[5] The ecclesiastical courts, like all other branches of the Church in

---

[1] *Recopilación de Leyes de Indias*, ii. xv. 147; Orozco y Jiménez, *Colección*, vol. ii, p. 35.

[2] For a general account of the Ecclesiastical Courts and their relation to the secular jurisdiction see Marta, *Tractatus de jurisdictione inter judicem ecclesiasticum et laicum exercenda* (Avignon, 1669).

[3] C. H. Lea, *The Inquisition in the Spanish dependencies* (New York, 1908), p. 241.

[4] Solórzano, *Política Indiana*, v. ii. 11.

[5] Sandoval, for instance, held a commission as inquisitor. C. H. Lea, op. cit. p. 196.

Spanish territory, were controlled by the Crown. Royal legislation limited the powers of the courts, but at the same time
strengthened them by recognition and support. To the audiencias
fell the thankless task of enforcing the limits of the episcopal
jurisdiction; and this was yet another source of inevitable conflict.

Spanish jurists in defining the powers of bishops habitually drew
a distinction between *jurisdicción propia* and *jurisdicción privilegiada*.
The first, inherent in the episcopal office, entitled bishops to try
spiritual offences and to inflict spiritual penances. By the second,
the bishops might impose civil penalties also upon spiritual
offenders, whether laymen or clerics, and might try disputes
between clerics and all charges brought against them, whether on
secular or spiritual grounds.[1] *Jurisdicción privilegiada* was in theory
delegated to the bishops by the Crown; it might be defined, altered,
or abolished by secular legislation. In practice it was never clearly
defined in the sixteenth century. The elaborate enactments contained in the *Recopilación de Leyes de Indias* were laid down, for the
most part, in the early seventeenth century. They follow earlier
Castilian precedents, however, and represent fairly the experience
of the sixteenth-century courts, to whose proceedings they furnish
a valuable key. Their principal rulings are summarised briefly
below.

The bishops held a recognised, though limited, civil jurisdiction.
The Church claimed, indeed, that the plaintiff should seek the
defendant's law and that all suits brought by clerics against clerics,
or by laymen against clerics, should be heard in the ecclesiastical
courts.[2] Spanish law limited these claims in many ways. The royal
jurisdiction was defended against encroachment by general legislation[3] forbidding ecclesiastical judges to hear disputes over the
property of laymen or over property or privileges granted to the
Church by royal favour or lay gift or bequest. Litigation concerning
the temporalities and the boundaries of sees and livings, encum-
brances on property bequeathed to the Church by laymen,
trusteeships, wardships, entails and so forth, went before the
secular courts. Disputes concerning appointments to livings and
other ecclesiastical preferments belonging to the royal patronage

[1] J. Escriche, *Diccionario razonado de legislación y jurisprudencia* (Madrid, 1847), vol. I,
p. 450.
[2] Marta, *De jurisdictione*, II. xxvii; II. xxxix.
[3] J. Escriche, loc. cit.; *Nueva Recopilación de Leyes de España*, I. iii. n. 28; I. vi. 2;
IV. i. 3, 4, 6; *Recopilación de Leyes de Indias*, I. x. I.

LIBRARY
EISENHOWER COLLEGE

in the Indies were to be decided by the officials—viceroys, governors, or presidents—who exercised the patronage in the provinces concerned.[1]

The ecclesiastical courts held between them a monopoly of criminal jurisdiction over the clergy, in accordance with Canon Law.[2] This principle was endorsed by royal legislation.[3] The audiencias had no jurisdiction over criminous clerks as such. They could issue writs requiring the episcopal courts to proceed against criminous clerks;[4] and clergy convicted of the most serious crimes would be unfrocked and handed over to the 'secular arm' for punishment. To meet the case where an episcopal court failed or refused to do justice upon a priest accused of serious crime, a curious but very necessary procedure was provided. A priest enjoyed benefit of clergy only in his capacity as priest. In another capacity, as a subject of the king, he enjoyed the right to reside and to own property within the king's dominions, and this privilege, which the king conferred, might be withdrawn by the king or the royal courts. An audiencia might not try a priest, but it could draw up information against him out of court, to be forwarded to the Council of the Indies,[5] and in case of contempt or obstinate resistance might condemn him to exile and loss of all his goods, without trial, by an administrative act under the royal seal,[6] sending both his person and the charges against him to the Council of the Indies.[7] The revenues of bishoprics were specifically included in the goods which might be confiscated in such a case.[8]

These were extreme measures. In general, in normal circumstances the clergy enjoyed immunity from arrest by secular authority. This immunity might also cover laymen who placed themselves under clerical protection in consecrated places. Not only churches, but convents also were exempted from entry by the constables of the secular courts, and criminals seeking sanctuary therein were immune from arrest, for a short time at least, except in flagrant cases of serious crime. Respect for all the forms of

---

[1] *Recopilación de Leyes de Indias*, I. vii. 17; I. vi. 38, 39.
[2] Marta, *De jurisdictione*, I. ii. 6: 'Privilegium fori clericorum esse de jure divino et ideo neque clericos posse se submittere jurisdictioni laicorum.'
[3] *Nueva Recopilación de Leyes de España*, I. iii. 5.
[4] *Recopilación de Leyes de Indias*, I. xii. 8.
[5] Solórzano, *Politica Indiana*, IV. xxvii. 34.
[6] Ibid. IV. xxvii. 9, 11, 12. *Recopilación de Leyes de Indias*, II. xv. 143.
[7] *Recopilación de Leyes de Indias*, II. xv. 144.   [8] Ibid. II. xv. 145.

ecclesiastical immunity was repeatedly enjoined upon the secular judges.[1] Safeguards were imposed, however, against the abuse of immunity. Among the many duties laid upon the *fiscales* of the audiencias was that of watching the proceedings of the episcopal courts and of representing before them the interests of royal justice.[2] In cases where clerical immunity was lawfully claimed, the *fiscal* might prosecute the offender in the episcopal court. If a layman accused of any secular crime sought sanctuary the Church authorities were required to surrender him upon demand made in due form by the secular magistrates;[3] the right of sanctuary merely protecting him from mob violence in the heat of the chase.

No sixteenth-century Spaniard would have denied the justice of ecclesiastical jurisdiction over the clergy in all ordinary cases. Jurisdiction over the laity in ecclesiastical causes, however, produced numerous problems and conflicts, since no exact definition was possible, either of laymen or of ecclesiastical causes. Certain general rules were laid down: ecclesiastical judges were ordered to co-operate with the royal justices, and were forbidden to take such proceedings against officials, as might interfere with the general administration of justice;[4] they might not cite officials before them, for offences whose ecclesiastical nature arose solely from breach of an oath of office;[5] they held no jurisdiction over unconverted heathens.[6] In dealing with persons offending against both civil and spiritual codes, a careful distinction was made; for example, a layman who assaulted a priest was to be tried by the episcopal court for sacrilege, and by the nearest secular court, for assault.[7] In all cases in doubt between bishops and secular judges, decision rested with the audiencias, by means of the *recurso de fuerza*.

Episcopal courts might not arrest laymen, except by the *auxilio real*—the help of the secular arm—which was to be requested and not demanded; the secular judges being instructed to provide constables for the purpose in all lawful ecclesiastical causes.[8] Fees might be charged for the arrest of Spaniards on behalf of the episcopal authorities, but not for the arrest of Indians.[9]

---

[1] Ibid. i. v. i; i. vii. 54; ii. xv. 150; ii. xxxi. 16.
[2] Ibid. ii. xviii. 30; Solórzano, *Política Indiana*, v. vi. 23.
[3] *Recopilación de Leyes de Indias*, i, v. 2, 3.
[4] Ibid. i. x. 1, 2, 3.   [5] Ibid. i. x. 5.   [6] Ibid. i. x. 4.
[7] Solórzano, *Política Indiana*, v. xviii. 16.
[8] *Recopilación de Leyes de Indias*, i. x. 12, 13; ii. xv. 153.
[9] Ibid. i. x. 14.

The lack of exact definition in the matter of ecclesiastical jurisdiction over the laity, was naturally a source of anxiety to the secular authorities, in view of the severe penalties which might be inflicted. During the period in which they acted as inquisitors, the armoury of the bishops contained all the forms of penance, including imprisonment, flogging, galleys, and 'relaxation' for heresy. These more serious penalties, of course, required the co-operation of the secular arm; but that would never be refused, in dealing with the dreaded taint of heresy. In lesser causes, certain exceptions limited the power of the episcopal courts; the imposition of fines upon laymen was discouraged, though—according to Solórzano—not absolutely prohibited;[1] the Crown in this matter being concerned to discourage the cupidity displayed by most ecclesiastical institutions at that time. Episcopal judges, finally, were forbidden to fine Indians, or to condemn them to forced labour.[2]

In all cases, the bishops could employ the various degrees of excommunication, anathema and interdict, in order to secure the enforcement of their sentences. Excommunication alone might not be particularly effective, if the victim were otherwise in good standing with authority and with his neighbours; in the loosely organised dioceses of the New World, friars could be found who would administer the sacraments to an excommunicate in defiance of episcopal authority. If, however, a bishop went so far as to lay a general interdict upon the town where an offence took place, disorder would certainly break out among a superstitious and turbulent population, and a serious situation might arise, unless the offender submitted, or the bishop could be persuaded to lift the ban. The interdict was therefore the bishops' most potent weapon, in defending their jurisdiction against the civil courts.

Co-operation and good feeling between civil and ecclesiastical judges was clearly essential for the effective working of a system in which such powers existed. This necessity was emphasised by the existence of certain classes of cases recognised as de mixto fuero[3] and shared between the two jurisdictions. Of these, the most important was probate. The proving of wills belonged, as might be expected,

[1] Recopilación de Leyes de Indias, I. vii. 47. Solórzano, Política Indiana, IV. vii. 40.
[2] Recopilación de Leyes de Indias, I. x. 6, 7, 8.
[3] For the Canon Law rules concerning Mixtum Forum see Marta, De Jurisdictione, Pt. II.

to the episcopal judges; but they were forbidden by law to hear disputes over the property of laymen. Accordingly the work of enforcing the provisions of wills and of dealing with litigation concerning them fell to the audiencias. In every audiencia one of the *oidores*, in rotation, was nominated by the president or the viceroy to serve as *juez de bienes de difuntos* in his province for two years.[1]

From his decisions litigants might in certain cases appeal to the audiencia itself.[2] Immediately upon the death of any owner of property, the local *corregidor* or *alcalde mayor* was required to send to the *juez de bienes de difuntos* an inventory of all the goods involved.[3] After the proving of the will, the heirs might apply in the audiencia for a writ, ordering the executors to make over the property,[4] the *juez* being responsible for the prevention of fraud on the part of the executors. In the case of a testator leaving heirs in Spain, the *juez* might direct his property to be sold and the proceeds to be paid into the *caja de bienes de difuntos*, the chest kept for this purpose by the treasury officials of the province; the contents of the *caja* were supposed to be audited annually, and were shipped, along with the royal silver, at regular intervals to the *Casa de Contratación* in Seville, where the heirs might hope, eventually, to claim their inheritance.[5] When owners of property died intestate, the *juez* discovered, through the local authorities, the identity of the nearest relatives of the deceased, and awarded the inheritance to them according to law,[6] or, if no heirs could be found, declared the property vacant, the same procedure being followed whether the deceased had been cleric or layman.[7] All this work on the part of the *juez* depended upon speedy and reliable probate procedure in the episcopal courts, as well as upon accurate accounting. Both these desiderata were too often lacking, and the situation was further complicated when the ecclesiastical judges insisted on collecting the dues of the Church 'at source' from the property of the deceased. In such cases the assessment made by the ecclesiastical judges had to be revised, and often reversed, by the audiencias as guardians of the rights of the heirs.[8]

---

[1] *Recopilación de Leyes de Indias*, II. xxxii. 1.
[2] Ibid. II. xxxii. 4.
[3] Ibid. II. xxxii. 18.
[4] Ibid. II. xxxii. 45.
[5] Ibid. II. xxxii. 48.
[6] Ibid. II. xxxii. 43. Solórzano, *Política Indiana*, v. vii. 26, 27.
[7] *Recopilación de Leyes de Indias*, II. xxxii. 8.
[8] Ibid. II. xv. 146.

Apart from the complicated procedure prescribed in these cases of *mixto fuero*, the ordinary decisions of episcopal judges might be reversed in some cases by superior spiritual courts, in others by the audiencias. Appeals from the decisions of a bishops' court might be made to the metropolitan, and from the metropolitan (with Royal permission) to Rome. A Bull of Gregory XIII,[1] in 1573, recognising the difficulty and expense of appeal to Rome from the Indies, laid down that if the sentences of bishop and metropolitan agreed, the second decision should be final; if they disagreed, then recourse should be allowed to a neighbouring bishop, to settle the case. This was not interpreted as abolishing the right of recourse to Rome, but only as permitting the enforcement of the sentence, pending further appeal.[2] The Bull did not in any case alter the law concerning 'reserved' suits. Cases concerning the deposition and deprivation of bishops were reserved for the Pope.

Appeal to a superior ecclesiastical court involved the tacit admission that a case was lawfully within the episcopal jurisdiction and had been tried in due form, even though the sentence given might be reversed. If an episcopal judge committed an injustice which could not be remedied by an ordinary appeal, the litigant might seek redress from the royal courts by means of the *recurso de fuerza*. The word *fuerza* means simply an injury; in the technical language of lawyers, however, it acquired the special meaning of an illegality in the conduct of an ecclesiastical court, and included three principal forms of injustice: failure to observe the rules of procedure laid down by Canon Law in the conduct of a case; denial of lawful appeal; and trespass upon the jurisdiction of the secular courts.[3] The *recurso* might be invoked in two ways: an aggrieved party, sentenced in an episcopal court, might appeal to the nearest audiencia, in which case the bishop was required to permit the appeal and to hand over the papers in the case to the notary of the audiencia.[4] Alternatively the *fiscal* of the audiencia might intervene to stop the hearing of a case pending before an episcopal court. If the episcopal judge demurred, the appellant or the *fiscal* might secure a writ of *recurso* from the 'oidor of the week',[5]

---

[1] F. J. Hernáez, *Colección de Bulas*, vol. I, p. 188.

[2] Ibid. p. 189.

[3] J. Escriche, *Diccionario razonado de legislación y jurisprudencia* (Madrid, 1847), vol. I, p. 838; F. Martínez Alcubilla: *Diccionario de la administración española, peninsular y ultramarina* (Madrid, 1868), vol. V, p. 807.

[4] *Recopilación de Leyes de Indias*, I. x. 10.   [5] See p. 40, above.

demanding the surrender of papers. With the papers before it, the audiencia debated in *acuerdo*[1] whether a *fuerza* had been committed. If the proceedings had been according to law, the suit was returned to the episcopal court; if the necessary forms had been neglected or lawful appeal denied, a court order was issued requiring the bishop to remove the cause of complaint; if the secular jurisdiction had been invaded, the case was retained to be tried by the audiencia in the ordinary course of its work, with the exception that in certain cases the *oidor* who had issued the original writ might not sit in judgement.[2] The episcopal judge was required, when the audiencia intervened in a case, to revoke all censures and excommunications pronounced in connection with it[3]—a necessary provision, since an *oidor* in the course of his work might himself incur excommunication, and be disqualified thereby from hearing ecclesiastical appeals until he received absolution.[4] Should the judge resist the intervention of the audiencia, the *fiscal* or the appellant might 'seek the royal help'—invite the audiencia to make his quarrel its own, to repeat its writ a second, third and fourth time, and finally to take disciplinary action.[5]

The audiencias occupied a very strong legal position in dealing with cases of *fuerza*. The audiencia in each province represented the king and sealed its writs with the royal seal. To resist the royal authority was sedition, and seditious clerics could be shipped to Spain without trial and all their goods confiscated, by the order of an audiencia.[6] In New Galicia the bishops contended that the audiencia, since it was a subordinate court and held no royal seal during the first twenty-four years of its existence, had no power to enforce these laws against extensions of the episcopal jurisdiction. This contention was vigorously supported by the audiencia of Mexico. A decree of 1561,[7] however, settled the question in favour of the audiencia of New Galicia, confirming to it the same powers in ecclesiastical matters as other audiencias enjoyed.

[1] I.e. sitting in its advisory, as distinct from its judicial capacity.
[2] *Recopilación de Leyes de Indias*, II. xv. 135, 136, 140, 141.
[3] Ibid. I. x. 9, 10; I. vii. 18.
[4] See, for example, *A.G.I.* Auda. de Guadalajara 230, Z 1, fol. 214: 'Vos...el Licenciado Contreras...siendo reaisado en los negocios tocantes al obispo...no os entrometáis en conocer de las fuerzas eclesiásticas.'
[5] *Recopilación de Leyes de Indias*, II. xv. 143.
[6] Solórzano, *Política Indiana*, IV. xxvii. 9, 11, 12.
[7] *A.G.I.* Auda. de Guadalajara 230, Z 1, fol. 61 verso. 31 de Marzo 1561. Cited Orozco y Jiménez, *Colección*, vol. I, p. 401 (Pleito...1565).

New Galicia was made a diocese and the district of an audiencia at the same time; a new secular and a new ecclesiastical jurisdiction were thus created simultaneously, as the *visitador* Lorenzo de Tejada had suggested.[1] Contrary to Tejada's recommendations however, the first bishop, Pedro Gómez Maraver, was not a friar, nor was he a person likely to assist the audiencia greatly in finding a solution for the Indian problems which were at that time so pressing. He was known to have advocated a general enslavement of the Indians after the Mixton war,[2] and seems to have harboured a personal dislike for Lebrón de Quiñones, whom he regarded as a troublemaker. His own relations with the Indians of New Galicia were confined to the mass 'conversion' of the people of Tlaxomulco, who are known as the Maraveres to this day.[3] The chroniclers do not relate how the conversion was achieved. Most of Maraver's short incumbency was occupied in travelling, and in acrimonious litigation with the bishop of Michoacán concerning the boundary between the two dioceses.[4] He never resided in Compostela, and so never came into prolonged direct contact with the audiencia, though his letters contain much virulent criticism of the court.[5] The episcopal court was established from the first in the more populous town of Guadalajara, and being better staffed with advocates—since clergy with legal training were more plentiful than civil lawyers—probably handled some litigation which would otherwise have gone to the audiencia. No cases of *fuerza* are recorded.

The see of New Galicia remained vacant for seven years after the death of Maraver. Several bishops-elect died before reaching their post, while the dean and chapter carried on the routine work of the diocese. Fray Pedro de Ayala, the second effective bishop, took up his duties in 1559. He was a Franciscan, and Tello (for whom a Franciscan could do no wrong) recorded his devotion to conventual life and his strict observance of the rule of his Order.[6] Pride in the name and privileges of the Order was indeed the key to many of his actions, though he did not share the concern over

---

[1] See p. 30, above. [2] See p. 48, above.
[3] F. J. Hernáez, *Colección de Bulas*, vol. II, p. 72.
[4] *A.G.I.* Justicia—Audiencia de México 148, no. 3, 1551: 'D. Pedro Gómez Maraver...con D. Vasco de Quiroga...sobre demarcación de límites. El obispo de Michoacán...contra el obispo de la Nueva Galicia, sobre que éste le satisfaga los perjuicios que le causó en haberse introducido a exigir diezmos en la juridicción del dicho obispo de Michoacán', etc.
[5] See p. 47, above. [6] Tello, *Crónica miscelánea*, cap. clxxxiv.

the fate of the Indians which distinguished so many of the leading Franciscans. The audiencia occasionally attempted to compel him to perform his ecclesiastical duties towards the Indians; a *requeri-miento*[1] issued by the *oidores* in January 1565 complained of the number of Indian villages left without clergy, and the small number of priests who could speak Indian languages. The bishop was ordered to remedy this state of affairs as best he could; he did nothing, however, beyond sending a routine request to the king for more friars.[2] Later in the year, when a small band of Augustinians attempted to establish a house in Guadalajara, Ayala opposed their project on the grounds that no more clergy were needed in so thinly populated an area; that the Council of Trent discouraged the entry of a second Order into a province where one was already established; and that the Augustinians had incurred severe penalties by celebrating mass in a place forbidden by law—their lodging, which they called a monastery, and Ayala an inn. Ayala complained bitterly that the audiencia refused to 'lend the royal help' to eject the newcomers.[3] The needs of the Indians, conventionally supposed to be thirsting after the Gospel, were forgotten in a maze of legal dispute, in which Ayala showed himself hot-tempered, litigious, and absolutely uncompromising in matters touching his dignity and jurisdiction.

This dispute occurred some time after Ayala's arrival in New Galicia; during the first three years of his incumbency, while Morones was still alive, relations between the bishop and the audiencia were peaceful. Ayala, indeed, showed himself friendly towards Morones and supported the Chiametla project in his letters to the king. His first official activities, in collaboration with Morones, concerned the movement to transfer the seat of government, both secular and spiritual, from Compostela to Guadalajara. The lengthy memorials and petitions which he drew up and dispatched to Spain[4] no doubt weighed with the Council of the Indies

---

[1] Orozco y Jiménez, *Colección*, vol. II, p. 35: 'Requerimientos de los oidores al obispo que ponga sacerdotes donde no los hay...10 de Enero 1565.'

[2] Ibid. vol. I, p. 280: 'Carta del Ilmo. Sr. Ayala en que trata varios asuntos de su obispado, 6 de Febrero 1565.'

[3] Ibid. vol. I, p. 302: 'Carta del Ilmo Sr. Ayala en la que comunica al Rey, entre otras cosas, la falta de justicia que se nota en la Nueva Galicia. 10 de Nov. 1565.'

[4] *A.G.I.* Patronato 181, R°. 36: 'Información recibida en México a petición de D. Pedro de Ayala sobre si convendría que la iglesia catedral del Nuevo Reino de Galicia, que estaba en Compostela, se trasladase a Guadalajara, y en cuál de estas dos ciudades debía residir la audiencia de aquel Reino. 1559.'

in 1560, when it reversed its unfavourable decision of 1552, and authorised the establishment of the audiencia and the episcopal seat at Guadalajara.[1] Ayala answered the decree in a letter full of thanks, expressing the hope that the audiencia would soon be increased to its full strength and would co-operate with him in his efforts to beautify the city of Guadalajara by building, and to spread the Faith throughout the province.[2] These amiable hopes were not to be fulfilled; the restoration of effective audiencia rule from 1564 onwards was to produce acute dissension between the bishop and the *oidores*.

Meanwhile Ayala's quarrelsome nature found vent in controversy with his own colleagues. Throughout the year 1563 he was endeavouring (without success) to secure the removal of the archdeacon, Bernardo de Quiroz, whom he accused of crimes and failings ranging from illiteracy to murder.[3] The archdeacon appealed to the metropolitan court and to Rome, the provisor in Mexico allowing the appeal, much to Ayala's annoyance. The bishop asserted not only that Quiroz's crimes rendered him unfit for ecclesiastical preferment, but that the local recommendation upon which the king had acted in appointing him came not from the dean and chapter, but from the dean alone, pretending illegally to act in the name of the chapter on behalf of Quiroz, a personal friend; Quiroz's preferment, according to the bishop, had been a piece of jobbery, and was invalid. Some of the charges against Quiroz may well have been justified; but the suit led to an undignified quarrel with the dean, a venerable man, much respected, who had presided over the see during the whole period of the vacancy without any complaint being voiced against him.[4] On 14 July 1564, in the course of an angry discussion in the sacristy of the cathedral, the bishop set upon the dean, and chased him down the length of the nave, striking him, in full view of the inevitable crowd of idlers in the porch and the plaza. The incident naturally caused great

[1] Orozco y Jiménez, *Colección*, vol. 1, p. 261: 'Cédula Real en que se manda que la sede episcopal de esta diócesi y la Audiencia se trasladen de Compostela a esta ciudad de Guadalajara. 10 de Mayo 1560.'

[2] Ibid. vol. 1, p. 250: 'Carta del obispo a S.M....hace constar el regocǐjo con que han recibido la merced que S.M. le hizo...27 de Enero 1561.'

[3] Ibid. vol. 1, pp. 267, 270, 273, etc.: 'Cartas del Ilmo Sr. Ayala...respecto del proceso formado al arcedeano D. Pedro Bernardo de Quiroz. 31 de Enero, 17 de Feb., 24 de Sept. 1563.'

[4] Ibid. vol. 1, p. 244: 'Carta de Sr. D. Bartolomé de Rivera, exponiendo los servicios prestados a S.M. como Deán de la Catedral de Nueva Galicia. 20 de Enero 1562.'

scandal; the audiencia at once assembled, and collected the evidence of all those present, in order to send an attested statement to the king.[1] The *oidores* themselves took no judicial action, however, being no doubt uncertain of the powers of a secular court in so awkward a case, and having regard to the fact that most of the witnesses were Indians, whose unsupported testimony carried little weight in a court of law.

Shortly afterwards a case arose which, though trivial in itself, necessarily involved the intervention of the audiencia.[2] The cathedral chapter of Guadalajara employed a scrivener, one Calixto de León, not himself in orders, to do the secretarial work connected with the cathedral. In August 1564 the chapter issued a *requerimiento* to the diocesan treasurer, to release certain funds for necessary repairs to the cathedral fabric. The secretary León conveyed these requirements by word of mouth to the treasurer, who demanded a certified copy of the chapter's decision in writing. Whether through idleness or dishonesty, León failed to produce the copy, and after waiting a few days the treasurer complained to the bishop, who issued a writ ordering León to comply with the treasurer's demand; León ignored the writ, and was sentenced to pay a fine of 12 *pesos*, remaining excommunicate until the fine should be paid. León thereupon appealed to the audiencia, on the ground that he was a layman and that a suit concerning a money order was clearly not an ecclesiastical cause. The bishop countered with the assertion that the fact of León's employment by the chapter made him legally a cleric, and so subject to the episcopal jurisdiction in criminal charges, such as negligence and disobedience; the appeal was therefore disallowed. This contention, though ingenious, was very unsound law; and the audiencia at León's petition issued a writ of *recurso*, citing the case before its tribunal, ordering the bishop's notary to transfer the relevant papers, and calling upon the bishop to absolve León while his case was under consideration.[3] As a result of the hearing in the audiencia, León undertook to comply with the treasurer's demands and the bishop allowed the prosecution to drop. This

[1] Ibid. vol. II, p. 37: 'Acusación contra el Ilmo. Sr. Ayala por faltas graves al Sr. Deán. 14 de Julio 1564.'
[2] Ibid. vol. II, pp. 55–61: 'Autos que pasaron en lo de Mateo de Villanueva mayordomo de la Iglesia con Calixto de León secretario del Cabildo eclesiástico, sobre mandar el obispo que entregase cierto requerimiento, 16 de Sept. 1564.'
[3] Ibid. vol. II, p. 56. Auto. 2 de Sept. 1564.

typical case of a minor *fuerza* was thus settled without serious disturbance.

The following year a much more serious case arose out of an alleged breach of sanctuary, in which the audiencia itself was implicated. Sanctuary was a form of ecclesiastical immunity which continually gave trouble to the secular authorities, since the more extravagant claims of the clergy tended to exempt not only churches and convents, but houses and property of clerical persons, from entry by secular officers, and attributed to the priests the right to shelter any criminal from arrest. The case of Lope de Cisneros arose from just such an extravagant claim. In the spring of 1565 the audiencia held in its prison a number of Indians who had been taken while engaged in plundering raids along the roads leading from the city. Some of the culprits were headmen of nearby villages, and in order to prevent local disturbances their trial had been postponed for some months, until the excitement over their capture had died down. On 10 May three of these banditti escaped from prison and fled to the convent of St Francis in the hope of finding sanctuary.[1] The chief constable of the audiencia, Juan Sánchez, promptly raised the hue-and-cry and, entering the convent with a small body of followers, recaptured the fugitives without much trouble. The commotion, however, attracted the attention of the bishop, who came down to the convent gate as the party was leaving and demanded that the captives be released and restored to sanctuary. One of the Indians, understanding the situation if not the words, flung himself at the bishop's feet, clasping his protector's knees. A scuffle ensued in which one of the constable's assistants, Lope de Cisneros, a shopkeeper in the town, thrust the bishop violently aside, cursing him for his interference, while several others dragged the Indian away, to be tried with his companions and in due course, hanged.

The result of this encounter was a sentence of excommunication and penance pronounced in the episcopal court against Juan Sánchez, Lope de Cisneros, and Cristóbal Ponce de León.[2] The cases against Sánchez and Ponce de León were not pressed—the charge of breach of sanctuary by itself would certainly have been

[1] Orozco y Jiménez, *Colección*, vol. I, p. 385: 'Información testimonial. 10 de Mayo 1565.'
[2] Ibid. p. 387: 'El Ilmo. Sr. Ayala declara excomulgados a Cisneros y Ponce de León. 2 de Junio 1565.'

dismissed upon appeal, in view of the serious criminal charges under which the refugees lay. Cisneros, on the other hand, had committed an assault and the case against him was pursued vindictively; his penances were extremely heavy—excommunication alone was a disaster for a shopkeeper—and he was illegally denied the right to appeal. He placed his case in the hands of an advocate,[1] however, and entered two appeals against the episcopal sentence: one to the audiencia for *recurso de fuerza*, on the grounds that he had committed no offence against ecclesiastical law for which he could be tried in the bishop's court, and that the bishop, having assumed a jurisdiction which he did not possess, had denied the right of appeal from his decisions to the metropolitan;[2] the other, in the alternative and despite Ayala's prohibition, to the archbishop of Mexico for reversal of the bishop's decision, if the case proved after all to fall under the episcopal jurisdiction.[3] The audiencia, regarding the case as an interference upon Ayala's part with the course of justice, willingly furnished Cisneros with a writ of *recurso*, calling on the bishop to send his notary with the relevant papers to explain the case before the court, to allow appeal, and to absolve Cisneros until it should be decided to whose jurisdiction the case belonged.[4] The bishop rejected the writ, which was repeated three times on three successive days; on the fourth day Cisneros appeared before the audiencia and demanded the *auxilio real*.[5] A delay of ten days ensued, after which the audiencia repeated its writ a fourth time, threatening the bishop with exile and the confiscation of all his goods in case of further disobedience;[6] the following day, no reply having been received, the bishop was formally declared an exile.[7] Ten days more elapsed before Cisneros appeared again before the audiencia to request the enforcement of this last writ; he duly secured a court order requiring Ayala to

[1] Ibid. vol. I, p. 388: 'Poder de Lope de Cisneros a Cristóbal de Rivera. 2 de Junio 1565.'
[2] Ibid. vol. I, p. 392: 'Petición de Lope de Cisneros a la Real Audiencia de la Nueva Galicia. 6 de Junio.'
[3] Ibid. vol. I, p. 391.
[4] Ibid. vol. I, p. 393: 'Primeras providencias de la Real Audiencia en el pleito contra el Ilmo. Sr. Ayala. 6 de Junio.'
[5] Ibid. vol. I, p. 399: 'Petición de Lope de Cisneros al Rey de España. 10 de Junio.'
[6] Ibid. vol. I, p. 404: 'Amenazas de la Audiencia neogallega al Ilmo. Sr. Ayala. 19 de Junio.'
[7] Ibid. vol. I, p. 406: 'Auto de la Real Audiencia de Guadalajara declarando al Sr. D. Fray Pedro de Ayala por ageno, extraño de todos los Reinos de Su Magestad, y se le secuestren las temporalidades. 20 de Junio.'

leave New Galicia within ten days[1] and authorising the sequestration of the bishop's goods.[2] The constables visited the bishop's lodgings, but found no property of his except the negro slave-woman who cooked his meals; she was taken and lodged in the prison of the audiencia.

This high-handed action on the part of the *oidores* so enraged Ayala that he went at once to the royal house, followed by a crowd of minor clergy and casual onlookers, and publicly declared the judges excommunicate, abusing them violently in the crowded street.[3] Oseguera and Alarcón, who had come down cap in hand and with all the forms of deference, to greet the bishop, politely informed him that a public quarrel would lead only to scandal; that an excommunication must be declared in due form, in writing, and a copy supplied to the victim; and that they would appeal to the king if the bishop persisted in his action against them. After the bishop's departure they took sworn statements from a number of the onlookers (who all professed themselves greatly shocked by the unseemly manner of the quarrel) for dispatch to the king.

The formal writ of excommunication was served the same evening, followed the next day by the publication of an anathema against the *oidores*,[4] and the day after by a general interdict upon the city of Guadalajara.[5] Representations made in the bishop's court by a *fiscal* appointed *ad hoc* by the *oidores* merely elicited the reply that since the case involved the removal of a bishop, absolution could come from the Pope alone. The *oidores* were placed in a somewhat awkward position; only two of them were in residence at the time, and since both were excommunicate they could not legally sit in judgement in ecclesiastical cases. They would not willingly resort to force to expel the bishop from his diocese, since Ayala would certainly resist and call upon the townspeople for help. The interdict upon the city, under these circumstances, was a standing invitation to malcontents to commit what disorders they chose.

---

[1] Orozco y Jiménez, *Colección*, vol. I, p. 409: 'La Audiencia de Guadalajara señala al Sr. Obispo Ayala un plazo de diez días para que salga de su obispado. 4 de Julio.'

[2] Ibid. vol. I, p. 410: 'Secuestro de bienes del Sr. obispo. 4 de Julio.'

[3] Ibid. vol. II, p. 45: 'Información sobre los requerimientos del Ilmo. Sr. Ayala a los oidores, en las calles. 4 de Julio.'

[4] Ibid. vol. II, p. 4: 'Carta de participantes y anatema contra los oidores Oseguera y Alarcón. 5 de Julio.'   [5] Ibid. vol. II, p. 6: 'Entredicho. 6 de Julio.'

Deliverance from the dilemma came in letters to the bishop from Mexico, summoning him to a provincial council which was about to meet in that city, and ordering him in the name of the archbishop to absolve Lope de Cisneros, whose case had been heard in appeal and who had been acquitted of the charge of sacrilege.[1] The *oidores* remained excommunicate; but the problem of lawfully removing Ayala from Guadalajara had been settled for them, and the problem of the excommunication and interdict was to prove easier of solution in his absence. The bishop left for Mexico on 16 July, twelve days after the issue of the order for his expulsion, having delegated his jurisdiction to a provisor, the cathedral treasurer Jorge Pérez.[2] Pérez was given no power to absolve the *oidores*, the case being reserved, according to his instructions, to the Pope. Upon the bishop's departure, however, the audiencia bombarded Pérez with its writs, threatening him in turn with exile if he should not comply; after the third repetition he yielded to threats of the royal displeasure, absolved the *oidores* and lifted the interdict.[3] The victory of the *oidores* was thus complete. They never troubled to exercise their right, over which the whole suit had been fought—the right to try (and presumably acquit) Cisneros on a charge of assault; they celebrated their victory, however, by prosecuting the Franciscan prior, Fray Angel de la Valencia, for preaching a highly abusive sermon in support of the bishop, against the audiencia.[4] Fray Angel had on previous occasions supported the *oidores*, especially over questions of Indian policy; but in this matter he was concerned for the immunities of his House and Order. A noticeable feature of the Cisneros case was the intemperate language constantly used by the churchmen concerned in the quarrel, contrasting sharply with the formal courtesy and dignity of the *oidores*. The law significantly allowed considerable latitude to the secular authorities in dealing with seditious and abusive sermons;[5] and the prior was fined.

Ayala, upon his arrival in Mexico, was called upon to answer charges of sedition brought against him by the *fiscal*—that licentiate

---

[1] Ibid. vol. ii, p. 11: 'Provisión del Juez Metropolitano communicando al obispo Ayala que absuelva a Lope de Cisneros. 28 de Junio (recibida 10 de Julio).'

[2] Ibid. vol. ii, p. 26: 'Facultades que el Ilmo. Sr. Ayala otorga a su provisor. 16 de Julio.'

[3] Ibid. vol. ii, p. 29: 'El provisor levanta el entredicho a la ciudad de Guadalajara y absuelve a los excomulgados. 20 de Julio.'

[4] Ibid. vol. ii, p. 67: 'Información referente a un sermón del P. Fray Angel de la Valencia, O.F.M. 16 de Julio 1565.' [5] *Recopilación de Leyes de Indias*, i. xii. 19.

Contreras who had been expelled from New Galicia by Morones and was shortly to return there. The viceregal audiencia threatened to enforce the sentence of the subordinate court by shipping Ayala to Spain, and to add on its own account a fine of 500 *pesos*, if he did not at once absolve the *oidores alcaldes mayores* and comply with the writs issued by them.[1] Ayala at length submitted, though he dispatched a bitter letter of complaint to the king,[2] containing a grossly exaggerated account of the original quarrel, according to which the licentiate Oseguera in person assaulted the bishop, having entered the convent 'with half the city at his back', in order to lynch a number of innocent Indians. Ayala declared also his intention of going to Spain to state his case in person. He returned to Guadalajara the following year, however, entering the city at night and causing the cathedral bells to be rung in celebration of his return.[3] The *oidores* made no further attempt to expel him, 'for fear of public disturbance'; relations between bishop and audiencia remained hostile, however, especially after the return of Contreras as senior *oidor*.

The cases of León and Cisneros, with their attendant complications, have been examined at some length and with detailed references, as examples of the results which might follow typical cases of *fuerza*, when the litigants decided to go to extremes. Besides the ill-feeling which such suits produced, the time and labour involved were often out of all proportion to the nature of the complaint, which might be a merely technical offence. Writs might pass daily for months; each writ, even though merely a repetition of a previous one, had to be sued out in person by the interested party or his advocate and paid for at the official rate. Such conflicts were made inevitable by the very existence of an episcopal jurisdiction, the boundaries of which were left so vague. Cumbrous procedure and the professional interests of the lawyers turned each conflict into a protracted suit, the result of which the Law could not predict.

No other major quarrel arose between the audiencia and the bishop during the remaining three years of Ayala's incumbency. The *oidores* had frequently to mediate, however, in the constant

---

[1] Orozco y Jiménez, *Colección*, vol. II, p. 30: 'Auto de la Real Audiencia de México para que el obispo absuelva. 7 de Sept. 1656.'

[2] Ibid. vol. I, p. 302: 'Carta del Ilmo. Sr. Ayala en la que comunica a Rey, entre otras cosas, la falta de justicia que se nota en la Nueva Galicia. 10 de Nov. 1565.'

[3] Ibid. vol. I, p. 321: 'Carta de los oidores de la Nueva Galicia sobre varios negocios. 2 de Agosto 1566.'

disputes between the bishop and the chapter, arising for the most part from Ayala's attempts to remove canons of whom he disapproved.[1] On one occasion the bishop went so far as to send his proctor with armed support to expel some of the canons from their stalls in the cathedral, and to break up a meeting of the chapter. The dean and chapter presented a petition, and the bishop a counter-petition to the audiencia;[2] but the *oidores* wisely declined to give judgement in a case concerning the royal patronage, and the suit was dropped. The following year (1568) Ayala complained to the king against the action of Contreras, who had ordered him to release Indians summarily imprisoned by his court, and had reminded him that an episcopal court might not arrest either Indian or Spaniard without the help and approval of the audiencia.[3] The law in this matter was clear and no lawsuit followed; but the tone in which the circumstances were reported was no more friendly than that of three years before.

The constant stream of embittered correspondence concerning the episcopal jurisdiction in New Galicia must have convinced the Council of the Indies of the necessity of providing to that see a man who could be trusted to co-operate with the audiencia and prevent any further disturbance. Fortunately local opinion after Ayala's death in 1569 showed a remarkable unanimity; the audiencia, the dean and chapter, and a number of private individuals presented petitions begging the king to elevate one of the *oidores*, the licentiate Mendiola, to the bishopric.[4] Mendiola was a nephew of the first

[1] Ibid. vol. I, p. 310: 'Carta a S.M. del Lic. Alonso de Oseguera, el Doctor Alarcón, y el Lic. Mendiola, oidores de Guadalajara; confirman la relación hecha acerca de la conducta de D. Pedro de Ayala, obispo del reino, desavenencias con el cabildo de la iglesia, y sus prebendados, y mediación que han procurado de tener en pro de la concordia. 16 de Feb. 1566.'
Ibid. vol. I, p. 329: 'Carta del obispo de la Nueva Galicia a S.M. en la cual se trata varios asuntos 16 de Mayo 1567.'
[2] Ibid. vol. I, p. 346: 'Peticiones de D. Fray Pedro de Ayala, obispo de Nueva Galicia, y de los capitulares de aquella Santa Iglesia sobre que no llevase vara un fiscal que el dicho obispo tenía nombrado. 23 de Agosto 1567.'
[3] Ibid. vol. I, p. 351: 'Carta a S.M. de Fray Pedro de Ayala obispo de Nueva Galicia—dice que aunque escribió a S.M. lo que le pareció ser necesario, lo vuelve hacer porque siempre se ofrecen cosas que suplicar....9 de Marzo 1568.'
[4] Ibid. vol. II, p. 99: 'El V. Cabildo propone a S.M. nombre por obispo de Guadalajara al meritísimo Licenciado D. Francisco Gómez de Mendiola, oidor de la Nueva Galicia, 15 de Octubre 1569.'
Ibid. vol. II, p. 107:-'Carta de la Real Audiencia de Guadalajara pidiendo por obispo al Licenciado Mendiola. 20 de Marzo 1570.'
Ibid. vol. II, p. 102: 'El Doctor Alarcón, oidor alcalde mayor de la Real Audiencia de Guadalajara, propone por obispo al Licenciado Mendiola, 15 de Marzo 1570,' etc.

archbishop of Mexico, Fray Juan de Zumárraga; he had served three years in New Galicia, being occupied during half that time upon a *visita* in Zacatecas and other mining centres; he had been active in preventing and punishing the abuse of native labour, and had drawn up a series of ordinances regulating labour conditions in the mines.[1] The petitioners, in urging his elevation, significantly mentioned, in addition to his piety and learning, his wide acquaintance with Indian customs.

Mendiola was elevated to the bishopric in 1570. The choice was a singularly happy one; he made without difficulty the transition from the position of a judge who happened to be in Holy Orders to that of a priest who happened to have had legal experience; in both capacities he displayed all Lebrón de Quiñones's hatred of oppression without his genius for unpopularity. To be loved and respected by all classes, in so heterogeneous a society, was an achievement little short of marvellous, yet the chroniclers are unanimous that Mendiola was so loved, and cite in proof the names given to him by his contemporaries—'apostle of New Galicia', 'friend of the poor' and so forth. He co-operated loyally with the audiencia in the encouragement of Indian agriculture and handicrafts, supported the mission friars in their desperate journeys, and sternly punished the petty exactions practised by many of the secular clergy. After his death in 1576 his tomb became a place of pilgrimage and remained so until the eighteenth century, when a movement was set on foot to secure his beatification, and pious research recovered some of the story of his life along with many curious accounts of miracles attributed to his dead body.[2]

The elevation of Mendiola was important in the history of the audiencia, in putting an end to a period of miserable bickering between the secular and episcopal jurisdictions. Another event which occurred at the same time, and which affected the whole history of the Indies, was to prevent such bickering from recurring in the old form. On 16 August 1570, a royal decree[3] authorised the Inquisitor-General to establish a regular tribunal of the Holy Office in New Spain. The official reason given was the danger to

---

[1] *A.G.I.* Auda. de Guadalajara 5: 'Averiguaciones del Lic. Contreras y Guevara sobre lo tocante a la visita del Real Consejo de Indias fols. 122–137.' (Text of Mendiola's decrees.)

[2] Orozco y Jiménez, *Colección*, vol. ii, p. 130: 'Causa de la beatificación del Ilmo. Sr. Mendiola. 1714.'

[3] *Recopilación de Leyes de Indias*, i. xix. i. See C. H. Lea, op. cit. p. 200.

the Faith from Judaising New Christians settled in the Indies, and above all from English and other Protestants who carried on illicit trade with the Spanish colonial ports. The voyages of John Hawkins, and his encounter with Enríquez at San Juan de Ulúa had opened the eyes of the Council of the Indies; a large number of men captured from his ships were living in more or less rigorous servitude in New Spain, and one of the first duties of the new inquisitors was to send for these men and revise their sentences. Apart from the Lutheran menace (which in practice appears to have been negligible), it had long been clear that many duties of the ecclesiastical courts in the Indies could not be performed adequately by overworked episcopal provisors. Lebrón de Quiñones himself had advised the establishment of the Holy Office in New Spain, not upon the ground of any alleged danger to the Faith, but simply because the existing courts were insufficient to maintain discipline among the clergy.[1] From the point of view of the audiencia, the decree of 1570 meant that much of the jurisdiction which had formerly given so much trouble was transferred from the episcopal courts to the far more powerful Inquisition. The bishops were left with powers to try matrimonial causes, cases of perjury, and sacrilege (though the Inquisition soon claimed that as part of its own province) criminal charges against the clergy (with the exception of solicitation, which was extremely prevalent and was always tried by the secret tribunal) and the offences of Christian Indians—apostasy, idolatry, and the holding of forbidden dances; Indians were exempted from the activities of the Holy Office, on the ostensible ground of their feeble understanding. The episcopal courts were still in a position to dispute cases with the audiencia, therefore, but their authority was considerably weakened, and they had lost the power to impose the severer penalties, which the bishops had formerly held when acting as Inquisitors. On the other hand, the audiencias had to face in the new Holy Office formally installed in 1571, a competent, highly centralised ecclesiastical jurisdiction, wielding immense power and responsible, like the audiencias themselves, to the king alone. The years 1571–72 saw not only the opening of a new chapter in the history of the audiencia of New Galicia itself, but a revolution in its relations with the Courts Christian of New Spain.

[1] *A.G.I.* Auda. de Guadalajara 51: 'Licenciado Lebrón de Quiñones al Rey, de Tlaximoroa en Michoacán. 10 de Sept. 1554.'

CHAPTER VI

THE REORGANISATION OF
THE AUDIENCIA, 1570–72

The paternal government of the Spanish Indies demanded constant reference to Spain over comparatively trifling matters, and quickly accumulated, in consequence, great stacks of papers—reports, orders, recommendations, account books, petitions—which defied adequate classification and to some extent defeated the very purpose of record-keeping, since in any general inquiry, references to the archives proved far too slow and laborious a task for overworked officials. Special summaries and testimonies had to be prepared for individual cases, therefore, by persons having direct knowledge of the facts. In 1568 a commission was issued to Fray Juan de Ovando, of the supreme council of the Inquisition, to conduct a general *visita* of the Council of the Indies. In order to avoid the superhuman task of reviewing the whole body of records of the Indies administration, the *visitador* secured decrees in 1569, commanding the senior *oidor* of each audiencia to draw up an attested summary of the manner of government in his district, the *cédulas* and orders issued to the court of which he was a member since its foundation, and the measures taken to give effect to those orders. The *Averiguaciones* compiled in answer to Ovando's questionnaire by the licentiate Contreras, then senior *oidor* at Guadalajara, form a substantial vellum-bound volume.[1] They make no mention of the miserable conflicts with the second bishop, which had occupied so much of the *oidores'* time and attention during the 1560's, and which ended only with the elevation of the *oidor* Mendiola to the See; naturally, also, they contain no revelations of serious incompetence or dishonesty on the part of the *oidores*. They supply, however, a clear account of the institutional arrangements of New Galicia, and of the official activities of the audiencia, especially in the years following the move from Compostela to Guadalajara.

Contreras claimed that the audiencia had successfully enforced

---

[1] *A.G.I.* Auda. de Guadalajara 5: 'Averiguaciones hechas por el ilustre Señor Licenciado Miguel Ladrón de Contreras y Guevara, sobre lo tocante a la visita del Real Consejo de Indias 1569–1570.'

the greater part of the legislation addressed to it, though his testimony was deliberately vague on some points, indicating that a number of decrees had been lost during the period of the *visitas* in New Spain, and that no complete register had been kept. A few failures were recorded: offices could not be found at once for all those who brought *cédulas* of favour from Spain; the bridge over the Río Grande remained half constructed, owing to lack of funds; arrangements for instructing the clergy in native languages were admittedly inadequate; and the members of the legal profession in Guadalajara had successfully resisted Contreras's efforts to enforce decrees reducing the fees payable by Indian litigants. These, however, were comparatively minor omissions and could not be attributed to negligence on the part of the *oidores*. Contreras could, on the other hand, point to several instances in which useful work undertaken by the audiencia had been hampered by lack of support at home. The Council of the Indies had never recognised the ordinances issued by members of the audiencia regulating the exploitation of mines and salt-beds,[1] the use of Indian labour in mining, and the marketing of food in the towns of New Galicia. Contreras included copies of these ordinances, and others of less importance, in the *Averiguaciones*, and asked that they should be confirmed or revised as the king might command.

In reporting upon matters of organisation, the *Averiguaciones* entered into greater detail. The Spanish population had increased rapidly since 1548, and with it the complexity of the administrative and judicial organisation.[2] There were in 1570 about fifteen hundred Spanish householders in New Galicia, distributed among two cities, six towns, and fifteen established mining settlements. Fifty-five of them held *encomiendas*, or parts of *encomiendas*, the rest being miners, ranchers, merchants or officials. The number of Indian householders living peacefully under Spanish rule was estimated at twenty thousand, distributed among some fifty *encomiendas* and an equal number of *corregimientos* of Crown *pueblos*. Many Indians, of course, remained unsubdued and without

---

[1] Contreras was mistaken about the salt-bed regulations. Cf. A. F. A. and F. R. Bandelier, *Historical Documents relating to New Mexico*, vol. I, p. 92: 'Respuesta a los oidores alcaldes mayores de la Nueva Galicia sobre lo de la Sal. 22 de Sept. 1562.' Salt was used instead of quicksilver in the extraction of silver, and was much sought after for that and other reasons.

[2] See J. López de Velasco, 'Geografía de las Indias 1571–1574,' *Boletín de la Sociedad geográfica de Madrid*, 1864.

permanent settlements. Forty-five *corregidores* and fifteen *alcaldes mayores* were appointed annually by the audiencia; the appointments were for one year only, the *corregidores* receiving from 200 to 300 *pesos* in salary, the *alcaldes mayores* from 500 to 600,[1] paid from the Indian tributes of the province. Most of these offices had been created by the audiencia, with the approval of the viceroy. The Crown had rarely refused to sanction the creation of a post by the audiencia, though on several occasions it had issued warnings against a too liberal appointment of deputy-*corregidores*, since the small size of the *corregimientos* rendered such offices superfluous. A decree of 1570 revoked the appointment to a *corregimiento* of a man who already held the office of notary (*escribano de cámara*) to the audiencia.[2]

Specimens of the commissions issued by the audiencia to *corregidores* and *alcaldes mayores* were included in the *Averiguaciones*.[3] *Corregidores* received orders to enforce the New Laws, to expel aliens and undesirable Spaniards, and to compel the recognition by Spaniards of their children by native women; married Spaniards who had left their wives in Spain were to be offered the alternative of arranging for their wives' passage to New Galicia, or of being themselves deported to Spain; all Spaniards travelling through the country were to pay for the hospitality they received, at rates which the *corregidores* might determine; Indians were to be protected in the possession of their lands and instructed in the arts of stock-raising and chicken-farming; missionaries were to receive all possible support and assistance from the *corregidores*. *Alcaldes mayores* received more general instructions to do justice and preserve the Indians from molestation; like the *corregidores*, they held office nominally for one year, and were forbidden to pass sentence in cases involving death or mutilation, or in suits between Indian chiefs, 'because such questions are difficult and their solution must be left to trained and learned persons'. These serious cases the audiencia reserved for itself.

Of the fifty-odd *encomiendas* of New Galicia, forty-two were based upon formal grants made by Nuño de Guzmán, copied by

[1] *A.G.I.* Auda. de Guadalajara 5: 'Averiguaciones', fol. 91. The appointment of *corregidores* for one year was an unusual feature. In most provinces, *corregidores* held office for three years. (*Recopilación de Leyes de Indias*, v. ii. 10.)

[2] *A.G.I.* Auda. de Guadalajara 230, Z 1, fol. 222. 26 de Agosto 1570.

[3] *A.G.I.* Auda. de Guadalajara 5. Averiguaciones, fols. 144, 145. A specimen commission is appended (Appendix B).

de la Marcha in his *visita* of 1549, and preserved in the register of the audiencia.[1] The six or eight *encomenderos* who could display no title-deeds were deemed to hold their Indians by prescriptive right. All the surviving deeds contained the old clause, which had now become illegal, empowering the *encomenderos* to employ the labour of their Indians without wages. None of the deeds had been revised and no new grants had been made. The audiencia, of course, had no authority to commend Indians; its duties, in the matter of the succession to *encomiendas*, were confined to reporting vacancies. No vacancies had been reported; possibly none had occurred, since the official 'two lives' might easily cover thirty-six years. More probably, the audiencia had prudently refrained from enforcing the unpopular law concerning the 'two lives', with the result that *encomiendas* had been treated as hereditary fiefs. Certainly some and probably all of the *encomenderos* of 1570 were descendants of the first conquerors. Contreras claimed, however, that within the *encomiendas* the New Laws had been rigorously enforced; personal servitude had been abolished and tributes duly assessed.

Of the offices outside the patronage of the audiencia, the most important were the treasury posts—treasurer, auditor and overseer, and their deputies. The recommendations made by de la Marcha concerning the distribution of these officials had received tacit royal approval, and since 1550 the treasurer and the overseer, with the auditor's deputy, had resided in Zacatecas, while the auditor and the other two deputies had remained at the seat of the audiencia. After the move to Guadalajara, the *oidores* had issued orders for the concentration of the treasury organisation in that city; the Zacatecas officials had refused to comply, without an order from Spain, alleging as their reason the danger of loss by fraud or robbery if the royal silver had constantly to be brought across the Río Grande to Guadalajara. The Council of the Indies, upon the advice of the audiencia of Mexico, had upheld the officials in a decree of 1563;[2] a further decree of 1571 established a separate royal chest in Zacatecas.[3] The *oidores* had always been defeated in their attempt to control the policy and the personnel of the provincial treasury; their temporary appointments, such as

---

[1] Ibid. fol. 157. A specimen is appended (Appendix A).
[2] *A.G.I.* Auda. de Guadalajara 230, Z 1, fol. 145. 27 de Junio 1563.
[3] Ibid. fol. 231. 23 de Junio 1571.

those of Gaspar de Morones as auditor, and of Domingo de Mendiola as treasurer, were never allowed to become permanent. The old treasurer, Pedro Gómez de Contreras, indicted for peculation during the *cuenta* begun by Oseguera in 1558, never made his peace with the government; an order of 1562[1] commanded the audiencia to distrain upon his person and his goods, but he died still owing a large sum to the treasury. The *cuenta* never became the routine annual event contemplated by the ordinances, or more than an occasional upheaval, and even the salaries of the justices were not always punctually paid by the treasury officials.[2] In general, however, complaints after 1562 were not serious, and reasonably good relations prevailed between the audiencia and the treasury, especially since the officials depended, for the collection of tribute, upon the co-operation of the constable and his deputies.[3]

Relations with the various municipal bodies had been rather less friendly. The councillors of the principal towns were usually among the wealthier *encomenderos*, ranchers and mine-owners, and the *cabildos* of Guadalajara and Compostela had always shown a marked hostility towards reformers such as Lebrón de Quiñones and Contreras. In Guadalajara, conflicts between the audiencia and the *cabildo* were frequent. In 1563 the councillors complained of the action of the audiencia in allotting building sites and gardens within the city to individuals—a right which they claimed for the *cabildo*. The Crown on this occasion decided in favour of the *cabildo*,[4] and the decision held until 1572, when a joint committee was set up.[5] Later in the same year the *oidores* were commanded to regulate the sale of foodstuffs in the city, to inspect meat-markets and to prevent the raising of prices by monopolists—duties which again brought them into conflict with some of the more influential councillors.[6] They were forbidden, at the same time, to interfere in the election of municipal magistrates, or to trespass in any other way upon the privileges of the municipality. Such prohibitions failed to satisfy the councillors, whose attitude towards the audiencia was reflected, in the early years, by constant petitions

[1] *A.G.I.* Auda. de Guadalajara 230, Z 1, fol. 104. 4 de Mayo 1562.
[2] Ibid. fol. 115 verso. 8 de Nov. 1562. Royal officials to pay salaries at four-month intervals.
[3] Ibid. fol. 112 verso. 8 de Nov. 1562. The *alguacil mayor* to assist the treasury officials.
[4] Ibid. fol. 143 verso. 2 de Enero 1563.
[5] Ch. VII, p. 146.
[6] *A.G.I.* Auda. de Guadalajara 230, Z 1, fol. 140 verso. 15 de Mayo 1563.

for the abolition of the court, and later, after 1561, by requests that the minimum sum, over which lawsuits might be carried to Mexico, should be reduced. The townsmen of Guadalajara apparently never lost their faith that the distant audiencia would deal more justly with them than the one nearby.

Civil appeals from one audiencia to the other were in practice very rare, partly because comparatively few lawsuits in New Galicia involved more than 500 *pesos*, but chiefly because few litigants could afford the time and expense involved in a special journey to Mexico; most of the civil cases heard in appeal by the viceregal audiencia concerned the property of *oidores* of New Galicia or of their children.[1] Some Spaniards who held land or Indians in New Galicia, however, either resided in Mexico or had frequent business there. Such men preferred to bring their suits directly before the viceregal audiencia; the judicial records therefore contain a few cases concerning property in New Galicia, decided without reference to the subordinate court.[2] The *oidores alcaldes mayores*, though they occasionally protested against this direct recourse to Mexico,[3] had no means of preventing it; nor was there any reliable evidence that they hindered lawful civil appeals from their own decisions. Their permission was not required for a civil appeal to Mexico; it was for the higher court to decide whether it would receive an appeal, and the influence of the legal profession encouraged prolonged litigation wherever possible. The absence of examples of civil appeal can only mean either that the need for appeal was not felt, or that the expense and trouble of travelling acted as a natural deterrent.

[1] E.g. Archivo General de la Nación, México, D.F.: Ramo de Tierras, tit. 2971, exp. 8: 'Catalina de Figueroa y Diego de Medrano sobre evaluo de sus bienes.' (Medrano was an *oidor* in the audiencia of New Galicia.) Ramo de Civil, tit. 430, exp. 1: 'Proceso de Felipe de Vargas contra Gerónimo Baéza de Herrera su hermano, sobre los alimentos.' Defendant was the son-in-law of the *oidor* Hernán Martínez de la Marcha. He and his wife were sued for failing to support his younger brother out of the revenues of an *encomienda*. Plaintiff appealed to the audiencia of Mexico.

[2] *A.G.I.* Justicia—Audiencia de México:
205, no. 7. 'Con Cristóbal Romero, vecino de la ciudad de Guadalajara, sobre el derecho a la mitad de la encomienda del pueblo de Indios de Malinalco (1560).'
208, no. 1. 'El fiscal con Dā Francisca Ferrer, vecina de México, sobre el derecho a la encomienda del pueblo de Atotonilco (de Nueva Galicia) (1566).'
179. 'Gobernador y Consejo de los pueblos de Chachaliutla, Mecatlán, y Coavitlán (de Nueva Galicia) con el gobernador y consejo del pueblo de Chila y los Indios de la estancia de Xapala, sobre demarcación de límites (1575).'

[3] *A.G.I.* Auda. de Guadalajara 51: 'Audiencia al Rey. 2 de Feb. 1562.'

The situation in the realm of criminal jurisdiction was rather different, since a criminal under arrest could not easily appeal to Mexico without the knowledge and consent of his judges; on the other hand, a criminal in danger of exile or execution would undoubtedly appeal if he could. In so disorderly a society the criminal work of the courts was naturally very heavy, and serious criminal cases, in which appeal was legally permitted, occurred much more frequently than civil suits involving large sums. From the small number of the recorded criminal appeals from New Galicia to Mexico, it seems probable that the *oidores alcaldes mayores* deliberately hindered such appeals, perhaps under colour of the fourth clause of their ordinances which permitted a re-trial (*suplicación*) before the full court of the subordinate audiencia, instead of an appeal to Mexico, with the consent of the prosecutor and the accused. 'Consent' might no doubt be extorted. The colonists of New Galicia certainly complained of the restriction of appeals during the first few years of audiencia rule.[1] The records, however, are very incomplete. Criminal appeals went before a different bench of judges in Mexico, since the viceregal audiencia was divided into two chambers, the *oidores* hearing civil suits and the *alcaldes del crimen* hearing criminal charges. The records of the criminal chamber—unlike those of land and other civil disputes, which are still a source of fees to the Mexican government—have suffered by fire, flood, and the carelessness of early archivists.[2] In the Spanish archive the records for New Galicia are scanty in both civil and criminal departments. There are only five bundles of judicial papers concerning New Galicia for the period before 1572,[3] and only one record of appeal to Mexico, that of Francisco Moro, sentenced to death in 1569 for the murder of a Spaniard.

Some of the unpopularity of the audiencia in its early days no doubt arose from the fact that the *oidores alcaldes mayores* were frequently compelled to act both as prosecutors and as judges in criminal matters, since the only regular prosecuting authorities were the minor justices—themselves often venal and negligent—and the constables, who acted under the orders of the audiencia.

[1] E.g. *A.G.I.* Auda. de Guadalajara 51: 'Oficiales Reales del nuevo reino de Galicia al Rey. 20 de Diciembre 1549.'

[2] Archivo General de la Nación, México D.F.: Ramo de lo Judicial. Only about a hundred volumes survive.

[3] *A.G.I.* Justicia—Guadalajara 335–9.

In 1568, however, the criminal work of the court was rendered more effective and more impartial by the creation of the office of *fiscal*,[1] or public prosecutor. Such an official had been greatly needed in New Galicia; before the appointment of the first *fiscal*, the licentiate Morante, the audiencia employed any attorney it could find to prepare prosecutions. A large number of cases, in the names of three different prosecuting attorneys, were pending in 1569, the year of Morante's actual arrival in Guadalajara. Contreras included a list of cases in the *Averiguaciones*;[2] the commonest charges were murder, ill-treatment of Indians, and tax evasion; negroes were frequently arrested for acts of violence, Indians more rarely. The most usual sentences passed upon Spaniards were heavy fines for fraud; fines, exile or mutilation for ill-treatment of Indians; and exile for brawling or for contempt of the audiencia. Indian and negro criminals were more commonly punished by flogging or mutilation. Sentence of death almost always followed a conviction for murder, or for robbery with serious violence, whatever the race of the culprit, and the most powerful offenders were not immune (if Contreras was to be believed) from prosecution for breach of the Indian laws.

Such was the tenor of Contreras's report; but critics of the *oidores* were never lacking, and they, as well as the official spokesman of the audiencia, were given an opportunity of deposing before the *visitador* of the Council of the Indies. In 1569 the chapter of the cathedral of Guadalajara (the See being at the time vacant) was commanded to draw up a survey of conditions in New Galicia, with an account of the civil and ecclesiastical government. The canons had never shown themselves particularly sympathetic towards the audiencia, partly perhaps on account of the close relations between some of the *oidores*, and the friars of the Orders. Their report,[3] however, though carping in tone, bore indirect testimony to the relative efficiency of audiencia rule. It contained no really serious specific complaints; most of the accusations against the *oidores* were concerned with minor personal scandals. Contreras,

---

[1] *A.G.I.* Auda. de Guadalajara 230, Z 1, fol. 185. 18 Feb. 1568. Appointment of Licentiate Morante. For duties of Fiscal see *Recopilación de Leyes de Indias*, II. xviii. 1–48; J. de Solórzano, *Política Indiana*, v. vi. 1–49.

[2] *A.G.I.* Auda. de Guadalajara 5. Averiguaciones, fol. 168.

[3] J. García-Icazbalceta (ed.), *Documentos para la historia de México*, vol. II, p. 484: 'Informe al Rey por el Cabildo eclesiástico de Guadalajara acerca de las cosas de aquel Reino. 20 de Enero 1570.'

as might be expected, received most of the abuse; his hasty temper, which had served him so ill on previous occasions, was still the talk of Guadalajara, and references to his vindictiveness against leading Spaniards indicated that the campaign against the *encomenderos* still continued. Contreras, also, was said to be ruled by his wife, a formidable lady who insisted upon occupying a seat in the cathedral, which stood in the way of the processions; the *oidor* publicly offering to thrash any one who dared to move his wife from her chosen seat. For these reasons, the canons protested against the practice of restoring to office *oidores* who had once been condemned and deprived; they assumed without question that the charges brought in 1556 had been well founded, and piously thanked God that Contreras's friend Lebrón de Quiñones had died before he could return to New Galicia.

Orozco, Mendiola and Alarcón were described as learned and active, at least in their professional capacities. Mendiola was comparatively unknown; he had been much occupied since his appointment in inspecting and regulating labour conditions in the mines of Zacatecas. No mention was made in the chapter's report of the proposal to elevate him to the bishopric; but he was already beginning to impress his contemporaries with the saintly and commanding character which he later displayed as bishop. Alarcón was accused of exploiting the powers possessed by the *oidores*, of regulating the prices of important commodities, in order to establish a profitable personal monopoly in the manufacture of candles. He was an eccentric and irritable old man, possessed of two leading passions—for gardening and for judicial disputes. He had secured exemption from the rules against *oidores* possessing land, in order to amuse himself by growing vegetables, to the neglect of his judicial duties;[1] and had been more determined and more tactless than any of his colleagues, in quarrelling with the late bishop, Pedro de Ayala, though this was not held greatly to his discredit by the canons, whose own relations with that litigious prelate had not been altogether harmonious. Of the licentiate Orozco, rumour said that he owed his appointment to the influence of his elder brother, Doctor Orozco, *oidor* of the audiencia of Mexico. It was held to be a particularly serious judicial scandal, that appeals from the decisions of the audiencia in which the younger brother sat, should be heard in the higher court of which

[1] *A.G.I.* Audà. de Guadalajara 230, Z 1, fol. 225 verso.

the elder brother was a member, and the removal of one or other of the Orozco brothers was the only specific reform recommended by the chapter to the Crown.

The information submitted to the Crown from all these various sources in 1570 formed the first complete survey of conditions in New Galicia, and testified on the whole to the efficiency of audiencia rule. The royal treasury accounts corroborated this testimony. New Galicia was growing rapidly in importance as a source of revenue.[1] It seemed probable that the court would soon be released from its subordination to Mexico, and be given an independent authority within its province. The Crown in making decisions for the future, however, had to consider the situation of the viceroyalty of New Spain as a whole. New Galicia, though no longer a frontier province, still contained numerous warlike and unsubdued Indian tribes, especially in the Sierra de Nayarit and in the area which now forms the State of Zacatecas. Travel between the Spanish settlements was fraught with danger. Responsibility for suppressing revolts rested ultimately with the viceroy as captain-general, but his actions were often hampered by the audiencia, which resented his interference and claimed the right, as the chief administrative authority in the province, to organise military expeditions of its own, in spite of royal prohibitions of such undertakings.[2] As late as 1570, Contreras wrote to the king, describing a punitive expedition which he himself had led against a marauding Chichimec band.[3] The viceroys, for their part, sometimes trespassed upon the preserves of the audiencia, by assuming judicial authority in cases where military objectives were involved. Velasco had intervened in Guanajuato in 1561.[4] In 1567 some of the inhabitants of Zacatecas—probably miners aggrieved by the proceedings of Mendiola while on *visita* there—complained to Falces of the prevailing state of disorder in the mines. The viceroy dispatched a judicial commissioner, one Enciso, to investigate the trouble, without however warning the audiencia of his intention. The *oidores*, hearing of Enciso's arrival, sent orders to the *alcalde*

---

[1] *A.G.I.* Patronato 182, R⁰. 4: 'Relación del valor que han tenido los diezmos y quintos de plata que se han sacado en la gobernación de Nueva España y Minas de Zacatecas en los años de 1562 a 1572.' The royal officials of New Galicia accounted for 12,000 marks of silver in 1562 and 21,640 marks in 1572.

[2] E.g. *A.G.I.* Auda. de Guadalajara 230, Z 1, fol. 200 verso. 4 de Nov. 1568.

[3] *A.G.I.* Auda. de Guadalajara 5: 'Contreras al Rey. 16 de Marzo 1570.'

[4] See ch. IV, p. 87.

mayor to eject him, as an unauthorised and unqualified intruder upon their jurisdiction—one of the complaints against him apparently being that he held only a bachelor's, not a licentiate's degree. The Council of the Indies on this occasion supported the viceroy and reprimanded the audiencia.[1] Doctor Orozco, the elder brother, received a royal commission to go to Zacatecas and investigate the whole situation there; his report,[2] compiled at about the same time as the *Averiguaciones* of Contreras, exculpated the *oidores* on the ground that they had not been officially informed of Enciso's commission, but emphasised the disturbed state of the country round the mines and recommended a unified military control.

The reprimand administered to the audiencia was on a point of order, not a point of law. The *oidores* continued to exercise their appellate jurisdiction in litigation arising from military operations, as they had every right to do. The *Averiguaciones* record one such case, of a Spanish renegade tried and condemned to death in the audiencia.[3] The institution of martial law was not recognised by the professional lawyers.

Enríquez, Falces's successor, dealt more tactfully but no less firmly with the audiencia. Himself a soldier, he had no wish to assume the functions of a judge; but neither would he tolerate any interference on the part of the judges with his military authority. In his first year of office, he secured a royal decree commanding the audiencia of New Galicia to obey his orders in matters concerning the well-being of the whole viceroyalty, and to support and assist his agents.[4] His policy was to maintain the autonomous courts of justice, to restrict them to purely judicial functions, and to centralise administration in the interests of military efficiency; a policy which, for a few years, he persuaded the Council of the Indies to support.

In 1572, upon Enríquez's advice, the whole structure of the audiencia was reorganised. The Ordinances of 1548 were repealed; the audiencia lost all its administrative authority; the viceroy was made supreme governor of the whole of New Spain and New Galicia, with sole power under the Crown to appoint minor officials and judges, to supervise public works, and to authorise

---

[1] *A.G.I.* Auda. de Guadalajara 230: Z 1, fol. 231. 23 de Junio 1570.
[2] *A.G.I.* Auda. de Guadalajara 5: 'Dr Orozco al Rey. 14 de Abril 1571.'
[3] Ibid.: 'Averiguaciones—Procesos fiscales', fol. 168.
[4] *A.G.I.* Auda. de Guadalajara 230, Z 1, fol. 200. 31 de Diciembre 1568.

emergency expenditure from the royal chest.[1] The audiencia, on the other hand, was elevated to the status of a royal chancellery consisting of a president and three (later four) *oidores*, armed with a royal seal and holding independent and final jurisdiction in its district, under the Council of the Indies.[2] The salaries of the *oidores* were raised from 650,000 *mrs.* to 2,000 ducats (750,000 *mrs.*), while the president received 3,500 ducats (1,312,500 *mrs.*).[3] All subordination to Mexico in judicial matters was ended; the inferior title of *oidor alcalde mayor* disappeared and the audiencia received in addition, a year later, a considerable accession of territory.[4] Further decrees followed, extending to New Galicia the general audiencia ordinances known as the ordinances of Monzón, already in force in the provinces of Quito and Los Charcas. These ordinances, though amended in some details, were never superseded, and their main provisions were repeated in all the editions of the *Recopilación de Leyes de Indias*.

The administrative arrangements of 1572 quickly proved unsatisfactory. Great distances and bad communications made government by the viceroy intolerably slow and difficult, and after the successes of Enríquez's frontier campaigns the need for unified authority seemed less pressing. The Council of the Indies, with its insistence on centralisation, preferred a centre in Spain to a centre in Mexico City, and Philip II could never bring himself to trust a powerful and able viceroy for long. To revert to the state of affairs which existed before 1572, however, would merely have restored the old confusion between judicial and administrative authority. New Galicia needed a governor as well as a court of appeal. In 1574 a solution was provided by a decree[5] depriving the viceroy of

---

[1] 'Don Martín Enríquez, Nro. Capitán-General...vos solo tengáis el gobierno de todos los distritos de esa audiencia y de la provincia de la Nueva Galicia, en todo lo que se ofreciere...y mandamos al Nro. presidente y oidores de la Nra. audiencia que no se entremetan ni se puedan entremeter en el gobierno del distrito de la dicha audiencia.' *A.G.I.* Auda. de Guadalajara 230, Z 1, fol. 258. 11 de Junio 1572.

[2] 'En lugar de los dichos cuatro oidores alcaldes mayores que hasta aquí ha habido y hay, de aquí adelante haya un presidente y tres oidores, y sea audiencia formada, y tenga la misma autoridad y preeminencias que tienen las Nras. audiencias que residen en la villa de Valladolid y ciudad de Granada destos Nros. reinos, y las otras audiencias que residen en las Nras. Indias, islas y tierra firme del mar océano, para lo cual mandamos hacer y enviar a la dicha provincia nuestro sello real.' *A.G.I.* Simancas—Guadalajara 230, Z 1, fol. 259. 11 de Junio 1572.

[3] Ibid. fol. 241. 30 de Abril 1572.

[4] See ch. IV, p. 96, and accompanying map.

[5] *A.G.I.* Auda. de Guadalajara 230, lib. Z 2, fol. 13. 21 de Abril 1574.

direct administrative authority in New Galicia and conferring upon the president of the audiencia the title of governor, with most of the powers which had been taken from the *oidores* in 1572. By 1574, therefore, the audiencia had assumed the form and authority which it was to retain throughout the colonial period,[1] and which was more or less common by that time to all the audiencias of the Indies. The first governor-president under the new arrangements was Doctor Orozco, late *oidor* of the audiencia of Mexico, and *visitador* in Zacatecas.

[1] *Recopilación de Leyes de Indias*, II. xv. 7.

PART II

THE AUDIENCIA AND ROYAL CHANCELLERY, 1572–1600

CHAPTER VII

ADMINISTRATION

One of the leading characteristics of Spanish government in the sixteenth century was its interest in legal codification. In the sphere of colonial administration, particularly, a number of impressive codes were compiled, of which the most important were the New Laws of 1543, regulating the relations between the Indians and their conquerors; the Ordinances on Discoveries of 1573, laying down the conditions of future exploration and settlement; and the Ordinances of the Audiencias, which were promulgated at Monzón in 1562 and which for the sake of brevity may be called the Ordinances of Monzón.

The Ordinances of Monzón were designed to organise the audiencias of the Indies (except the two viceregal audiencias, which were necessarily different in constitution and powers) according to a common pattern, and so to counteract the growing influence of local custom in the various provinces. They applied originally to the two new audiencias of Quito and Los Charcas and were subsequently extended to cover the other lesser audiencias. When the audiencia of New Galicia was reorganised in 1572 and declared independent of the audiencia of Mexico, it received the Ordinances of Monzón as its charter[1] in place of the original loosely worded and experimental ordinances of 1548.

A closer definition of powers and duties was badly needed. The authority of the audiencia, like that of most other administrative organs in a centralised empire, rested not upon local support but upon royal appointment and the letter of royal decrees. As a court of appeal enforcing known law, the audiencia had proved itself

---

[1] *A.G.I.* Auda. de Guadalajara 230, lib. Z 1, fol. 259, 11 de Junio 1572. The entry in the Guadalajara register of *cédulas* merely commands the audiencia to observe the same ordinances as the audiencia of Quito. These are in *A.G.I.* Auda. de Quito, 211, lib. 1, fol. 30. The text of the ordinances is published in R. Levillier (ed.), *Correspondencia de la audiencia de Charcas* (Buenos Aires, 1910), Appendix.

reasonably just and efficient; as an administrative board exercising a wide discretion it had been less successful. The *oidores* had been uncertain of the extent of their own powers. They had received little practical guidance from Spain and had been compelled by circumstances to work out policies for themselves; but since each had an equal vote in *acuerdo* meetings, they had seldom managed to agree. In particular, they had failed to make adequate provision for the defence of the province against Indian raids.

After several decades of frontier disorder, an attempt had been made to disentangle judicial from administrative authority. In 1572 the administration of New Spain and New Galicia was centralised in the hands of the viceroy. The audiencia retained only its judicial powers, and those clauses of the Ordinances of Monzón which dealt with administration became inoperative in New Galicia. It was obviously impossible, however, to administer the province from Mexico City, and in 1574 New Galicia again became a separate government. The viceroy retained a general right of supervision, as he did over all Spanish territories north of Panama,[1] and certain matters were specifically reserved for his decision; but he was not to govern New Galicia directly.[2] The governor was to be the president of the audiencia, a school-trained lawyer; and the administrative clauses of the Ordinances of Monzón came into force, except in so far as they were modified by the 1574 decree itself and by subsequent legislation. Throughout the empire, general codes designed to bring all the provinces into a common plan conflicted repeatedly with *ad hoc* legislation intended to solve the problems of particular provinces. New Galicia was no exception.

In the Ordinances of Monzón, as in the ordinances of 1548, the space devoted to administration was comparatively small; the section headed 'Casos de gobierno' contained fifteen clauses out of three hundred and eleven. The powers granted were wide. There was a recognised right of legislation—the audiencia might make ordinances for the area under its control; the ordinances must, of course, be submitted to the Council of the Indies for approval, but meanwhile, until the reply of the Council was received, the

[1] *Recopilación de Leyes de Indias*, II. xv. 50, 51, 52.
[2] *A.G.I.* Auda. de Guadalajara 230, lib. Z 2, fol. 13 verso. 21 de Abril, 1574: '…sin embargo de lo contenido en aquella cédula (de 1572) la gobernación de esa provincia la tenéis vos toda, y en vuestra ausencia el audiencia, y al visorrey solamente le está reservada la gobernación de guerra y gratificación de servicios.'

audiencia might enforce them on its own authority. Examples of the type of ordinances contemplated in this clause are to be found in the various codes of mining regulations issued by the audiencia[1] and in the regulations for the manufacture and marketing of salt.[2] The audiencia had, in practice, issued ordinances before 1572; but only in that year did it receive express authorisation to do so.

The audiencia might authorise *repartimientos*; this clause, again, confirmed officially a power which the audiencia had previously exercised with only tacit permission. In this context the word *repartimiento* clearly meant the levy of gangs of Indians for compulsory, though paid, labour. The clause stipulated that the *repartimientos* were to be for works of public importance and were not to be made in favour of persons who held *encomiendas*, the general principle being that individual Spaniards could not expect to enjoy both tributes and the use of forced labour.

The word *repartimiento* occurs again in the next clause in a different sense—the distribution of land. Land for farms and ranches in New Galicia was to be granted by order of the audiencia, having due regard both to the preservation of Indian rights and to the special claims of 'old conquerors and settlers' and of the councillors of the corporate towns of the province. Since many town councillors bought their places from the Crown, it was a matter of financial importance to make municipal offices attractive, by giving their holders preference in the distribution of land. Grants of land made to persons in any of these privileged classes were officially limited to three *caballerías*; but in the absence of reliable surveys the audiencia adopted the rough and ready method of measuring grants in terms of radius from a given point—two thousand paces for sheep farms, three thousand for cattle ranches.[3] Additional land might also be purchased from the Crown, and one of the duties of the president was to arrange and supervise auctions of unoccupied land. In theory both grants and purchases required royal confirmation, but this rule was seldom enforced.[4]

[1] *A.G.I.* Auda. de Guadalajara 5. Averiguaciones del Lic. Contreras y Guevara (1570), fols. 105–21; *A.G.I.* Patronato 182, Rº. 52: 'Ordenanzas hechas por el Lic. Santiago de Riego, oidor de la audiencia de la Nueva Galicia, sobre el buen régimen y gobierno de las minas de Zacatecas y Pánuco. 1576.'

[2] A. F. A. and F. R. Bandelier, *Historical documents relating to New Mexico*, vol. i, p. 92: 'Respuesta à los oidores alcaldes mayores de la Nueva Galicia sobre lo de la sal. 22 de Septiembre 1562.'

[3] *A.G.I.* Auda. de Guadalajara 6: 'Lic. Pinedo al Rey. 30 de Marzo 1585.'

[4] León-Pinelo, *Tratado de confirmaciones*, ii. xxiii. 5.

The audiencia was charged, as it had always been, with the assessment of Indian tributes, both those payable to *encomenderos* and those due to the Crown. In each province a flat rate of tribute was fixed, to be paid by every adult male Indian; the assessment for a bachelor being half that for a married man. The unit of taxation was the village, the headman of each village being responsible for the delivery of an assessed total every year. It was necessary, therefore, to keep careful record of the frequent shifts of population which occurred in the sixteenth century; the necessary information being supplied to the audiencia by the *corregidores*. A royal letter of 1575 complained that the assessments had not been kept up to date and that Indians living in the new settlements which had sprung up near the Spanish towns were not paying tribute, though they could afford to do so.[1] The president was reminded of the importance of constant revision of assessments and told to maintain close correspondence with the viceroy on the amount to be paid and the method of levy.

An institution empowered to distribute royal favours such as land and labour *repartimientos* was naturally empowered also to exact the services due to the Crown. The inhabitants of New Galicia were solemnly charged in the Ordinances to obey the order and summons of the audiencia in peace and in war, under pain of incurring 'the displeasure and punishment which falls upon vassals who fail to obey the summons of their king and lord'. The phrase 'in peace and in war' appears to conflict with the viceroy's monopoly of military command; no doubt the use of the phrase was a mere formality. In normal circumstances audiencias were restrained from undertaking military adventures not only by respect for the viceroy's authority, but also by the difficulty of persuading the treasury officials to release funds.

The administrative authority of all the audiencias was carried into the various districts of their jurisdiction by the *visitas* or official tours which the *oidores* undertook in turn, theoretically every third year,[2] but in practice much less frequently. The Ordinances of Monzón, like the ordinances of 1548, contained a list of the duties of *oidores-visitadores*; but while the earlier list included chiefly judicial duties, the later code prescribed more detailed administrative action. The duties were very varied. *Visitadores* were to

[1] *A.G.I.* Auda. de Guadalajara 230, lib. Z 2, fol. 23 verso. 15 de Febrero 1575.
[2] *Recopilación de Leyes de Indias*, II. xxxi. 1.

inspect shops and markets and to enforce reasonable prices and correct weights and measures; they were to pay particular attention to the sale of medicines and to destroy 'corrupt' preparations. (Doubtless many horrible specifics were employed against tropical fevers.) They were to make detailed investigations into the state of industry and agriculture, the condition of the roads, the treatment of the natives, the prevalence of idolatry. They were to discover whether the local officials performed their duties conscientiously; whether adequate provision was made for the religious instruction of the natives; and what new churches and other public buildings were required. In minor matters, and in cases where delay might prove dangerous, they were to make administrative orders on the spot; otherwise they were to refer their recommendations to the audiencia. Both the *visitadores* and the audiencia itself necessarily exercised a wide discretion in performing their administrative duties. As in military affairs, however, they were restrained by the fact that they had normally no power to authorise the spending of royal funds. The treasury officials were always reluctant to release money from the royal chest without express order from Spain.

The Ordinances of Monzón entrusted administrative duties to the audiencia as a whole—president and *oidores*. The ordinances were modified for the province of New Galicia, however, by special legislation in 1574. The decree of 1574, which repealed the grant of administrative powers to the viceroy, laid down that the administration of the province should be in the hands of the president alone, to the exclusion of the *oidores*.[1] The *Recopilación* a century later reiterated this exclusion in the most emphatic terms.[2] The *oidores* retained, however, the right to be consulted on all important matters in the *acuerdo* meetings, just as did the *oidores* of the viceregal audiencia, and their votes upon such matters were recorded. Royal letters, whether or not they concerned administration, were normally addressed to the president and *oidores* and were opened and read at *acuerdo* meetings. Since in the event of the death or prolonged absence of the president the *oidores* had to administer the province, it was necessary for them to be kept informed. The president was not expressly bound to follow the advice of the *oidores*, but in practice they must have exercised a considerable influence upon administration, however able or autocratic the

---

[1] *A.G.I.* Auda. de Guadalajara, fol. 13 verso. 21 de Abril 1574.
[2] *Recopilación de Leyes de Indias*, II. xv. 7.

president might be; the *acuerdo* as a whole making decisions and the president in his capacity of governor enforcing them.

The administrative authority of the president (or in his absence, of the *oidores*) was confined to the area of New Galicia proper. Colima and the *pueblos* of Avalos[1] remained under the administration (though not the jurisdiction) of New Spain. The great northern province of New Vizcaya from 1562 had its own governor appointed by the Crown and responsible in administrative affairs to the viceroy; though appeals from his judicial decisions lay to the audiencia of New Galicia. Governors were subsequently appointed in New León (Coahuila) and New Mexico.

Within the administrative area of New Galicia the president was empowered to deal with all classes of administrative business except two, which the 1574 decree specifically reserved to the viceroy. These were defence, and *gratificación de servicios*—the rewarding of services. Defence had always been the concern of the viceroy, in New Galicia as in New Spain, and remained in his hands until the eighteenth century, when a separate military command was established for the frontier zone. Military authority was never entrusted to the president or the audiencia in New Galicia, though emergencies sometimes compelled them to assume command without warrant. Orozco, the first president, was also the last to take the field in person, and indeed met his death in a skirmish with raiding Indians.[2] Orozco was occasionally described as 'captain-general' in official documents,[3] but this was probably due to a mistaken analogy with the constitutional arrangements in Santo Domingo and Guatemala, where the presidents held that title. The viceroy of New Spain was the captain-general of New Galicia. Sometimes the viceroy delegated his command to a prominent local *encomendero*, after consultation with the audiencia;[4] but this arrangement, since it included no provision for the raising of troops in an emergency, did not lift the

---

[1] See ch. IV, above.

[2] Orozco y Jiménez, *Colección*, vol. V, p. 168: 'Cabildo eclesiástico de Guadalajara al Rey. 6 de Abril 1583.' (Begging the Crown to provide for Orozco's widow and children.)

[3] *A.G.I.* Patronato 182, R°. 53: 'Ordenanzas que formó y dió a los oficiales reales de la Nueva Galicia el capitán-general de ella, el Doctor Gerónimo de Orozco 1579.'

[4] Orozco y Jiménez, *Colección*, vol. II, p. 111: 'Audiencia de Guadalajara al Rey 20 de Marzo 1570: Vuestro virrey envió a esta real audiencia...una real cédula...por la cual le hace capitán-general de este reino...y lo cometió con comunicación desta audiencia su parecer a Vicente Zaldívar vecino deste reino, persona muy suficiente para ello.'

load of anxiety from the president's shoulders. The correspondence of the audiencia in the 1570's and 1580's is full of reports of Indian raids and of the dangers besetting travellers, including the judges upon circuit and the royal silver trains, which may be presumed to have been well escorted. The audiencia complained constantly of the impossibility of keeping down banditry without the power to spend money, and these complaints prevailed upon the king in 1580 to modify the ordinances of Monzón by a letter authorising the president and the treasury officials, with the concurrence of the viceroy, to release 'moderate sums' from the royal chest for operations against the tribesmen when necessary.[1] This was a rare and generous concession, and indicates the seriousness of the situation; in 1584, for instance, the Guaynamota Indians rose, not for the first time, and killed several missionaries. The audiencia raised a local force under Juan de Salas, which suppressed the revolt and took some hundreds of prisoners, of whom twelve were hanged and the remainder given as slaves to their more loyal neighbours.[2] Two years later the audiencia was ordered by the viceroy to call out the *encomenderos* of New Galicia against the English privateer Thomas Cavendish, who was then cruising off the Pacific coast of New Spain. Both these enterprises were apparently organised entirely by the audiencia and financed by the local treasury. Such episodes, however, were becoming less frequent as the century drew to a close and the Indian frontier moved further north.

The second 'reserved' power, the rewarding of services, was even more debatable. The usual rewards for unpaid service in the Indies were either *encomiendas*, or appointments to minor judicial offices such as *corregimientos* and *alcaldías mayores* which were salaried but not purchasable, and which were regarded as the perquisites of 'deserving conquerors and settlers'. The right to grant *encomiendas* in New Spain and New Galicia was legally reserved to the Crown and usually exercised by the viceroy. The president's power was confined to forwarding reports, recommendations, and the petitions of applicants. The audiencia sometimes obliged *encomenderos* by conniving at infractions of the law governing the succession to *encomiendas*, but it never presumed to commend Indians. The

---

[1] *A.G.I.* Auda. de Guadalajara 230, lib. Z 2, fol. 47 verso. 26 de Mayo 1580: 'Respuesta a la audiencia de la Nueva Galicia.'

[2] V. Riva Palacio, *México a través los siglos* (Mexico, 1888), vol. II, p. 438.

ADMINISTRATION

right of appointing *corregidores*, however, left in the viceroy's hands in 1574, had belonged until 1572 to the subordinate audiencia of New Galicia. Evidently there were doubts in the mind of authority as to the wisdom of withholding these powers from the president-governor on the spot, for the decree of 1574 promised that the question should be reviewed later and that a definite decision should be made according to reports received of the president's conduct and ability.[1] No decree has been found making such a decision; but the president did unquestionably appoint *corregidores* and *alcaldes mayores* and at the end of the century it was not doubted that he did so lawfully.[2] Apparently the question was decided by local custom and convenience, not by a legislative act. All the *corregimientos* and *alcaldías mayores* of New Galicia except one—that of Zacatecas—were annual offices; neither the salaries nor the duties were particularly attractive.[3] None of the viceroy's entourage in Mexico would be likely to covet such offices. The viceroy, on the other hand, could not be expected to know the deserts and abilities of the settlers of New Galicia who were the usual applicants for *corregimientos*; he would be compelled to seek information from the authorities in New Galicia, and in practice he left appointments in the hands of the president. The duty of reviewing the *residencias* of local magistrates and of punishing their irregularities was in any case entrusted to the audiencia of New Galicia.[4]

The town and surrounding district of Zacatecas called for special treatment because of its size (it had a larger Spanish population than Guadalajara), its importance as a silver-mining centre, and its reputation for disorder. Up to 1580 the administration of the area was entrusted to an *alcalde mayor* appointed annually by the president; in 1580 this official was replaced by a *corregidor* responsible to the president but appointed by the Crown.[5] This

---

[1] *A.G.I.* Auda. de Guadalajara 230, lib. Z 2, fol. 13 verso. 21 de Abril 1574: '...según la cuenta y buena orden que diéredes en lo demás que toca a gobernación que como está dicho es a vuestro cargo, y en vuestra ausencia a cargo del audiencia, se platicará sobre si estos dos casos reservados al virrey se os remitirán a vos y esa audiencia.'

[2] A. de la Mota y Escobar, *Descripción geográfica de los reinos de Galicia, Vizcaya y León* (1603): '...Todas las justicias que gobiernan los pueblos de la Galicia son alcaldes mayores o corregidores, y los provee el presidente y paga su Majestad.'

[3] See ch. VI, p. 131.

[4] *A.G.I.* Auda. de Guadalajara 230, lib. Z 2, fol. 25 verso. 24 de Enero 1575: 'Mandamos que las tales residencias se tomen por comisión vuestra y se traigan a esa audiencia y en ella se vean y determinen y no en la dicha cuidad de México.'

[5] Amador, *Bosquejo histórico de Zacatecas* cap. xlii, *Recopilación de Leyes de Indias*, v. ii. 1.

140

was a much bigger appointment than the petty *corregimientos* of Indian villages elsewhere in New Galicia; it ran for three years and carried a salary of 1,000 *pesos* a year. Its dignity was emphasised in 1585 by the grant of arms and the title of 'city' to the town of Zacatecas.[1]

Apart from offices such as *corregimientos* which were bestowed as rewards for service, a large number of administrative offices in the Indies were habitually sold. 'Public offices. . .' so ran the decree on the subject 'are of two sorts: those involving the exercise of jurisdiction; and those which, while not themselves judicial in character, are connected with the administration of justice. Public and general necessities have compelled Us (while reserving those of the first class) to sell those of the second for the benefit of Our Royal revenue.'[2] The sale of offices, with the devices which the Crown adopted to mitigate its evil results, formed a vital and characteristic element in the administration of the Indies, and one which deserves separate and detailed description. The financial straits of the Crown towards the end of the sixteenth century led to constant and ingenious attempts to increase the number of offices which might be sold. Some of the places so created were mere dignities; others carried the right to levy fees or to exercise a minor patronage. They included principally police offices (*algùacilazgos*), a great variety of notaries' practices (*escribanías*) and most municipal offices. The work of notaries and police officers belongs to a later chapter on judicial procedure; it remains now to describe the municipal councils, the degree of control which the president-governor exercised over their composition and conduct, and the procedure for the sale of municipal and other offices.

By the second half of the sixteenth century the practice of election or local appointment of town councillors had disappeared in the more important towns of the Indies and the *cabildos* were being filled with councillors who bought their *regimientos* for life. The significant decree of 1554 has already been described.[3] This decree—the first to deal generally with the question—mentions sale as the normal method of appointing *regidores*. Its wording seems to leave to the *cabildos* the right to elect suitable householders to *regimientos* which found no purchasers; but in practice

---

[1] Amador, op. cit. cap. xliii.
[2] *Recopilación de Leyes de Indias*, VIII. xx. 1.
[3] Ibid. IV. x. 6. See ch. I, p. 33.

this right existed only by express permission in exceptional cases, and *regidores* so elected held office for only one year. The right of nominating *regidores* for life was reserved to the Crown, which sold the posts either directly to intending emigrants before they left Spain or, more commonly, indirectly to residents in the Indies. An office once sold was the property of the purchaser, and if serious local complaints were made against him the Crown could, in strict law, remove him only by buying him out.[1] In 1606 the proprietary character of *regimientos* and many other offices was emphasised by legislation[2] making them *renunciable* in law, as they had been in practice for some time before that date. This meant that the holder of a *regimiento* might resign it in favour of a successor chosen by himself, the Crown claiming at the first *renuncia* one half of the purchase price of the office, at the second one third. Elections of *regidores*, and choice by lot, were finally and categorically forbidden in 1620.[3]

Certain municipal offices—*alguacil mayor* or chief constable, *alférez mayor* or standard-bearer, *depositario general* or public trustee, *fiel ejecutor* or inspector of weights and measures, and *receptor de penas* or collector of fines—carried with them seats in the *cabildo*. These offices were a source of fees to their holders and were usually purchasable. In some *cabildos* in the sixteenth century—notably in Mexico City—certain of these municipal offices were granted by virtue of a royal *merced* to the proprietary *regidores* to be divided among themselves at annual or biennial intervals. The tendency, however, was to withdraw such local rights, where they existed, from the *cabildos* and to sell the offices separately for life. The purchaser in each case then became a *regidor de oficio* if, as usually happened, he was not already a *regidor*. The senior treasury officials of a province (*tesorero, contador* and *factor*) who did not purchase their posts, but were appointed, might also hold seats *ex officio* in the capital city of their province, at least until 1622.[4] A sixteenth-century *cabildo* might thus contain three classes of *regidores*—*regidores cadañeros* appointed or elected (i.e. co-opted—the word *elegir* may have any of these meanings) for one year; *regidores perpétuos* who bought their places from the Crown for life; and

[1] For an example of the procedure see *D.I.I.* vol. xix, p. 145.
[2] *Recopilación de Leyes de Indias*, VIII. xxi. 1. *Escribanías* were made renunciable in 1581. Solórzano, *Política Indiana*, V. xiii. 12.
[3] *Recopilación de Leyes de Indias*, VIII. xx. 7.
[4] Ibid. VIII. iv. 53.

regidores de oficio. The total number of *regidores* varied from six in small towns to twelve in large ones.[1] In Guadalajara there were officially eight; but usually several of the *regimientos* were vacant.

One important municipal official, the *escribano de cabildo* or town clerk, never held seat or vote and was always regarded as a servant of the *cabildo*, though he too purchased his office from the Crown. He was simply a secretary, not a town clerk in the modern sense; and in his spare time he usually practised as a licensed notary public. The rules concerning unsuitable applicants for the post were the same as those governing *regimientos* and were as loosely applied in practice. In 1528—to name a notorious example—the *cabildo* of Mexico refused to admit one Pedro del Castillo (presumably the purchaser) as *escribano de cabildo* because he was (so they said) a convicted thief. They nominated in his place one of the other public notaries of the city; but the audiencia intervened on Castillo's behalf and compelled the *cabildo* to reinstate him.[2]

In New Galicia the *cabildos* were smaller and less varied than that of Mexico City. They had no special rights, so far as is known, in the allocation of offices. The treasury officials do not appear to have exercised municipal privileges either in Guadalajara or in Zacatecas. The more ornamental posts such as that of *alférez* existed only in Guadalajara and rarely found purchasers. The sale of *regimientos* for life in the *cabildo* of Guadalajara, however, became a recognised practice in the second half of the century. A petition from the *cabildo* of Compostela in 1557 for permission to elect annual *regidores* was refused.[3] The city of Zacatecas in its charter of 1585 received permission for its *cabildo* to elect *regidores*, but within ten years of that date proprietary *regimientos* in the city had been created and were being sold.[4]

The Council of the Indies was naturally concerned to ensure that sales of municipal and other offices should be properly supervised and should be held in places where the highest bids might be expected. Eight authorities in the Indies were empowered to supervise sales and to issue provisional titles pending royal confirmation. These were the viceroys of New Spain and Peru and the presidents of Santo Domingo, New Granada, Manila, Panama,

[1] Ibid. IV. x. 2.
[2] *Actas del Cabildo de México*, vol. I, p. 128; vol. II, pp. 16, 18.
[3] *A.G.I.* Auda. de Guadalajara 51. 28 de Julio 1557.
[4] Amador, *Bosquejo histórico de Zacatecas*, cap. xlii.

Guatemala and New Galicia.[1] Upon these authorities lay the responsibility of ensuring that the purchasers of offices, or the successors by way of *renuncia*, were persons competent to discharge their duties. Vacancies were reported to the president concerned, by the town clerks of the various towns in his province, and were advertised in the towns where they occurred and in the capital city of the province. Intending purchasers made their bids to the treasury officials at the capital; the highest bidder, or in the case of *renuncia*, the designated successor, might enter upon his duties as soon as the purchase price was paid, but was required to obtain a provisional title from the president within four months and confirmation from the Crown within four, later six, years. Viceroys and presidents were forbidden as a general rule to issue even temporary titles to saleable offices, except to the purchasers. If no purchaser appeared the office remained technically vacant. The colonial authorities were particularly discouraged from appointing notaries except by the prescribed procedure of sale and confirmation; the public auction of *escribanías* being considered (as León-Pinelo explained) not only as a source of revenue but as a safeguard against nepotism.[2]

These rules, if strictly obeyed, caused considerable inconvenience, particularly in remote provinces, where the purchase of legal offices was a risky investment. Sometimes, indeed, purchasers arrived direct from Spain; in Mexico such arrivals were common; but in New Galicia both *escribanías* and *regimientos* often remained technically vacant for years. In 1585 the *fiscal* reported that there were only two *regidores* in Guadalajara, of whom one was old and blind, the other constantly absent on private business.[3] The audiencia repeatedly broke the laws governing the sale of *escribanías*, since the court could not function without clerical staff. It was reprimanded in 1576 for entrusting pleas to unlicensed notaries, to the detriment of those who had bought practices, or might be induced to buy them, through the proper channels;[4] and again in 1582 for appointing minor municipal officials in Zacatecas without warrant. On that occasion the offices in question were *depositario general*

---

[1] León-Pinelo, *Tratado de confirmaciones*, ii. xi. 3, 10. The legislation governing the sale, renunciation and confirmation of offices is in *Recopilación de Leyes de Indias*, lib. viii, tits. xx, xxi, xxii.

[2] León-Pinelo, *Tratado de confirmaciones*, ii. xix. 6.

[3] *A.G.I.* Auda. de Guadalajara 6. 30 de Marzo 1585.

[4] *A.G.I.* Auda. de Guadalajara 230, lib. Z 1, fol. 294 verso. 4 de Mayo 1576.

(public trustee) and *fiel veedor de carnicerías* (inspector of meat market and slaughter-houses), and the complaint came from the *corregidor*, who himself claimed a prescriptive right to appoint these officials. The royal reply, in demanding a detailed report, clearly implied that if the offices were necessary, they should be sold and not given away.[1] The viceroy, to whom was entrusted a loose and general supervision over the audiencia in this as in other administrative matters,[2] was too far away to supervise effectively, and complaints continued throughout the sixteenth century. In 1636 the power to issue titles to offices was taken from the president by royal decree and entrusted to the viceroy;[3] though the authorities in New Galicia continued to supervise the sale of offices.

The usual purchasers of municipal offices in New Galicia were local *encomenderos*, ranchers and mine-owners. Already in the sixteenth century the wealthier Spaniards were developing the habit of the modern Mexican *hacendado*, of keeping a town and a country house and dividing their time between the two. Their attention to municipal affairs was necessarily intermittent. Each town was governed by its small oligarchy of local dignitaries, highly respected in the town but drawing their income from the country, firmly entrenched in their offices and responsible to nobody except a distant king. Though not representative in any modern sense, the *cabildos* sometimes displayed considerable vigour and independence, and were always determined defenders of the interests of the local Spanish community. Conflicts between *cabildo* and audiencia were frequent; yet the *cabildos* could do little without the approval of the president. The *repartimientos* of native labour needed for public works could be authorised only by him. He presided, moreover, in the meetings of the *cabildo* of Guadalajara. It was a general rule throughout the Indies that in corporate towns which were the seats of governors or *corregidores*, those functionaries presided in the *cabildos*, either in person or by means of deputies.[4] The president might not vote or canvass for votes in elections of municipal magistrates, but all such elections had to be confirmed by him[5] and under the Ordinances of Monzón he presided over the most

---

[1] *A.G.I.* Auda. de Guadalajara 230, lib. Z 1, fol. 381 verso. 7 de Mayo 1582.
[2] *Recopilación de Leyes de Indias*, II. xv. 52.
[3] Ibid. VIII. xx. 23.   [4] Ibid. IV. ix. 5.
[5] Ibid. v. iii. 2, 10. Municipal magistracies, being judicial offices, were never sold.

important of the municipal committees—a standing committee of the president and two councillors which allocated plots of land (*solares*) in the city for building sites and gardens. This arrangement was probably designed deliberately to prevent quarrels between audiencia and town council over the allocation of building lots. The *oidores* were in strict law excluded from municipal government;[1] the duty of scrutinising audits of municipal accounts was, however, entrusted to each of the *oidores* in turn,[2] and in this as in many other ways they could find excuses for interfering in the affairs of the town, despite repeated royal decrees forbidding such interference.

The president exercised an extensive ecclesiastical patronage. Provision to the more senior ecclesiastical dignities such as bishoprics and deaneries in the Indies was made in Spain; and at the lower end of the scale of preferment, clergy in the *encomiendas* were provided by the *encomenderos* as patrons (though the president fixed the salaries which the *encomenderos* were to pay). All other livings in the province were filled by the president, exercising the royal patronage in his capacity of governor. On this point the law was clear, having been decided in his favour, and against the viceroy, in 1575.[3] The *oidores* were strictly forbidden to hear disputes over provisions to livings. If the complaints of the cathedral chapter of Guadalajara are to be believed, the presidents guarded their authority with a petty insistence, even obstructing the arrangements made by the bishop for the administration of the sacraments in villages where the livings were temporarily vacant;[4] but the Crown was intensely jealous of its patronage, and such complaints from ecclesiastical bodies received little sympathy.

The president supervised the provincial treasury administration. The principal royal chest was at Guadalajara; the senior officials, treasurer, auditor and factor, had their offices there and all the dues of the Crown—proceeds of the sale of offices, tributes, silver tax, customs, sales tax, and so forth—were collected at this chest for transmission via Mexico to Spain. The treasurer at Guadalajara also made all disbursements from the chest—the salaries of president, *oidores*, *fiscal* and treasury officials, and the occasional

---

[1] *Recopilación de Leyes de Indias*, IV. ix. 8.   [2] Ibid. IV. ix. 21.
[3] *A.G.I.* Auda. de Guadalajara 230, lib. Z 2, fol. 28 verso. 27 de Abril 1575.
[4] Orozco y Jiménez, *Colección*, vol. v, p. 163: 'Carta del deán y cabildo de la santa iglesia catedral de Guadalajara sobre la penuria de la dicha iglesia. 11 de Marzo 1579.'

authorised payments for defence or public works. There was a subsidiary royal chest at Zacatecas, with a similar, but junior, staff; this office was concerned mainly with the collection of the silver tax—the *quinto*, actually one-tenth in New Galicia. Silver was refined, taxed and stamped at the mines. Once stamped, privately-owned silver might be taken wherever the owners wished; but the royal silver, whether the product of the *quinto* or metal actually mined on the king's behalf, was taken under escort at frequent intervals to the Guadalajara chest and ultimately to Spain. The treasury offices were busy enough to need the services of a proprietary *escribano* in each.

Among the mass of legislation affecting New Galicia in 1574 was a new and detailed code of ordinances for the provincial treasury.[1] These rules emphasised the responsibility of the president in supervising all treasury transactions. He conducted the annual audit (*cuenta*) with the assistance of two of the *oidores*. He held one of the four keys of the royal chest, and was required to be present on all occasions when money was paid into or withdrawn from the chest. He was to accompany the factor in all inspections of silver refineries and all sales of tribute in kind brought in from the royal *pueblos*. He was to be present at the stamping of silver as it issued from the refineries, to ensure that the royal tenths were duly paid; and was to countersign all entries in the treasury ledgers. Only he could grant leave of absence to the treasury officials. All questions of local treasury policy were to be referred to him, and at least one president issued local ordinances regulating the conduct of the officials.[2]

These duties, if performed conscientiously, were extremely irksome and occupied a great deal of the president's time. It was, indeed, impossible for him to supervise the stamping of silver, since that operation was performed at Zacatecas. The inclusion of such a requirement was a flagrant example either of careless drafting, or of culpable ignorance in the office of the Council of the Indies. Even if the president confined his attention to the Guadalajara chest, the supervisory responsibility laid upon him was unduly heavy. The protests of the treasury officials were

[1] *A.G.I.* Auda. de Guadalajara 230, lib. Z 2, fol. 15 verso. 26 de Mayo 1574: 'Ordenanzas a los oficiales de la Nueva Galicia para el buen recaudo de la Real Hacienda.'

[2] *A.G.I.* Patronato 182, R⁰. 53: 'Ordenanzas que dió a los oficiales reales...el Doctor Gerónimo de Orozco. 1597.'

inspired, no doubt, by their own desire to be free from supervision; but they told no more than the truth when they pointed
out to the king, in a strongly worded letter in 1575,[1] that treasury
transactions occurred every day and at all hours; that serious
delays and denials of justice ensued if the president were constantly
called away from the court-room to deal with routine financial
business; and that the paying of sums of money into the chest could
not be allowed to wait upon the rising of the court, since both
general considerations of safety and specific royal ordinances
required such sums to be paid in as soon as they arrived. The
president, in fact, was constantly required to be in two places at
once. The royal answer to this complaint came in a decree issued
three years later, which emphasised the president's responsibility,
but authorised him to nominate one of the *oidores* to deputise for
him at the royal chest if he were unable to be present himself[2]—
but one more example of the tendency to employ judicial officers
in administrative work.

The president was never authorised to spend royal funds without
consulting the viceroy, and when time allowed, the king; and the
treasury officials were instructed to refer all demands to the viceroy.
In the seventeenth century this insistence on viceregal approval
became much more definite.[3] The president could in practice,
however, direct the proceeds of fines and court fees to be devoted
to specific local objects instead of being paid into the chest,[4] and
could seek royal approval afterwards. It is clear, also, from
repeated complaints[5] that the president often bullied the treasury
officials into releasing small sums, and it is difficult to see how he
could have carried on the administration without doing so.

Throughout the period the president wielded administrative
powers much wider than those conferred on him by express decrees,
and the *oidores* participated much more freely in those powers than
strict law allowed them to do. The Ordinances of Monzón, the
subsequent legislation amending them, and the frequent com-

[1] *A.G.I.* Auda. de Guadalajara 230, lib. Z 2, fol. 35 verso. 'A S.M. los oficiales de
la Nueva Galicia. 15 de Septiembre 1575.'

[2] Ibid. fol. 46 verso. 5 de Julio 1578.

[3] *Recopilación de Leyes de Indias*, II. xv. 526.

[4] A fine of 2,000 *pesos* imposed on Francisco de Urdiñola in 1598 was devoted to
improving the Guadalajara water supply. See ch. IX, below.

[5] *A.G.I.* Indiferente General 1087. Registro de peticiones de 1580, fol. 159 verso:
'Petición de los oficiales Reales de Nueva Galicia por diferencias con el Presidente.'
A.G.N. Ramo de Duplicados, tit. 2, fol. 24 (1583).

plaints of their non-observance, all taken together, show how a sixteenth-century colonial audiencia—officially a court of appeal—worked in practice as a general administrative board. Such a development was inevitable in so wild and remote a country, and from time to time its inevitability was recognised, even by the Council of the Indies. The royal decree of 1574, which entrusted the administration of New Galicia to the president of the audiencia, commented significantly upon his complaints of the small amount of litigation in the province and the consequent lack of employment for the judges.

The principal task of the audiencias is to watch over the peace and prosperity of the Indies, to encourage discovery and settlement and to see that the natives are converted and instructed in agriculture and stock-raising. You will find sufficient occupation in performing these duties. As for litigation, it is to be discouraged as much as possible. When lawsuits are unavoidable, deal with them without delay. If natives appear before you, give them summary justice and protect them from lawyers and others who might cheat them.[1]

The practical common sense of this royal reply, however, is in startling contrast with the letter of the Ordinances of Monzón, and is not really typical of the Indies government in Spain. The Council of the Indies was a predominantly legal body. Its members were far more interested in jurisdiction than in administration, except where administration directly affected the royal revenue, and placed an exaggerated reliance upon judicial provisions for safeguarding the rights of Indians, of Spaniards, and of the Crown. In the Ordinances of Monzón the longest, most detailed and most emphatic sections are those which deal with jurisdiction. Next in length is the section on financial administration, with its supplementary code of instructions to the royal officials. The section on general administration is short and loosely worded, leaving much to the discretion and energy of the judges. Although the audiencia of New Galicia was admittedly the chief administrative organ of its province, the Council of the Indies established it, and continued to regard it, primarily as a court of appeal, and assumed, in ignorance of conditions on the spot, that it could usefully apply the elaborate procedure used in the audiencias of Spain.

[1] *A.G.I.* Auda. de Guadalajara 230, lib. Z 2, fol. 13 verso: 'Respuesta al presidente de la Nueva Galicia. 21 de Abril, 1574.'

CHAPTER VIII

JURISDICTION AND PROCEDURE

Under the Ordinances of Monzón the audiencia was empowered to hear both civil and criminal appeals from the decisions of all other secular courts within its province. It held also first-instance jurisdiction in the ancient *casos de corte*,[1] in criminal charges arising within five leagues of the capital city, and in all cases of debasement and counterfeiting. From the audiencia's decisions in criminal cases there was no appeal; in civil cases involving large sums[2] aggrieved parties might appeal to the king in the Council of the Indies *en grado de segunda suplicación* on questions of law, but not on questions of fact, and always provided that they appeared before the Council within one year. In such cases the decisions of the audiencia were to be executed pending the findings of the Council; but the parties in whose favour the audiencia had decided were required to furnish security, in case the Council should reverse the audiencia's decisions. In cases involving less than 10,000 *pesos*, but more than 200, the aggrieved parties might, as under the 1548 ordinances,[3] demand a re-trial *en grado de suplicación* before the whole audiencia, provided that the appeal was on a question of law, or that new facts had come to light.

Civil cases involving less than 200 *pesos*, and criminal cases of a trivial nature (*casos de palabras ligeras*) might be decided by one *oidor* sitting alone. The normal custom was for the *oidores* in residence to serve in turn as '*oidor* of the week' (*oidor semanero*) for the purpose of hearing these petty suits and issuing writs of course. In more serious cases one *oidor* might conduct the preliminary stages of the hearing, but might not give a final judgement (*definitiva*); the final judgement required a quorum of two *oidores*, or in cases heard *en grado de suplicación*, the president and all the resident *oidores*. All these quorum regulations were intended as minimum requirements and did not, in theory, excuse the judges

---

[1] 'Muerte segura, muger forzada, tregua quebrantada, casa quemada, camino quebrantado, traición, aleve, riepto, pleito de viudas y huérfanos y personas miserables, o contra corregidor o alcalde ordinario o otro oficial de tal lugar.' *Nueva Recopilación de Leyes de España*, IV. iii. 8.

[2] The minimum sum varied from time to time. It was fixed in 1545 at 10,000 *pesos* (Puga, *Cedulario*, vol. I, p. 469) and in 1620 at 6,000 (*Recopilación de Leyes de Indias*, V. xiii. 1). [3] See ch. II, p. 37.

their statutory three hours in the court room every morning. All decisions of the audiencia were by majority vote; if the total number of judges were only two, and if the two should differ in their judgements, they might co-opt one of the licensed advocates (*abogados*) practising in the court, to give a casting vote.

Civil suits in which *oidores* were themselves parties were to be begun before the municipal magistrates and carried in appeal before the audiencia, the interested *oidores* being required to absent themselves from the hearing. Criminal charges against *oidores* were heard by a judicial committee of the president and the municipal magistrates of the capital city.

The audiencia might send officers (*ejecutores*) to compel local magistrates and others to obey its writs, and might appoint judicial commissioners (*jueces de comisión*) to investigate crimes and riots and to bring suspected persons before the *oidores*. A *juez de comisión* was usually a person not holding a regular judicial appointment, designated to act as a judge of first instance in a particular case. The audiencia was forbidden to appoint *jueces de residencia* or— except in urgent cases of serious crime or public disorder— *pesquisidores*.[1] *Residencias* of retiring officials were usually conducted by their successors. A *pesquisa*—an extraordinary inquiry con- ducted by a senior judge—normally needed the special authority of the Crown. The audiencia did, however, sometimes send members of its own Bench as *pesquisidores* to investigate serious charges against prominent people outside Guadalajara; and it regularly reviewed the *residencias* held within its district, according to law, and imposed penalties upon those against whom adverse reports were received.

The area of the audiencia's appellate jurisdiction was very much larger than that covered by the administrative authority of the president-governor. It included not only New Galicia proper, but Colima, the *pueblos* of Avalos, the kingdom of New Vizcaya, and subsequent conquests farther north. Throughout this great area the audiencia was the direct representative of royal jurisdiction. It issued writs and court orders in the name of the king and sealed them with a facsimile royal seal.[2]

---

[1] *Ordenanza* 14. For definitions of these various types of inquiry see ch. II, p. 38.

[2] 'Yten mandamos que las provisiones que dieren los dichos nuestro presidente y oidores que no sean para dentro de las cinco leguas y ejecutorias y otras cartas vayan libradas en nuestro nombre y con nuestro título y sello real.' *Ordenanza* 10.

The possession of a facsimile seal, the sign and prerogative of a royal chancellery, was naturally not granted lightly. The Laws of the Indies prescribed in some detail the ceremonies to be observed in connection with the seal[1] and the audiencia ordinances set definite limits to the uses which might be made of it. The court might not grant licences to *oidores* or others to return to Spain or to visit the viceroyalty of Peru; such licences were issued only by the Council of the Indies or by the *Casa de Contratación* in Seville. Similarly, applications for *privilegios de hidalguía*—patents of gentle birth—had to be remitted to Spain, to be considered by the audiencias traditionally empowered to issue these valuable documents. The audiencia of New Galicia might not use its seal to revoke sentences of exile, by whatever authority pronounced, and was forbidden—curious necessity!—to proclaim a general moratorium to debtors; though it might grant six months' grace to deserving individual debtors. Court orders addressed within five leagues of the court might not be sealed. The *oidores* issued these orders in their own names, presumably because within that radius the audiencia sat as a court of first instance. It was specifically stated, however, that all orders of the audiencia, sealed or unsealed, were of equal validity. A majority of the *oidores* might, in all lawful cases, make an order for the affixing of the royal seal, and the president had no power to override such an order. The seal was supposed to be kept by an official known as the deputy chancellor (*teniente de gran chanciller*) who was appointed by the Crown and who levied fees for sealing;[2] but no such office appears to have existed in New Galicia; there the seal presumably lay in the keeping of the president at his official lodging.[3]

All decisions of the audiencia were by majority vote. In important discussions—whether they concerned judicial decisions, or advisory recommendations in administrative matters—the votes of individual *oidores* were recorded by the president in a secret ledger (*libro de acuerdo*). It is unlikely that the Council of the Indies ever examined these ledgers, though the possibility was no doubt intended to be held over the *oidores* as a threat.

The hours of work in the audiencia and the list of miscellaneous duties were similar to those prescribed in the ordinances of 1548.

[1] *Recopilación de Leyes de Indias*, II. xxi. 1- .
[2] Ibid. II. xxi. 1- .
[3] Ibid. II. xv. 19.

All the restrictions hitherto placed upon the life of the *oidores* were summarised in the Ordinances of Monzón. The judges might not receive fees or gifts, plead as advocates, engage in trade or discovery without special permission, hold land or Indians, or even own their own houses. In 1575 a fresh prohibition was added; *oidores* might not contract marriage for themselves or for their children within the area of their jurisdiction.[1] Neither their relatives nor their servants might hold judicial office within their province. They might accept no hospitality save that allowed by the official *ayuda de costa*—expenses account—while on *visita*.

Such were the rules of conduct prescribed for the judges of every colonial audiencia. The whole system was designed to protect the judiciary from all personal contacts, to reduce the business of jurisdiction and government to a series of formulae provided by the Crown. This was true not only of the rules for the conduct of the judges, but also of the procedure employed in their courts. This procedure was so elaborated and divided among different officials, that important stages in all litigation (except that which called for summary treatment) were beyond the control of the judges altogether. No plea of importance could reach the court-room without elaborate preparation. Evidence produced before the bench was normally required to be in writing, signed by the witnesses, by the attorneys of the parties, and by an official notary. No sentence was valid unless witnessed and signed by a notary. The notary's signature was the guarantee, in theory, against the dishonesty of litigants and witnesses and the partiality of judges.[2]

Mention has been made of the court officials provided by the ordinances of 1548. The Ordinances of Monzón enumerated a much larger legal staff and prescribed its duties in much greater detail. Next to the judges in order of precedence was the *fiscal*, first appointed in 1568. This important official, whose full title was *Nuestro procurador fiscal y promotor de la nuestra justicia*, was appointed to protect the royal interests, primarily by punishing frauds against the treasury, but also by acting as public prosecutor. He

---

[1] Ibid. II. xvi. 82.
[2] 'La institución del Notariado es complemento necesario de la vida civil...asegura la legitimidad de los actos civiles...presta facilidad a los mismos...es causa, sobre todo, de su certeza y verdad, tanto en el orden moral, por las garantías que de ello prestan las condiciones exigidas al notario, como en el ordan legal, por la autenticidad que a su intervención se atribuye en virtud de su fe pública.' F. Sánchez Román, *Estudios de derecho civil*, II. 614.

sat in the *acuerdo* of the audiencia and consequently had a voice
(though not a vote) in the administration of the province.[1] He
could proceed against offenders either upon denunciation (*delación*)
or upon his own initiative in cases of 'notoriety' (*hecho notorio*). His
instructions particularly emphasised the duty of detecting and
punishing crimes and oppressions committed against Indians.[2] The
fiscales in New Galicia gained a reputation as devoted defenders of
Indian rights, in a province where the Indians stood in special
need of protection. No advocates' fees were paid in pleas of the
Crown, the *fiscal* being expected to appear in person for the
prosecution. This perhaps explains his generous salary. From the
point of view of the Crown, the cost of maintaining the office was
amply justified by the diligence of successive *fiscales* in protecting
the royal revenue from fraud and evasion, and even occasionally
in keeping watch and reporting on the *oidores* themselves.

There were no other salaried lawyers in the court. All the other
legal officials received payment in the form of fees and most of
them purchased their offices. The most important and responsible
fee-earning office was that of the *relator* (or *relatores*, for in some
audiencias there were more than one). A *relator* was required to be
a qualified advocate, though naturally debarred from advocacy
while holding office. His principal duty was to prepare from the
masses of evidence supplied by the litigants and their witnesses,
relaciones or summaries of the questions of fact involved in each
case, which were read to the judges at the beginning of the hearing.
Obviously partiality or incompetence on the part of the *relator*
might materially affect the fortunes of the litigants; an oath of
office was prescribed, and penalties ranging from fines to suspension
or imprisonment were imposed on *relatores* convicted of inaccuracy
in their summaries.

The routine legal work of the court was done by the group of
officials collectively described as notaries (*escribanos*). Every institution of importance employed notaries.[3] There was an *escribano de
cabildo* in every corporate town; there were *escribanos de minas*
(mines); *de casas de moneda* (mints); *de consulados* (chambers of
commerce); there was even, in Peru in the early days of settlement,
an official vaguely styled *escribano de la Mar del Sur*—notary of the

[1] *Recopilación de Leyes de Indias*, II. xviii. 4.
[2] Ibid. II. xviii. 34, 37.
[3] Ibid. VIII. xx. 1.

South Sea; there were, of course, *escribanos públicos*, or *del número*—licensed notaries public. Notaries who held office in the audiencias were distinguished by the title *escribanos de cámara*. They were, in theory, court officials, forbidden to undertake private business. They bought their practices from the Crown and made their living by the fees charged for their services. The number of notaries in any one audiencia in Spain was officially limited to twelve.[1] It is very unlikely that any colonial audiencia ever employed so many; certainly the audiencia of New Galicia did not. Notaries were expected to take their turn as clerk of the court (*escribano de guarda de la sala*) and as clerk to the *oidores* when on circuit (*visita*). There were in addition a number of more specialised duties entrusted to notaries. The *repartidor de pleitos* was responsible for seeing that the cases brought to the audiencia were fairly shared among the body of notaries, and kept a roster for this purpose. The *tasador* checked and approved the fees accruing in every case to each of the lawyers concerned in it; this was a mere matter of arithmetic, since all fees were prescribed in detail in the rate-book (*arancel*). Disputes arising from assessments made by the *tasador* were settled by the 'oidor of the week'. *Receptores* were collectors of evidence; their duty was to travel about the province interviewing witnesses who lived at a distance from the capital, and preparing certified copies of their testimony for production in court.

A litigant wishing to appeal to the audiencia against the decision of an inferior judge in a civil suit had first to give notice of his intention in the inferior court. If the appeal were allowed, a certified copy of the proceedings would be sent to the audiencia by the notary of the inferior court. The appellant's petition had to be filed with the audiencia within fifteen days of the notice of appeal. The inferior judge might attempt to hinder the appeal; in which case the appellant applied to the audiencia (in practice to the 'oidor of the week') for a writ *requisitoria* demanding the surrender of the papers in the case.

The next step was to engage an attorney (*procurador*). *Procuradores* advised litigants, served writs, presented petitions and in general dealt with the routine procedure of litigation on their clients' behalf. They were not necessarily trained lawyers; there was no professional class of solicitors. Their employment was largely a matter of convenience, to prevent crowds of litigants

---

[1] *Nueva Recopilación de Leyes de España*, II. xx. 1.

hanging about the court. The Ordinances of Monzón placed colonial *procuradores* in the proprietary class of officials by limiting the number practising in each audiencia and by requiring them to purchase licences to practise, from the Crown.[1] A *procurador* might not act in a suit without an authority signed by the party and witnessed by a notary public; and officially might not present any petition without the signature of a recognised advocate (*abogado*);[2] though it is unlikely that this rule was widely enforced in the smaller audiencias. It was frequently disregarded in New Galicia.

Abogados were always qualified lawyers and often candidates for judicial appointments.[3] In order to practise in the courts they were required to hold licences and to submit to professional examination by the *oidores* of an audiencia.[4] Their duty was to prepare litigants' cases and to argue them in court. Litigants were not debarred from conducting their own cases, but naturally were not encouraged to do so; for those who could not afford an advocate's fees it was usual to appoint a poor man's lawyer (*abogado de pobres*) who was paid a fixed salary out of the proceeds of fines.[5]

The papers prepared by the plaintiff's advocate consisted of a statement of the plaintiff's case (*petición*), a list of witnesses whom it was desired to call, and a list of questions (*interrogatorio*) to be put to the witnesses. The primitive practice of oath-helping had left its mark on procedure, even in those countries where the reception of Roman Law was most complete, and there was a tendency to call the largest possible number of witnesses to testify to the same set of facts; this tendency was later discouraged, though not very effectively, by the rule restricting the number of witnesses to whom any one question might be put to thirty.[6] The *interrogatorio* or list of questions was a highly formalised and obviously highly important step in the procedure and the skill employed in framing it might affect the result considerably.[7] It

[1] *Recopilación de Leyes de Indias*, II. xxviii. 1, 2; VIII. xx. 1.
[2] Ibid. II. xxviii. 11; II. xxiv. 13.
[3] The great jurist Solórzano argued strongly in favour of recruitment of the bench from the bar. *Política Indiana*, v. iv. 4.
[4] *Recopilación de Leyes de Indias*, II. xxiv. 1.
[5] Ibid. v. vi. 29. The *oidores* of New Galicia complained to the king in 1583 that the proceeds of fines were insufficient to cover the salaries of the *abogado de pobres*, the audiencia porter, and various other minor officials charged upon them. Tello, *Crónica Miscelánea*, vol. CCXVI.
[6] *Nueva Recopilación de Leyes de España*, II. xx. 32.
[7] See J. Escriche, *Diccionario razonado de legislación y jurisprudencia*.

consisted of three parts; the first a series of general questions prescribed by law and designed to discover the character of the witness being interrogated, his interest in the case, and the degree of credence to be given to his statements; the second, particular questions relating to the case, drawn up by the litigant or his advocate and arranged under the headings of the facts which it was desired to establish; the third, a general question concerning hearsay evidence, under the heading *de pública voz y fama*. The *relator* was responsible to the judges for seeing that the *interrogatorio* complied with the rules of evidence and contained no irrelevancies, leading questions (*preguntas sugestivas*) or questions otherwise inadmissible.

The *petición* with its accompanying *interrogatorio* and list of witnesses were all delivered by the plaintiff's attorney to the clerk of the court, who submitted them to the *oidores*. If the audiencia admitted the appeal, a notary was detailed for the case and the *relator* was instructed to prepare a summary for the judges. A writ was served on the defendant, ordering him to submit his reply (*contesta*), with his list of witnesses and *interrogatorio*, within nine days. In ecclesiastical courts it seems to have been a general practice for the parties to furnish one another with copies of their *interrogatorios*, but in the audiencias this practice was rarely, if ever, observed.

When the *petición*, the *contesta* and the *interrogatorios* of both parties had been received, the *relator* presented the case for its first hearing. To any one accustomed to English traditions of the day in court the most surprising feature of the conduct of the audiencia— and of most courts of the period in countries where Roman-Law procedure was used[1]—was the absence of judicial ceremonial. The procedure was complicated, but it was the procedure of a committee rather than that of a public hearing. The parties and their attorneys were not present at the deliberations of the court; the law merely required that they should be summoned to hear its judgement. The advocates in the case were present throughout the hearing, but they spoke only when invited to do so, and the proceedings never assumed the character, so familiar in English courts, of a public discussion between judge and counsel on points of law. Witnesses were not normally examined in person in court (though they might be). Probably there were never more than a dozen

---

[1] See Holdsworth, *History of English Law* (London, 1924), vol. IV, p. 170.

people in the court-room. Every one, including the *relator* and the advocates, remained seated while addressing the court. The danger that the privacy of the proceedings might lead to hole-and-corner methods and to sales of justice is indicated in the Ordinances of Monzón by the rule that *oidores* must hear *relaciones* in the court-room and not require *relatores* and counsel to attend them at their lodgings.

The first stage of the hearing was the preliminary *relación* (*relación para recibir a prueba*), a summary by the *relator* of the questions of fact at issue. At this stage verbal summaries were deemed sufficient, the *relator* merely being required to testify that he had discussed the *relación* with the advocates of both parties and that they agreed with his presentation of the case. After the *relación* counsel were permitted to open for their respective parties, presenting the points of law involved. As far as the main question at issue was concerned, their statements would merely repeat what was already before the judges in writing, in the *peticiones*; but if any interlocutory decision were required, the advocates might have a good deal to say. Interlocutory proceedings were normally conducted verbally; in difficult and protracted cases they might be of considerable importance and might form the subject of secondary *peticiones* and separate verbal *relaciones*. In suits concerning property, for instance, it was often necessary to give an interim judgement on the question of possession while the question of right was still *sub judice*. Any question of the competence of the court's jurisdiction or the admissibility of evidence might be the subject of an interlocutory decision. Such a decision might be given at any stage in the trial. The parties were not expected to attend in court to hear an interlocutory judgement unless it were of such a nature as to invalidate further proceedings, as a decision concerning the court's competence might do, or unless it imposed penalties on either party.[1]

When the necessary interlocutory decisions had been made, the main issue was admitted for proof (*recibida a prueba*). The notary of the case, armed with a writ *receptoria*, examined the witnesses, putting to them the questions contained in the *interrogatorios*. If any witnesses lived at a distance from the seat of the *audiencia*, a special *receptor* was appointed at the litigant's expense, to visit them and collect their testimony. Neither the parties nor their

---

[1] For a general discussion of *sentencias interlocutorias* see J. Escriche, op. cit.

near relatives were allowed to give evidence. Indian witnesses were not normally examined on oath, being supposedly ignorant of the nature of an oath; nor could they be indicted for perjury; groups of Indians might testify jointly, and the testimony of six Indians was commonly held equivalent to that of one Spaniard.[1] All other witnesses, however, were examined on oath; all statements were written in full, signed by the witnesses, and counter-signed by the notary to whom they were made. These writings were presented in court by the *relator* and had to be scrutinised by the judges, who were not allowed to take the notary's word for their contents. The considerable labour involved in this scrutiny, as well as the fear of forgery, no doubt dictated the minute detail of the ordinances on the subject; the notary was required to write legibly in his own hand, without abbreviations, emendations or erasures, and the number of lines to each page was prescribed.

The Laws of the Indies permitted the judges of an appeal court, if they wished, to summon witnesses in person for further examination; and indeed ordered them to do so in 'difficult and very serious cases'.[2] In such cases a limited form of cross-examination (*repregunta*) was allowed. An advocate who wished to cross-examine submitted a second *interrogatorio* containing the questions to be asked; the questions were then put to the witnesses by the judges. Cross-examination never developed in Roman-Law countries, of course, into the intricate art practised in English courts. In general the *oidores* seem to have preferred to confine themselves to written evidence in civil cases.

The term normally allowed for the presentation of evidence was eighty days.[3] At the end of that time (or earlier with the consent of both parties) the case was declared to be complete (*concluso*) and the *relator* presented to the court his final summary of fact (*relación para definitiva*). In minor cases this final *relación*, like the preceding ones, might be made verbally; but in cases involving more than 200 *pesos* the *relator* was required to produce a written summary, with full references, signed by himself and by the advocates of both parties. (Neither the parties themselves nor their attorneys were allowed to approach the *relator* directly.) Besides hearing the *relación* read in court, the judges were furnished with a copy; and

[1] J. de Solórzano, *Política Indiana*, II. xxviii. 34, 35.
[2] *Recopilación de Leyes de Indias*, v. x. 7.
[3] *Nueva Recopilación de Leyes de España*, IV. vi. 1.

with this summary of fact before them they proceeded to give judgement.

The law required the decisions of courts of appeal to be given within twenty days of the completion of the hearing.[1] The decisions had, of course, no binding force as precedents; reasoned judgements were not published, and nobody except the judges, the *fiscal* and the notary was allowed to remain in the court while a decision was being discussed.[2] Decisions were made by majority vote of the judges;[3] no record was kept of dissenting opinions, though the votes were recorded in a ledger kept by the president. The final judgement, besides being read to the parties in court, was embodied in a writ signed by the judges and by the notary of the case; copies were given to the parties in a civil suit, and the party in whose favour judgement had been given might, upon payment of a fee, employ the constables of the court to execute the court's writ.

In the viceregal audiencias of Mexico and Peru, as in the audiencias of Spain, criminal charges were tried before a separate bench of judges—the *alcaldes del crimen*. In the smaller colonial audiencias, however, the *oidores* heard criminal as well as civil cases, applying rules of criminal procedure based on the practice of the *salas del crimen* in Spain.[4] In so mixed and disorderly a society, great tenderness in safeguarding the interests of the accused was not to be expected; a single denunciation sufficed to set the law in motion and to justify an arrest. All persons arrested, whether at the instances of the *fiscal* or of the inferior judges, were entitled to a copy of their indictment and to the services of an advocate.[5] They were given three days to prepare their defence, during which time they might not be questioned or put to torture. The judges were required to inspect the prisons weekly, to ensure that these rules were obeyed, and were supposed to give priority of hearing to the cases of prisoners.[6] This rather vague enactment was the only guarantee against long imprisonment without trial; and prisoners did sometimes remain in prison for long periods, especially when conflicts of jurisdiction were involved.

The official prosecution, with its inquisitorial procedure, taken from Canon Law and adopted in secular courts in all Roman-Law

[1] *Nueva Recopilación de Leyes de España*, IV. xvii. I.
[2] *Recopilación de Leyes de Indias*, II. xv. 30.
[3] Ibid. II. xv. 97.   [4] Ibid. II. xv. 68.
[5] *Nueva Recopilación de Leyes de España*, II. vi. 6.
[6] Ibid. II. vii. 14.

countries by the sixteenth century, was far less favourable to the defence than was the accusatory procedure which it replaced.[1] Witnesses were examined in private and might not be cross-examined by the accused or by his advocate, though the accused had the right possessed by all litigants to object to the admission of evidence; and an elaborate and strict body of rules provided for the disqualification (*tacha*) of interested or untrustworthy witnesses.[2] When the accused was questioned, he was not shown a copy of the *interrogatorio*, but had to answer each question as it was put to him by the judges. He was examined upon oath, and no rule of evidence prevented his being compelled to testify against himself. He might be tortured if he refused to answer, if he were suspected of perjury, or—in order to extract a confession—if the evidence against him were considered nearly but not quite conclusive. Torture might again be used after sentence, to extract the names of accomplices. The use of torture required a written order from a magistrate, against which the victim might appeal. Certain classes of persons—men of gentle birth, men of learning, pregnant women, and children—were exempted from torture by the *Siete Partidas* and subsequent codes.[3] In a court which sat in private, however, the administration of torture was very much at the discretion of the judges, since a prisoner could easily be prevented from communicating with the outside world. There was a strong temptation to use torture, and it is clear from the repetitions of the rules governing its use that they were often disregarded.[4]

In the taking of evidence and the presentation of written statements the Ordinances of Monzón laid down the same procedure in criminal as in civil cases, except that in criminal cases the notaries were required to conduct their examination of witnesses in the presence of the local *alcaldes*, whose authority might be necessary to compel the witnesses to testify. The laws governing the *salas del crimen* in Spain prescribed the examination of all witnesses in person by the judges,[5] and this rule was binding by general

[1] F. A. Biener, *Geschichte des Inquisitions-Prozesses* (Leipzig, 1827), p. 208; A. Esmein (trans. J. Simpson), *History of Continental Criminal procedure* (London, 1914), Pt. ii, tit. ii, cap. i.

[2] *Nueva Recopilación de Leyes de España*, iv. viii. 1, 2.

[3] 'Menor de catorce anos, cavallero, fidalgo, maestro de las leyes o de otro saber, ome que fuesse consejero señaladamente del Rey o del común de alguna ciudad o villa del Rey, los fijos dessos sobre dichos, mujer que fuesse preñada.' *Partida* vii, tit. xxx, ley 2.

[4] *Nueva Recopilación de Leyes de España*, ii. vii. 13.   [5] Ibid. ii. vii. 15.

analogy upon the colonial audiencias. In practice the *oidores* appear to have admitted both written and verbal testimony, at their own discretion; in the case of a serious criminal charge or notorious riot, one of the *oidores* normally visited the scene of the crime as *juez pesquisidor* to conduct a preliminary inquiry and to hear the charge in first instance. The case would then be remanded to the audiencia, which would receive the evidence collected by the *juez pesquisidor* in writing.

The perpetrators of crimes of violence often evaded justice under cover of the sporadic guerrilla warfare waged by the unsettled tribes. The only police force consisted of the proprietary *alguaciles mayores*—the chief constables of the audiencia and of the corporate towns—and deputies recruited and paid by them. The chief constable of the audiencia was allowed two rural deputies (*alguaciles del campo*).[1] In order to make difficult arrests, the *alguacil* would have to organise a posse of local residents. The criminal records often bear the notes 'escaped from prison' or 'escaped from custody while being taken to prison'. An accused person could be tried and condemned in his absence, after the formality of crying his name through the streets;[2] but there was no effective machinery for pursuing a criminal who fled to another province. It is not surprising that people who had cause to expect prosecution, whether justly or not, often preferred flight to remaining behind— in the significant phrase of the time—to 'purge their innocence' (*purgar su inocencia*). It is fair to add that the audiencias were empowered to inflict summary punishment on false accusers and perjured witnesses.[3]

The special needs of Indian litigants formed the subject of a long series of enactments. The Crown was genuinely concerned to make justice readily available to Indians; but at the same time to discourage the needless litigation to which they were often incited by unscrupulous lawyers. It sought to achieve the first object by ordering the viceroys, and later all governors, as well as the inferior judges, to hear Indian suits in first instance;[4] and by requiring the colonial audiencias to set aside two days a week for hearing the appeals of Indians.[5] The second object could best be achieved by making Indian suits unprofitable for the lawyers, and by trusting

---

[1] *Recopilación de Leyes de Indias*, II. xx. 9.
[2] *Nueva Recopilación de Leyes de España*, II. vi. 7.   [3] Ibid. II. xxiii. 5; II. v. 57.
[4] *Recopilación de Leyes de Indias*, V. x. 13.   [5] Ibid. II. xv. 81.

to the integrity and acumen of the judges rather than to the safe-guards of formal procedure. Accordingly, when Indians appealed to the audiencia, their cases were to be dealt with summarily, according to the customs of the litigants' tribe, in so far as those customs were not repugnant to accepted notions of justice.[1] In some cases—particularly in interpreting native law on such vital subjects as water rights—the courts were specifically commanded to consult native opinion.[2] The importance of preventing delays in dealing with Indian litigation was repeatedly stressed in royal decrees. Formal *procesos* with their cumbrous procedure of *petición*, *interrogatorio*, and written proofs were forbidden to Indians except when specifically ordered by an audiencia in serious cases; in particular, in disputes over chieftainships.[3]

Nothing in theory prevented Indians from suing Spaniards, including their own *encomenderos* or *corregidores*;[4] and groups of Indians might litigate jointly.[5] They suffered, no doubt, from the small reliance placed upon their testimony by the courts; but on the other hand they enjoyed—again in theory—considerable privileges, defined in a series of decrees issued in 1591. Indian litigants were entitled to the legal services of the *fiscal* himself in suits against Spaniards;[6] in suits between Indians the *fiscal* appeared for one side and a lawyer nominated as *protector de Indios* for the other.[7] This official received no fees from his clients, but was paid a salary, which came later to be charged upon Indian contri-butions.[8] In 1623 a tax of half a *real* per head was imposed on the Indians of New Spain and New Galicia, to cover all the costs of Indian litigation, and it was then made a penal offence for any lawyer to demand legal fees from Indians.[9] In criminal proceedings against Indians, when the *fiscal* conducted the case for the Crown, the *protector de Indios* appeared for the defence.[10] Indians might not be prosecuted for offences consisting solely of words, or for unarmed brawling; for these offences they were merely to be admonished by the judges.[11] All the audiencias were required to employ salaried interpreters in Indian languages.[12]

[1] Ibid. II. xv. 83.   [2] Ibid. IV. xvii. 11.   [3] Ibid. V. x. 10.
[4] Solórzano, *Política Indiana*, III. xxvi. 43; II. xxviii. 39.
[5] *Recopilación de Leyes de Indias*, V. x. 14.
[6] Solórzano, *Política Indiana*, V. vi. 27; *Recopilación de Leyes de Indias*, II. xviii. 34.
[7] *Recopilación de Leyes de Indias*, VI. vi. 13.   [8] Ibid. VI. vi. 3 and 11.
[9] Ibid. VI. vi. 4.   [10] Ibid. II. xviii. 35.
[11] Ibid. V. x. 11.   [12] Ibid. II. xxix. 1- .

The mass of legislation concerning the procedure of the courts in dealing with Indian suits was emphatic and singularly comprehensive; yet Solórzano, who had long practical experience of the working of the law, and whose professional sympathies naturally lay with the audiencias and the system they represented, remarked gloomily that all the laws made for the protection of the Indians, in the long run worked to their disadvantage.[1] It was to some extent conventional for writers to deplore the wretchedness of the Indians. The truth was that the Crown, in seeking to protect Indians from the harshness of *encomenderos* and employers and from the rapacity of lawyers, had placed their interests in the hands of a small number of courts, each exercising an appellate jurisdiction over a vast area; and had given those courts wide discretionary powers in dealing with Indian affairs. Often, therefore, the remedy for injustice lay outside the Indians' reach. Everything depended on the accessibility of the audiencias and on the character of the judges; where Indians lived within easy reach of an audiencia, and where the *oidores* and *fiscal* were conscientious and sympathetic, the Indians had ready access to effective and inexpensive justice.

For Spaniards and *mestizos* on the other hand, litigation before an audiencia was normally an expensive and intricate business if the prescribed procedure were followed. Its intricacy and expense were due to the generous provisions for appeal and to the large number of legal officials responsible for the different stages of every suit. No doubt the system was intended to protect litigants against partiality or intimidation. All the traditions of the Crown and the legal profession were against entrusting summary powers either to judges or to administrators, and in all departments of the Empire there was a tendency to set one group of officials to watch and check another, and to insist on complete written records. Litigants paid the price of this solicitude in long delays and heavy expenses.

The multiplicity of minor legal offices had moreover another and more pressing cause, as we have seen—the need for raising revenue by the sale of offices. *Escribanías* figured prominently in the long list of saleable and renunciable offices,[2] and notaries were forbidden to practise without royal licence, for which, of course, they had to pay.[3] There is no doubt that the Crown multiplied

---

[1] Solórzano, *Política Indiana*, I. xii. 31.
[2] *Recopilación de Leyes de Indias*, VIII. xx. 1.
[3] León-Pinelo, *Tratado de Confirmaciones*, II. xix.

minor legal offices in order to sell them, and that audiencia procedure was to some extent designed to employ a numerous legal
staff. One inevitable consequence of this was a low standard of
skill and honesty among notaries employed in remote and sparsely
inhabited provinces. The total volume of litigation in New Galicia
was not very great, and much of it—criminal cases and pleas of
Indians—was unremunerative. Consequently, *escribanías* rarely
found qualified purchasers. The audiencia, in order to get its work
done, was compelled to employ any needy notary, whether
licensed or not, who cared to hang about the court in the hope of
occasional fees, and even to entrust pleas to unqualified *procuradores*.

It will be remembered that the *oidor* Morones had suggested an
increase in the number of *escribanías* in New Galicia as a means of
raising revenue.[1] At the time when Morones wrote (in 1561) the
audiencia's writs were being signed—or rather the *oidores'* signatures
upon them were being witnessed—by one Simón de Coca, who
described himself as *escribano de Su Majestad y de la audiencia Real.*
The phrase *escribano de Su Majestad* was merely a pretentious
synonym for *escribano público* or *escribano del número.* Coca was a
public notary whom the audiencia employed because it had no
proprietary *escribano de cámara* of its own. There was, therefore,
some point in Morones's suggestion; but little came of it. From
1560 to 1574 the register of royal *cédulas* for New Galicia contains
only two titles of *escribanos de cámara*, one in favour of Luis Méndez de
Haro, the other of Alonso Sánchez. The name of Méndez de Haro
does not occur again; presumably he never reached New Galicia,
or if he did he liked it so little that he went away at once. Alonso
Sánchez, however, signed all the audiencia's writs for about eight
years. He was described as *escribano de cámara de la real audiencia
del nuevo reino del Galicia y escribano mayor de la dicha gobernación.*
Escribano mayor was not a recognised title; its use can only have
meant that Sánchez, being the only proprietary *escribano de cámara*
in the province, regarded himself as officially senior to all the other
notaries. The signatures of a number of public notaries appear
upon witnesses' statements in *procesos* heard by the audiencia,
with the added phrases *escribano público*, *escribano del número* or
escribano de Su Majestad, indicating that the audiencia employed
these men as *receptores* to receive evidence when the amount of
litigation before the court made this necessary. The audiencia,

---

[1] *A.G.I.* Auda. de Guadalajara 51: 'Dr Morones al Rey. 4 de Enero 1561.'

indeed, never had more than one proprietary *escribano de cámara* in the sixteenth century, with occasional assistance from public notaries; the single *escribano* being frequently described simply as the Secretary of the Audiencia.

In 1582 fresh proposals were made by the Crown for selling offices of proprietary *receptores* and licences to practise as attorneys (*procuradores*). The audiencia's report in answer to these proposals forms a good illustration of the position with regard to legal offices in the province:

> In a recent decree Your Majesty commands us to exclude from practice in this audiencia all *receptores* and *procuradores* except those who hold titles from Your Majesty; and to report how many *receptores* and *procuradores* are needed, and what price their offices would fetch. We have to report that there are four *procuradores* in practice in the audiencia; they are local residents and their condition is poor and wretched. If responsible offices of this kind were put up for sale, nobody would buy them, because there is little litigation here, and what there is, is unprofitable. There are no *receptores* in the court; under present conditions only one is needed, and he would find difficulty in making a living.... Several *escribanos* have come here at various times with royal titles and claims to be admitted to practice in the audiencia; but having seen the poverty of the province and the impossibility of making a living they have gone away.[1]

It is clear that the law on the sale of legal offices was largely a dead letter in the smaller colonial audiencias. With the legal staff available it must often have been impossible to carry out the full procedure of the courts as officially prescribed. Consequently, in jurisdiction as in administration, the *oidores* held a much greater measure of real discretion than the law allowed. This fact no doubt gave a sharper edge to the constant local complaints against them.

One fruitful source of delays and denials of justice has so far been mentioned only incidentally. Litigants were often kept in suspense, sometimes in noisome prisons, while the audiencia and the other authorities of New Spain and New Galicia disputed the limits of their respective jurisdictions. Conflicts of jurisdiction were the curse of the Indies administration. It remains to describe the conflicts of the audiencia of New Galicia with the viceroy, the audiencia of New Spain, and the Inquisition.

---

[1] *A.G.I.* Auda. de Guadalajara 6, fol. 1. 17 de Octubre 1582: 'Audiencia de la Nueva Galicia a S.M.'

CHAPTER IX

CONFLICTS OF JURISDICTION

Throughout this detailed study of the judicial and administrative machinery of a Spanish American colony, the principal difficulty is to say where, in the Indies, real authority lay. This astonishing Empire displayed in the sixteenth century almost all the obvious weaknesses which a colonial empire can display. Its population—its quarrelsome and litigious Spanish settlers, its teeming Indians, many still unsubdued, its sullen and mutinous negro slaves—made an explosive mixture. It was beset by covetous enemies. It was governed by professional judges and officials responsible only to the Spanish Crown. It was separated from Spain by three thousand miles of ocean, a gap bridged only by the slow passage of infrequent convoys—rarely more than once a year and sometimes less frequently. All the circumstances conspired to make communications hazardous as well as slow. The ships were unhandy, overloaded, and overcrowded. The sailing-masters were often incompetent and usually subject to the orders of soldiers who knew little of the sea. The convoy lanes were beset with privateers and pirates and the convoy system itself imposed delay.

The most obvious policy in these conditions would apparently be to create a strong colonial government which could make rapid decisions and enforce them on the spot. On the contrary, the whole administrative system was devised deliberately to prevent the growth of such a government. The Spanish Crown never fully trusted its servants. Reference to Spain, with all its delays and uncertainties, was consistently encouraged. All important decisions were made in Spain. Naturally at such long range it was difficult to secure the prompt enforcement of royal decisions. The colonial authorities, great and small, temporised, appealed, or employed the formulae of obedience without compliance. There was no authority in the Indies which could be sure of obedience, no jurisdiction which could not be inhibited, and no decision which could not be reversed on appeal to Spain.

It is true that the viceroys within their respective provinces exercised a titular supremacy as the representatives of the royal person; that they commanded the available military force; and

CONFLICTS OF JURISDICTION

that audiencias and other bodies were repeatedly told to obey their orders. There was, however, no permanent body of professional troops in the Indies. A militia levy of *encomenderos* or casual mercenaries could be raised against invasion or Indian revolt, but was not to be relied upon for maintaining the viceroy's internal authority. The viceroys were admittedly the chief administrative officers of their provinces, and the decision as to what was, or was not, an administrative matter rested with them; but anyone who felt himself aggrieved by a viceroy's administrative action might seek redress from the courts by ordinary judicial process. Viceroys and governors were sternly forbidden to hinder this recourse to justice; and in entertaining such appeals the audiencias might reverse, alter or set aside the viceroy's administrative orders. 'But if', says Solórzano, 'the viceroy persists in his course of action despite the modestly worded protests of the *oidores*, and insists that the matter in dispute is purely administrative and not capable of judicial interpretation, then the *oidores* must give way, in order to avoid public scandal, and must send a full account to the Council of the Indies, in order that the matter may be settled there.'[1] In such cases the Council of the Indies did not by any means always support the viceroy; sometimes it supported the audiencia; but very often it merely told both parties, in effect, to be more polite to one another in future, and avoided giving a definite ruling. The complex balance of power between the various authorities in the Indies was thus assiduously preserved.

Not only audiencias but all kinds of minor bodies such as town councils and cathedral chapters corresponded directly with the Crown; they were indeed encouraged to do so, and to include in their letters accounts of the way in which their districts were governed. Some examples of this voluminous tale-bearing correspondence have already been quoted and more would be superfluous. The main point which they illustrate is that any public authority which received orders it disliked or which felt itself aggrieved by the actions of a superior authority in the Indies, could refuse compliance, usually on the grounds that the superior authority was in some way acting *ultra vires*. If pressed or compelled to obey, it could complain to the Council of the Indies that its jurisdiction or privileges were being invaded. It was sure of a hearing, and in the tangle of earlier legislation it could always find some excuse for

---

[1] Solórzano, *Política Indiana*, v. iii. 29, 30, 31.

turning its disobedience into a conflict of jurisdiction. In this way it could postpone action on the immediate subject of dispute for at least two years while awaiting the Council's ruling on the question of jurisdiction.

Apart from this technique of using conflicts of jurisdiction as a means to avoid or postpone the execution of unpopular orders, genuine conflicts constantly arose between authorities of approximately equal standing, about the geographical boundaries of their districts and the matters with which they were competent to deal. With the ingenuity of the legal profession so often employed in disputes of this kind, it is not surprising that a considerable body of legislation was needed to lay down the forms and rules whereby conflicts of jurisdiction were to be conducted. If any generalisations are possible concerning the power and standing of the various colonial authorities, they can best be drawn from the analysis of a series of conflicts, the manner of their conduct, and the resulting rulings.

To return to the restricted ground of New Galicia: the audiencia there was not called upon, of course, to sit in judgement on the viceroy's administrative acts, since the administration of the province was in the hands of the president, advised by the *oidores*. The loose and ill-defined powers of general supervision entrusted to the viceroy,[1] however, gave rise to a number of conflicts. The extent of viceregal supervision over the affairs of New Galicia varied greatly with the circumstances and with the character of the viceroy. Enríquez and Luis de Velasco I intervened energetically and effectively, Villamanrique with disastrous results. Most other viceroys were content, as a rule, to leave New Galicia alone; and in general the president refused to allow viceregal agents to enter his area unless they held a definite commission from the Crown. A *pesquisidor* sent by the viceroy to Zacatecas, at the request of some of the inhabitants, to investigate disorders there in 1570 was forcibly ejected by the local *alcalde mayor* acting upon orders from the audiencia;[2] an act of contempt which provoked a stern royal reprimand. In 1583 a royal letter ordered the viceroy to appoint a *pesquisidor* to investigate the conduct of the royal factor at Zacatecas, who was alleged to have embarked on various trading enterprises with capital embezzled from the royal chest.[3] A second

---

[1] *Recopilación de Leyes de Indias*, II. xv. 52.
[2] *A.G.I.* Auda. de Guadalajara 230, lib. Z 1, fol. 231. 23 de Junio 1571.
[3] *A.G.N.* Ramo de Duplicados, tit. 2, fol. 26, 1583.

letter of the same year acknowledged a report from the viceroy that
the audiencia of New Galicia was appointing *alcaldes mayores* without authority to do so, and in particular had appointed two entirely
unnecessary magistrates at the salt-beds of Santa María and Peñol
Blanco.[1] The viceroy was told to cancel these men's appointments
and to stop the payment of their salaries by the Zacatecas treasury.
As it happened, the viceregal throne was vacant when these letters
arrived. The audiencia of New Spain, governing during the interregnum, dispatched the licentiate Pablo de Torres, *corregidor* of
Mexico, to investigate the treasury accounts at Zacatecas, having
a royal commission for the purpose which the audiencia could not
disregard. Torres was treated with studied insolence while
carrying out his duties in Zacatecas; and in the matter of the
alcaldes mayores no action was taken.

The most striking instance of viceregal intervention in New
Galicia occurred in 1588 over the unlawful marriage of an *oidor*.
Viceroys and *oidores* were forbidden by a decree of 1575[2] to marry
or to allow their children to marry within their districts and were
automatically to be deprived of office if they did so. In 1588 Nuño
Núñez de Villavicencio, *oidor* in New Galicia, married the daughter
of Juan Bautista de Lomas y Colmenares, rancher and mine-
owner, *vecino* of Nieves in New Galicia.[3] It was the duty of the
president to deprive Núñez of his office and to order the treasury
officials to stop his salary; but the office of president was vacant,
and the *oidores* were administering the province. The senior *oidor*,
Altamirano, whether because of the wealth and influence of the
father-in-law, or simply because of a desire to avoid a quarrel
with his colleague, took no action. A peremptory order from the
viceroy (Villamanrique) to the audiencia, requiring Núñez to be
arrested and sent to Mexico, merely elicited a denial of the viceregal jurisdiction in New Galicia. Having at that time no effective
control over the New Galicia treasury, the viceroy could not stop
Núñez's salary. There followed an acrimonious correspondence,
which so enraged Villamanrique that he decided to reduce the
audiencia to obedience by force. Accordingly early in 1589 orders
were sent to all the *alcaldes mayores* of Michoacán, Colima and

---

[1] *A.G.N.* Ramo de Duplicados, tit. 2, fol. 24.
[2] *Recopilación de Leyes de Indias*, II. xvi. 82.
[3] The most complete account of the affair is in Mota-Padilla, *Historia de la Nueva Galicia*, cap. xliii.

Avalos to raise troops and to assemble them at Jacona on the boundary of New Galicia. A professional soldier and *encomendero* named Gil Verdugo was sent to Jacona to take charge; and having collected about three hundred armed Spaniards, he advanced upon Guadalajara with his little army and camped just outside the city, in the Indian suburb of Analco. He found barricades in the streets and the city prepared for siege, the *oidores* directing operations from the *casa real*. The audiencia had called out the *encomenderos* of the province with their servants and clients and had raised a force of two hundred Spaniards to defend Guadalajara, under the command of Rodrigo del Río, rancher and *alférez* of the city. All the local Indians had left their work and taken to the hills, and all business was at a standstill. A series of parleys ensued, in which it became clear that the men from Mexico had intended a demonstration rather than real fighting. Presently a solemn procession emerged from the city, including the bishop bearing the Host in his hands, the *oidores*, the canons of the cathedral, the magistrates and town councillors. Arrived at the camp, the bishop 'with sermons and showers of tears' exhorted Gil Verdugo to return to Mexico and to avert the horrors of civil war. Verdugo accordingly marched his men back to their homes and the 'little war of Guadalajara', as Tello called it, came to an end.[1]

It was too late, however, to stop reports of civil war reaching Spain. The *oidores* of New Galicia had written both to the audiencia of New Spain and to the Inquisition in Mexico, asking both authorities to dissuade the viceroy from using force.[2] The bishop and chapter of Guadalajara had sent similar messages to the inquisitors, and the *cabildo* of Guadalajara had written to the *cabildo* of Mexico.[3] Copies of these letters—which unanimously condemned the viceroy's ill-temper—were forwarded to the *Suprema* and to the Council of the Indies. The king, convinced that a real civil war had broken out, promptly appointed a new viceroy—Luis de Velasco the second, son of the great Velasco—to supersede Villamanrique and to restore order. All was quiet by the time Velasco arrived in Mexico; but it is significant that throughout his distinguished and successful reign he used the greatest tact and forbearance in dealing with the authorities of New Galicia.

[1] Tello, *Crónica miscelánea*, cap. ccxxviii.
[2] *A.G.N.*: Ramo de Inquisición, tit. 104, fol. 33.
[3] *Actas del Cabildo de México*, vol. IX, p. 330.

Villamanrique was placed under open arrest and a judicial commissioner—Diego Romano, bishop of Tlaxcala—was appointed to conduct his *residencia*.[1] The trial dragged on for two years in Mexico and was then removed to Spain; Villamanrique died before the findings were promulgated. Many charges were brought against him; but the 'little war of Guadalajara', if not the only cause, was certainly the occasion of his downfall.[2] As often happened in conflicts of jurisdiction, the original cause of the trouble escaped unpunished. Núñez de Villavicencio kept his wife and his judicial office. He remained at Guadalajara until 1596, when he was appointed one of the judges in the *Casa de Contratación* at Seville, and returned to the Indies in 1610 as president of the audiencia of Charcas. In a similar case in 1591, arising from the marriage of the daughter of the *fiscal* in New Galicia, the viceroy prudently referred to Spain for instructions; but the answer he received was non-committal.[3] In 1603 the viceroy Monterrey sent a commissioner to Guadalajara to deprive an *oidor* whose son had married locally; the audiencia insisted that the viceroy should show written authority from the Crown, and refused to admit the commissioner to the court-room. Again a ruling was sought; the resulting royal letter, addressed to the audiencia, was a mere admonition: 'Your duty is to obey the law; and you would have done better to have refrained from asking the viceroy to exhibit his authority.'[4] No action was taken, and the Council of the Indies never gave a clear answer to the question of whether the viceroy might enforce the law against the *oidores* of New Galicia, if their own president failed to do so.

In general, the sixteenth-century viceroys, despite the titular grandeur of their office, had very little real control over the affairs of New Galicia, except on the rare occasions when they intervened in person, as Enríquez did. Provincial particularism and jealousy was already beginning to play an important part in Latin-American politics. Even in the immediate administrative area of New Spain the viceregal audiencia was an effective check on the viceroy's

---

[1] *A.G.N.*: Ramo de Duplicados, tit. 2, fol. 207. Riva Palacio, *México a través los siglos*, vol. II, p. 439.

[2] *A.G.I.* Auda. de Guadalajara 47: 'Cargos de la visita secreta hacha por el obispo de Tlaxcala D. Diego Romano al virrey Marqués de Villamanrique—se refieren a la conducta del virrey con la Audiencia de Nueva Galicia.'

[3] *A.G.N.*: Ramo de Duplicados, tit. 2, fol. 258.

[4] Mota-Padilla, *Historia de la Nueva Galicia*, cap. XLVIII.

power, as Falces had discovered in 1568. In a formal conflict of jurisdiction a military governor was no match for the professional lawyers, and the viceroys could not rely with any confidence on the support of the Crown. Solórzano probably expressed both the official view and the general feeling when he declared, calling St Jerome to his support, that the viceroy who ill-treated a judge sinned most gravely: 'Why should I treat you with the respect due to a Prince, if you do not treat me with the respect due to a Senator?'[1]

After 1572 the audiencia of New Spain carefully avoided interference in the province of the smaller court, even when exercising the viceroy's authority during vacancies in the viceregal office; though in strict law its supervisory powers during such vacancies extended to New Galicia.[2] Relations between the two courts were not always cordial; but the conflicts between them arose for the most part from boundary disputes and are of little constitutional interest.[3] The nature of the occasional conflicts between the audiencia of New Galicia and the town council of Guadalajara has already been indicated. It remains to describe the relations of the audiencia with the most uncompromising and most closely organised of all the jurisdictions of the Spanish Empire—the Inquisition.

The tribunal of the Holy Office, formally established in Mexico by royal decrees of 1569 and 1570,[4] consisted originally of two inquisitors, a *fiscal* and a secretary. It was a far more formidable organisation than the ecclesiastical courts with which the audiencias had had to deal before that date. It was directly responsible to its own supreme council in Spain, which stood in the same constitutional relation to the king as did the Council of the Indies. There was no possibility of appeal from its decisions to any secular authority in the Indies; the familiar procedure of *recurso de fuerza* was expressly denied to its victims.[5] Apart from specific legislation, both the secrecy of the tribunal and the horror with which offences

[1] Solórzano, *Política Indiana*, v. xii. 30.
[2] *Recopilación de Leyes de Indias*, ii. xv. 47.
[3] E.g. *A.G.I.* Auda. de Guadalajara 48: 'La Auda. de Nueva Galicia informa al Consejo de Indias en virtud de Real Cédula de 20 de Junio 1596 si convendrá que las apelaciones de Colima y Zacatula vengan a dicha Real Audiencia.'
[4] H. C. Lea, *The Inquisition in the Spanish Dependencies* (New York, 1908), pp. 200 ff.
[5] *Recopilación de Leyes de Indias*, i. xix. 4.

against the Faith were regarded made the intervention of the secular courts extremely difficult.

The jurisdiction of the Holy Office was exclusively criminal and covered both clerics and laymen, including negroes but not Indians. It dealt with all offences against the Faith, principally heresy, blasphemy and sorcery; with various other spiritual offences such as bigamy and personation of priesthood which might, by a somewhat forced interpretation, be held to imply belief in false doctrine; with incest and homosexuality; and with certain offences committed by clerics which it was desired to punish secretly; of these the most important were solicitation in the confessional and the administration of sacraments by minor clergy not in priests' orders. The inquisitors let slip no opportunity of extending their jurisdiction, and were ruthless in punishing contempts of their own courts.

This wide and aggressive jurisdiction was made effective by the appointment of commissaries—ecclesiastical judges of first instance —in all important centres of population. These commissaries took over the inquisitorial duties which had been discharged before 1570 by the episcopal provisors. Having nothing else to do, and being closely controlled by the inquisitors at Mexico, they were naturally much more assiduous than the provisors had been.

In addition to the commissaries and a staff of chaplains and ecclesiastical notaries, the Inquisition employed a considerable number of laymen, including besides servants, warders and *alguaciles*, the important body of honorary lay agents known as *familiares*. The term familiar suggests a class of somewhat disreputable *sbirri* and secret informers; but in fact the *familiatura* was a coveted honour, and throughout the Indies men of wealth and position were proud to serve the Holy Office. The institution of the *familiatura* was a matter of grave concern to the secular authorities, for the Inquisition claimed and exercised a monopoly of criminal jurisdiction over its servants. Not only, therefore, were clerics in the service of the Inquisition exempt from the jurisdiction of the bishops; but a large number of wealthy and prominent laymen were partially exempt from prosecution in the secular courts. Legislation on the subject[1] restricted the *fuero* of the Inquisition in two ways: by limiting the number of familiars (in New Spain there

[1] C. H. Lea, op. cit. Appendix XII. Decree regulating the privileges of familiars in New Spain, 1570.

were twelve in Mexico, four in other cities which were the seats of bishops, and one in every other town); and by insisting that the *fuero* should not cover major crimes. The offences excepted from the inquisitors' jurisdiction were treason, unnatural vice, rebellion, rioting or inciting to riot, forgery of royal letters, rape, arson, house-breaking, highway robbery, robbery of churches, and 'other crimes greater than these'. Crimes committed by familiars against Indians were added to the list in 1572.[1] It is curious that murder, though clearly intended to be included, was not expressly mentioned. The attempts of the Inquisition to claim jurisdiction over familiars accused of one or other of these crimes, in a society where crimes of violence were common, gave rise to many conflicts with the audiencias. Other causes of trouble were failures, or alleged failures of the secular judges to provide the 'help of the secular arm' when required to do so by the inquisitors; failure of the inquisitors to supply the secular authorities with up-to-date lists of familiars; the appointment of familiars in excess of the statutory number; the proceedings of the Inquisition against laymen for alleged contempts; and the tendency of the inquisitors to use the threat of prosecution in order to secure petty economic privileges. It is important to notice that in any kind of conflict, the inquisitors' command of spiritual censures enabled them to take direct action against lay judges; but the secular courts could obtain redress against the Inquisition only by the circuitous way of appeal to Spain, to persuade the Council of the Indies to make representations to the Suprema.

Sixteenth-century New Galicia provided examples of nearly all the ordinary forms of conflict. Commissaries were appointed in Guadalajara and Zacatecas in 1572, the dean of Guadalajara filling the office in that city; and an enthusiastic heresy-hunt began. A number of survivors of John Hawkins's unlucky adventure at San Juan de Ulúa were living in New Galicia, employed apparently as slave foremen in mines or ranches. These men were hunted out and sent to Mexico for trial as heretics.[2] A few cases pending before the episcopal provisor were handed over to the commissary for remission to Mexico, and one of these revealed a conflict of jurisdiction with the audiencia. One Gaspar de Tapia had, as a result of a dispute with a cleric, been prosecuted by the provisor

---

[1] *A.G.N.*: Ramo de Inquisición, tit. 223, no. 5.
[2] Ibid. tit. 53, 54, 55.

for blasphemy. The 'oidor of the week'—the hot-tempered Contreras—had issued a writ of recurso and secured the papers in the case; taking them to his house, he had flung them into a corner and forgotten them. After his death his wife had sent the papers to the secretary of the audiencia, who had steadfastly refused to return them to the provisor; but a curt letter from the inquisitors secured their prompt remission to Mexico. Tapia was tried by the Holy Office and fined.[1]

The mixed and thriving community of Zacatecas provided much work for the resident commissary. Many of the denunciations forwarded to Mexico appear extremely trivial. In 1576, for instance, a wine merchant was denounced for blasphemy because, when accused of giving false measure, he protested that he was 'as innocent as any saint'.[2] The first conflict with the audiencia occurred in 1583: Pablo de Torres, corregidor of Mexico, had been sent to Zacatecas with a royal commission to audit the accounts of the local treasury. Torres was an unwelcome visitor, and one night an ill-wisher affixed to the window of his lodging a sheet of paper cut to represent a sanbenito—a penitential robe. This public insult, with its implication that Torres was a Jew, called forth a storm of protest both from Torres and from the Inquisition. The audiencia was urged to make a thorough inquiry (pesquisa) into the incident, and one of the oidores, Altamirano, went to Zacatecas in person; but whether through absence of evidence or lack of zeal, he made no arrest for several months. Exasperated by the dilatory proceedings of the juez pesquisidor, the commissary himself then started a proceso against the corregidor of Zacatecas, Félix de Zúñiga, whom Torres suspected of being the culprit. Zúñiga retorted that Torres had probably put the paper there himself in order to embroil him, Zúñiga, with the Holy Office; he being responsible for public order in the city. Altamirano, apparently anxious for peace at any price, eventually produced a scapegoat. One Felipe de Arandia was arrested, on the unsupported testimony of a negro named Vicente, and committed for trial before the audiencia. The records of Arandia's trial are lost; but apparently the Inquisition was satisfied.[3]

Another minor encounter occurred in 1589, this time at Guadalajara. The Inquisition had no prison of its own in that city and its

---

[1] A.G.N.: Ramo de Inquisición, tit. 74, no. 8.
[2] Ibid. tit. 81, no. 22.   [3] Ibid. tit. 139, no. 13.

prisoners, while awaiting escort to Mexico, were lodged in the prison of the audiencia building. Late one night one of the resident familiars brought in a prisoner and in handing him over, instructed the warder to take more than ordinary care of him. The warder told the familiar, with much abusive language, to take himself off and not to try to teach an honest warder his business. As a result, the commissary had the warder arrested for contempt.[1] The warder was not strictly a servant of the audiencia, being appointed by the *alguacil mayor*.[2] No secular authority intervened on his behalf.

From the year of its establishment, then, the Holy Office exercised a vigorous and effective jurisdiction in New Galicia and consistently had its way in a series of minor encounters with the secular authorities of the province. Not until 1594 did the audiencia make a stand in defence of its jurisdiction, over the trial of a prominent familiar indicted for murder. The case of Francisco de Urdiñola made a great stir at the time, and illustrates so many aspects of the relations between the two courts that its story is worth telling in detail.

During the viceroyalty of Luis de Velasco II (1590–5) elaborate and (for the first time) effective preparations were made for the long-discussed conquest of New Mexico, and great public interest was shown in the question of who was to command the expedition. There were two likely candidates, both resident in New Galicia. One was Juan Bautista de Lomas y Colmenares of Nieves, who was reputed to be the richest man in New Galicia and who moreover wielded considerable family influence. His two daughters had both married *oidores*; one, Dr Valderrama of Mexico, the other, licentiate Núñez de Villavicencio of Guadalajara, the cause of the troubles of 1589. Lomas had been negotiating for the New Mexico appointment for some years and seemed the most likely candidate. His rival was Francisco de Urdiñola, a Basque who had come to the Indies as a 'poor gentleman', but had acquired considerable wealth as a rancher and mine-owner. He was an able soldier and organiser, his principal achievements being the settlement of New León (Coahuila) and the foundation of the city of Saltillo.[3] Apart

---

[1] Ibid. tit. 130, no. 14.

[2] *Recopilación de Leyes de Indias*, II. xx. 13.

[3] For a full and clear account of Urdiñola see V. Alessio Robles, *Francisco de Urdiñola y el Norte de la Nueva España* (Mexico, 1931).

from their rivalry over New Mexico the two men were bitter enemies, their family enmity dating from a series of land disputes between Lomas and Alonso López de Loys, Urdiñola's father-in-law, from whom he had inherited his estate of Río Grande near Nieves. Both Lomas and Urdiñola were familiars of the Holy Office.

In February 1593 Urdiñola lost his wife, Leonor López de Loys, who died after a three weeks' illness. Urdiñola was away from home when Doña Leonor fell sick, and hurried home upon receiving the news, but arrived too late to see his wife alive. The cause of her death was diagnosed both by the physician who attended her, and by her mother, who nursed her, as erysipelas.

Six months later a mysterious incident occurred in the Urdiñola household; a Spaniard named Domingo de Landaverde, who was employed by Urdiñola as a mechanic and handy-man, disappeared from Río Grande. Rumour accused him of stealing silver; there may have been some suspicion of foul play, since the *alcalde mayor* of Nieves conducted an inquiry into the circumstances of his departure, but without discovering what had become of him. The written testimonies were deposited in the archive at Nieves and, for the time being, forgotten.

Shortly after Landaverde's disappearance Urdiñola was summoned to Mexico for consultations with the viceroy. His rival Lomas had made a proposal some time before, for undertaking the conquest of New Mexico; the proposal had been forwarded to Spain, and had been rejected, the Council of the Indies considering that the terms which Lomas demanded were 'outrageous' (*desaforadas*). The viceroy therefore sent for Urdiñola, whose demands apparently were more moderate, and by October 1594 the negotiations for Urdiñola's employment in the conquest were almost complete. They were interrupted by an order for his arrest on a charge of murder, issued by the audiencia of New Galicia.[1]

The case against Urdiñola began with an undated anonymous denunciation accusing him of poisoning his wife and of murdering his servant Landaverde, and alleging adultery between them as Urdiñola's motive. It is impossible to say when the audiencia

---

[1] The papers in the case are preserved as follows: *A.G.I.* Guadalajara: Escribanía de Cámara 380, legajo 1° de pleitos, 1562–1642: 'El capitán Francisco de Urdiñola y Alonso de León y consortes sobre la muerte de Leonor de Loys su mujer y Landaverde su criado y demás. Guadalajara, año de 1594.' See Alessio Robles, op. cit. pp. 217 ff.

received this document; but it took no action until October 1594, eighteen months after Doña Leonor's death and more than a year after the disappearance of Landaverde. The first steps were taken by Núñez de Villavicencio, the son-in-law of Lomas, acting as '*oidor* of the week'. On the strength of the denunciation and of some hearsay evidence in Guadalajara of quarrels between Urdiñola and Landaverde, Núñez promptly issued writs for the arrest of Urdiñola, of his younger brother, and of his steward, and for the sequestration of his property. The *oidor* Altamirano was dispatched to Nieves as *juez pesquisidor* to conduct a preliminary inquiry. The officers sent to Río Grande to enforce the writ of sequestration apparently gained admission to the property on the pretext of sightseeing, but failed to catch either young Urdiñola or the steward. Urdiñola himself was in Mexico; the writ for his apprehension was addressed to the audiencia of New Spain, and the *alguacil* of that court duly arrested him.

Urdiñola was determined at all costs to avoid falling into the hands of the audiencia of New Galicia. He applied first to the viceroy, who dispatched a courteous letter to the audiencia requesting that in view of the important negotiations in which Urdiñola was engaged, the trial might be removed to Mexico. The audiencia, having evidently decided to support Núñez, replied with an equally courteous but firm refusal. The viceroy, no doubt with the episode of Núñez's marriage in his mind, did not press his request; and Urdiñola next sought the protection of the Inquisition.[1]

The response of the inquisitors was prompt and emphatic. On 10 December, the day after the receipt of Urdiñola's plea, they issued a writ *inhibitoria* addressed to the audiencia of New Galicia, demanding that the case be remitted to them and that Urdiñola's property be released, he being a familiar of the Holy Office; the *oidores* were informed that if they wished to dispute the jurisdiction of the Holy Office they must give notice of their intention within fifteen days of receiving the writ and must proceed by way of a formal *competencia* or conference for the purpose. At the same time a *requisitoria* was served on the audiencia of Mexico, requiring its warders to hold Urdiñola's person at the disposal of the Holy

---

[1] The papers concerning the proceedings of the Inquisition are in *A.G.N.*: Ramo de Inquisición, tit. 214 and 215: 'Proceso...contra el capitán Francisco de Urdiñola ...familiar del Santo Oficio.' See Alessio Robles, op. cit. pp. 249 ff.

Office and not to send him to Guadalajara without the permission of the inquisitors.

The *inhibitoria* was read in court at Guadalajara by the commissary's notary on 28 December. The *oidores* replied that they could do nothing until a certified copy had been lodged with the *fiscal* and that in any case the Inquisition had no jurisdiction in charges of murder. This led to a second and more peremptory writ and finally to an ultimatum threatening the judges and their secretary by name with excommunication and heavy fines if they did not within six days either remit the case to the Holy Office or submit to a formal *competencia*. On 31 January 1595 the commissary reported that he had suspended the sentence of excommunication at the urgent entreaty of the bishop and the president, since the audiencia had agreed to a conference.

The rules governing *competencias* or conflicts of jurisdiction between the Inquisition and the audiencias in New Spain were laid down in a decree of 1572.[1] This decree provided that when a dispute arose over criminal jurisdiction the senior *oidor* of the audiencia concerned should attend a conference with the two inquisitors at the Inquisition building; if the conference failed to reach agreement the inquisitors and the audiencia were to forward their cases respectively to the Suprema and the Council of the Indies for discussion between the two authorities in Spain. Meanwhile, 'if the nature of the case permitted', the accused was to be released on bail. To such a conference the audiencia of New Galicia had now agreed; and the next few weeks were occupied by the shifts of the *oidores* to evade their undertaking. On 1 February they wrote stating that the work of the court would not permit the prolonged absence of an *oidor* and that they were sending instead a *receptor* named Tenorio with full power to act for the audiencia. They further complained that the delay caused by the inhibitions had allowed Urdiñola's accomplices to fly from justice; and that Urdiñola himself, according to reports, had been released from prison without their permission. To this the inquisitors replied that Urdiñola had been moved to his lodgings under close arrest to enable him to recover from a fever contracted in prison.

On 14 February Tenorio arrived and was granted an audience by the inquisitors. He stated that evidence had been found of

[1] *A.G.N.*: Ramo de Inquisición, tit. 223, no. 5: 'Orden para las cosas que se ofrecieren entre la Inquisición y la Audiencia Real...ano de 1572.'

Urdiñola's having poisoned his wife, murdered Landaverde, and buried the latter's body in the fields 'since alive or dead he has not been seen since'; and that the *familiatura* could not be allowed to protect murderers, especially in Urdiñola's case, since he had been appointed familiar less than a year before Doña Leonor's death, and had probably applied for the office with the deliberate intention of murdering her and then cheating justice. (In fact Urdiñola had first applied for the *familiatura* in 1588[1] though the audiencia could not be expected to know that.)

The inquisitors, after this speech, paid no attention whatever to Tenorio, and continued to insist on the presence of an *oidor*. Tenorio was left to spend his time in spying on Urdiñola and reporting on the conditions of his captivity. The audiencia finally gave way; the president, Doctor Santiago de Vera, wrote to the senior inquisitor on 5 March expressing regret that he could not go to Mexico himself but promising to send the senior *oidor* Altamirano. A few days later Altamirano wrote complaining of the rigours of the journey for one of his advanced years but congratulating himself on the prospect of kissing the inquisitor's hand. He made leisurely preparations and eventually arrived in Mexico in the middle of May.

Meanwhile, the officers of the audiencia had been proceeding against Urdiñola by the ordinary process of *receptoria*, examining witnesses before the magistrate at Nieves, in the absence of the *juez pesquisidor*, Altamirano. The Inquisition also began an inquiry on its own account, conducted by Juan de Morlete, familiar resident at Mazapil. Thus the officers of the two courts were examining the same set of witnesses in the same small town at the same time. It is remarkable that no affray occurred between them. Morlete reported in February that in his opinion there was no case against Urdiñola and that the whole affair had been trumped up at the instigation of Lomas y Colmenares to get Urdiñola out of the way while the expedition to New Mexico was being arranged.

Morlete's report introduced an element of cross-purposes into the conference in Mexico. Altamirano merely reiterated the plain law; that jurisdiction in charges of murder belonged to the royal courts whether the accused were a familiar or not. Peralta, the junior inquisitor, considered that since the Inquisition had no case

[1] *A.G.N.*: Ramo de Inquisición, tit. 196, no. 3: 'Información de limpieza de sangre y genealogía de Francisco de Urdiñola para familiar.'

against Urdiñola, whereas the royal judges claimed to have at least a *prima facie* case, his trial should be conducted by the audiencia. The senior inquisitor Lobo Guerrero, however, was resolutely determined not to allow Urdiñola to fall into the hands of the audiencia, though well aware that in strict law he had no good ground for intervention. He had to defend, as best he could, an indefensible position, in the interests of substantial justice; he made no reference in his judgement to the law governing *competencias*, but confined himself to an attack on the procedure followed in the audiencia. He said that the evidence against Urdiñola was purest hearsay, spread by persons known to be interested in Urdiñola's disgrace; that there was no solid ground even for believing that a murder had been committed; that the motive of jealousy imputed to Urdiñola involved the slanderous and baseless assumption that Doña Leonor had been an adulteress; that in view of the flimsy nature of the evidence Urdiñola's imprisonment had been unwarrantably harsh; and that a court which proceeded in such fashion ought not to be allowed to sit in judgement on the case. All this was probably true, but not really relevant to the *competencia*. The conference broke up without agreement and in June 1595 the conflict was referred to the *Suprema* and the Council of the Indies. The covering letters of the contending courts were both full of complaint, the audiencia's letter in particular containing a bitter attack on the institution of the *familiatura* and the use made of it by quarrelsome adventurers seeking to evade justice.

Almost exactly two years elapsed before a reply was received, and during part of that time Urdiñola was released on bail, with the consent of both courts, to visit his estates. The authorities in Spain, knowing nothing of the inner history of the case, decided the conflict according to strict law in favour of the audiencia. The letter of the Suprema conveying this decision to the inquisitors reached Mexico on 20 June 1597, and their writ remitting the case to the audiencia was issued on the same day. Urdiñola was furnished with copies of Juan de Morlete's report and the testimonies on which it was based, for use in preparing his defence. In September he was taken to Guadalajara for trial.

The composition of the audiencia, meanwhile, had changed. Santiago de Vera was still president, but Núñez de Villavicencio had returned to Spain and Altamirano was dead. The trial was started afresh from the beginning; a new *juez pesquisidor*, the *oidor*

Guillén Chaparro, was sent to Nieves; and the proceedings lasted a further year. Judgement was given in September 1598; Urdiñola was fined for being accessory to the death of Landaverde, but acquitted of all the murder charges and duly released. His fine was reduced on appeal *en grado de suplicación* early in 1599. From first to last the trial had taken four and a half years, most of that time being spent by Urdiñola in more or less close confinement.

Urdiñola's innocence of the charge of murder has been thoroughly established by his distinguished Mexican biographer. He was clearly the victim of a conspiracy between his rival Lomas and the judge Núñez de Villavicencio. It is unlikely that Núñez's colleagues were parties to the conspiracy, though they connived at some highly unjudicial proceedings, whether through fear of Lomas, or jealousy of the Holy Office, or simply professional *esprit de corps* and the desire to support one of their number. In fairness to the *oidores* it should be mentioned that Urdiñola had been convicted once before (in 1588) of harbouring murderers;[1] and that during the murder trial a jar of poisoned jam was found in his possession, bought by him (according to the evidence of the apothecary who supplied it) for the purpose of poisoning certain Indian chiefs who were leaders of disaffection and revolt.[2] Nobody, apparently, expressed any horror of this project. The poison was never used and was found with its seal intact; but clearly Urdiñola was no stranger to violence. That, however, might be said of almost any Spaniard in the troubled frontier region where he lived. Urdiñola himself was no murderer, and his record with regard to the treatment of Indians was comparatively good.

The president, Santiago de Vera, made tardy amends in his report on Urdiñola's 'merits and services'. In 1600 he wrote to the king: 'Captain Francisco de Urdiñola...is a distinguished gentleman of this Kingdom, a good soldier, and particularly experienced in Indian affairs.... He was selected by the viceroy for the conquest of New Mexico, but was prevented by the malice of his enemies from taking command.... I make this report in the hope that Your Majesty may find employment for him, as he is a most reliable and capable person.'[3] Urdiñola had missed his

---

[1] *A.G.N.*: Ramo de Inquisición, tit. 215.

[2] Alessio Robles, op. cit. p. 260.

[3] *A.G.I.* 66–6–17: 'Méritos y Servicios—el capitán Francisco de Urdiñola sobre que se le haga merced, 12 de Abril 1600.'

chance to command the New Mexico *entrada*; that went to Juan de Oñate; but in 1603 he was appointed governor of New Vizcaya, in which office he served with conspicuous success.

The Urdiñola case illustrates the power and confidence of the Holy Office in opposing the secular courts, even in defiance of the letter of the law; and the relative efficiency of the Inquisition machinery, contrasted with the somewhat dilatory and haphazard procedure in the audiencia. Probably the difference was due largely to the fact that the Inquisition was better staffed with notaries and clerks. Minor posts in the Inquisition were filled by appointment, not sold as in the audiencias. The case furnishes an example also of the indifference of the Spanish authorities to the personal character of judges, and of the solidarity of the legal profession. In 1588, by openly flouting a royal decree, Núñez de Villavicencio had come near to provoking civil war; in 1594 he had done his best to procure a gross miscarriage of justice; yet no question seems to have been raised of his fitness for judicial office. He was consistently supported by his colleagues, including Santiago de Vera who—if the chroniclers are to be believed—was one of the most distinguished and successful presidents of New Galicia.[1] Núñez returned to Spain with his official record unblemished, except for the indiscretion of marrying without permission.

A law degree and adequate seniority were the best qualifications for advancement in the Indies service. If a judge or an official possessed both and avoided quarrelling with his colleagues, he could rely on professional *esprit de corps* to conceal his failings. *Conquistadores* and military governors often incurred disgrace; *oidores* very rarely. The Law was second only to the Church in its solicitude for its servants, and the Council of the Indies was composed largely of lawyers. Hence no authority in the Indies, between 1572 and 1600, succeeded in calling the audiencia to account for its actions; and only one authority, the Inquisition, succeeded in maintaining a jurisdiction in New Galicia in the face of the audiencia's opposition. There were many things, including some necessary things, which the audiencia failed to do, or had no power to do; but it had ample power to prevent anybody else from doing them. In this negative sense the authority which it wielded under the Crown in its province may be called supreme.

[1] Mota-Padilla, *Historia de la Nueva Galicia*, cap. xlviii.

CONCLUSION

The only justification for breaking off the story of New Galicia arbitrarily at the end of the sixteenth century lies in the fact that a remarkably complete and instructive account of the province was written just at that time. The sixth bishop of Guadalajara, Alonso de la Mota y Escobar, was a great traveller. He visited almost every settlement of importance in his diocese and made careful notes of everything he saw. His *Descripción Geográfica*, written between 1601 and 1603, contains a record of his observations, with a wealth of descriptive detail. An account of the first half-century of audiencia rule may close appropriately with a summary of what an observant contemporary thought of the province—its natural features, its institutional organisation and the life of its people, both Spanish and Indian.[1]

The bishop's account of the government of New Galicia confirms the impression gained from the correspondence of the audiencia; that colonial society was top-heavy. An elaborate administrative, judicial and ecclesiastical organisation was superimposed upon a relatively sparse population. This is particularly evident in the description of Guadalajara. The city had grown considerably since the days of Lebrón de Quiñones, but as an administrative rather than commercial or industrial centre. It was laid out rather lavishly on a formal rectilinear plan, as it is to-day; it had two main squares, one containing the audiencia buildings, the president's lodging, the treasury, the prison and the arsenal, the other the municipal buildings and the great new stone cathedral, half built in 1600. There were, in addition to these public institutions, five monasteries; a Jesuit college, in which the fathers of the Company taught Latin and rhetoric; and a hospital of twenty beds, employing a staff of nine—physician, apothecary, barber, chaplain, and five negro servants. The total Spanish population was about five hundred and about half the *vecinos* were officials of one sort or another—'hombres de plaza y de hábito cortesano' (and yet the audiencia complained of being under-staffed). According to the bishop, hardly a single Spaniard in the city was employed by another Spaniard. The domestic service and the unskilled labour

[1] A. de la Mota y Escobar, *Descripción geográfica de los Reinos de Galicia, Vizcaya y León* (1603); J. Ramírez Cabanas, ed. (Mexico, 1930). The MS. is in the British Museum.

of the city were performed for the most part by negro slaves, while the more skilled trades were in the hands of Indians. These Indian craftsmen enjoyed considerable prosperity and the suburb of Analco, with its own well-appointed parish church, had grown up outside the city bounds to accommodate them. A market was held every five days at which the local Indians sold their produce. Other merchandise was brought from Mexico by mule trains, the roads being unfit for carts, and nearly all the merchants trading in Guadalajara had their homes and headquarters in Mexico. Apart from Indian crafts and husbandry the only mention of local productive activity is a reference to four water-mills for grinding the city's corn.

Guadalajara, of course, was not typical of the province as a whole. Zacatecas was a larger and busier town, though less impressively planned. The description of this mining centre, with its long main street winding through a narrow valley, its short steep side streets, its small and cramped houses, suggests comparison with the towns of the Welsh coal-field. The hills surrounding it were dotted with mine workings and for miles in every direction the forests had been felled to provide fuel for smelting, so that wood had to be brought to the city in carts over considerable distances and was sold at high prices.

The European population of Zacatecas must have been over a thousand. There were three hundred Spanish *vecinos* and a dozen or so foreigners, Italians and Portuguese. The number of officials was very much smaller than at Guadalajara. The salaried officials were the *corregidor*, the municipal magistrates, and the treasury officials with their staff of clerks and assayers. Proprietary officials included the town councillors, the usual municipal officers—*alguacil* and the rest—and four notaries: the treasury notary and three notaries public, of whom one served as town clerk. Purchasable offices at Zacatecas commanded relatively high prices, considerably higher, on the whole, than at Guadalajara.[1] Constables and

---

[1] The *Descripción Geográfica* gives average prices in silver *pesos* as follows:

	Guadalaraja		Zacatecas	
Secretary to the audiencia	(1)	12,000	—	
Chief constable to the audiencia	(1)	4,000	—	
Municipal chief constable	(1)	2,000	(1)	19,000
Town clerk	Office performed by public notaries			
Notaries public	(3)	2,000	(3)	6,000
Town councillors	(8)	500	(6)	400

notaries, in particular, did better in a place where there was plenty of business activity, than in the capital where they relied on litigation for their livelihood. There was a shortage of clergy (according to the bishop) and only one church, the priests of which fared badly, since the neighbourhood produced few crops of which tithes might be taken, and the civic charter exempted the *vecinos* from money contributions to support the parish clergy. Of the *vecinos* who were not officials, most were concerned either directly or indirectly with mining. About fifty owned shops, and some of these shopkeepers were prosperous enough to employ Spanish assistants. In addition, over a hundred Spaniards living elsewhere had business connections in Zacatecas and visited the place regularly. As at Guadalajara, unskilled labour was done by negroes, while most of the craftsmen were Indians or *mestizos*. In the mines also, negroes were employed, when they could be obtained, to do the pick-and-shovel work; though their health suffered so severely when they worked underground that Indians had frequently to be employed instead. Indians in any case performed all the skilled operations of silver extraction, whether by smelting or by the mercury amalgamation process. Spaniards were employed chiefly as foremen and overseers, and usually knew less about the technical aspects of mining than their Indian workmen.

It is clear from the bishop's description of Guadalajara and Zacatecas that the nature of Spanish society in the towns had changed greatly in fifty years. The frontier area of conquest and Indian warfare had moved north and the day of the *conquistador* was over. The older towns of New Galicia had long ceased to be military camps; they had developed their ruling oligarchies of wealthy miners and ranchers, their middle class of Spaniards employed as officials, shopkeepers, or overseers of native labour, their artisan class of Indians and *mestizos*. The mountain Indians, with their constant banditry and occasional armed revolt, were becoming a nuisance rather than a pressing menace. The bishop commented on the decline of warlike exercise and accomplishments, resulting from the comparative peacefulness of the times. Peace and poverty together, he considered, had turned the soldier-*conquistadores* into miners and shopkeepers. Few of the *vecinos* of either city possessed body armour or kept any arms other than a sword and possibly a musket for shooting game. A small royal arsenal was maintained in Guadalajara from which arms could be distributed in an

CONCLUSION

emergency. This was controlled by the audiencia; but the role of the *oidores* was changing too. In the sixteenth century they had been at need leaders in war as well as administrators and judges. It was now over twenty years since an *oidor* had taken the field in person. In the seventeenth century they were to have more litigation to deal with, but were to exercise less administrative power and no military leadership.

The smaller towns of New Galicia call only for passing mention. The numerous mining settlements in the northern and eastern parts of the province, and in New Vizcaya, were developing in much the same way as Zacatecas, though the existence of some of them was precarious. Of the older settlements planted by Nuño de Guzmán, Compostela had changed little in size since the foundation of the audiencia; it was a predominantly agricultural community, surrounded by wheat fields and orange groves, and fairly prosperous. Purificación had shown early promise of prosperity through the possession of a harbour at Navidad. Legaspi's first expedition to the Philippines had sailed from there; but Acapulco, being nearer to Mexico city, had soon afterwards monopolised the small seaborne trade of the north Pacific and partly for this reason, partly through the diminution of the local Indian population, Purificación had failed to develop. The town contained forty Spanish households in 1600. The decline of the native population along the Pacific coast had affected the isolated settlement of Culiacán even more seriously. The bishop visited Culiacán, and wrote a vivid description of a primitive frontier community. There were thirty Spanish families, who lived by hunting, fishing and horsebreeding 'dressed in the same fashion as the settlers whom Nuño de Guzmán planted there, neither knowing nor caring whether there were war or peace in the world, nor whether the convoys came and went; nobody except the single notary having any use for ink or paper'. The audiencia had concerned itself very little with Culiacán and no *oidor* had ever been there.

Not only in the towns, but in the country also, the nature of the Spanish community was changing. The original *conquistadores* had settled as military overlords. The *encomienda* system had enabled the more fortunate among them to live in Spanish settlements exacting services or drawing tribute, but otherwise taking little interest in rural economic activities. By the turn of the century, however, the leading Spaniards had become proprietors of estates,

188

dividing their time between those estates and the towns where many of them held *regimientos* and other offices. While the Indian village communities still cultivated their traditional crops, maize, beans and *maguey*, the frequent references in the *Descripción Geográfica* to fields of wheat and herds of cattle indicate that large areas of land were under direct Spanish management; though the wheat was often watered by irrigation works of Indian origin. New Galicia was already becoming—as much of it has been ever since—a country of large self-contained *haciendas*.

The most profitable rural occupation was cattle-breeding. Vast herds were grazed in the upland valleys of Jalisco, and since those valleys were both fertile and sheltered, still further herds were driven in from the neighbouring provinces of New Spain for wintering. There was a thriving export trade in fat cattle from New Galicia to the towns of New Spain, which drew complaints from people who thought that it kept up the price of beef in New Galicia. Some of the loudest objections to the trade were raised by the ecclesiastical hierarchy of Guadalajara, whose tithes were directly affected. A joint letter of bishop, dean and chapter in 1606 stated that among leading ranchers, Rodrigo del Río and Francisco de Urdiñola had sent more than twenty thousand head to Mexico in the previous year and that the valleys of New Galicia were being emptied of cattle.[1]

The cattle industry was the subject of constant complaint, litigation, and often actual fighting. An intelligent and responsible observer, the *fiscal* Pinedo, in a report to the king in 1585,[2] summarised the chief complaints: the unreasonably large area of the principal ranches; the practice of measuring land grants in terms of radius from a given point, which gave rise to endless boundary disputes; the wasteful use of pasture when cattle were allowed to graze at will over the open range; the indiscriminate slaughter of cattle, including cows and heifers, often merely for the sake of the hides or the tallow; cattle rustling, trespass, and quarrels over water rights. The *Descripción Geográfica* echoed most of these complaints, and added the depredations of bandits and roving Indians. The author attributed the trouble to the lack of an *Hermandad*—a rural security organisation such as existed in both Old and New Spain. The audiencia was the responsible authority;

[1] Orozco y Jiménez, *Colección*, vol. v, p. 194.
[2] *A.G.I.* Auda. de Guadalajara 6: 'Lic. Pinedo al Rey. 30 de Marzo de 1585.'

it granted or sold unoccupied land for ranches; it issued the licences which were officially necessary for the export or the slaughter of cattle; it was the court of appeal for disputes; but its only agents for enforcing the law in these respects were the two statutory *alguaciles del campo*,[1] and in practice it failed lamentably to maintain order on the cattle ranges. Nevertheless, the industry throve; the ranchers grew rich and the price of cattle remained surprisingly steady. According to the *Descripción Geográfica* a bullock on the hoof cost 6 *pesos* in 1600. The price had been 5 *pesos* in 1550. The prices of most other commodities had risen far more in the same period—sheep, for instance (much less plentiful than cattle) from 4 to 16 *reales*; the *fanega* of maize (rather more than a bushel) from 1 to 4 *pesos*.

The rise in the price of maize has a special significance, since maize was the principal crop and the staple food of the settled Indians. Indian rural society was also changing in character. The sedentary tribes of New Galicia had suffered severely, first from the brutalities of Nuño de Guzmán's *entrada*, then from the secondary effects of contact with Europeans. Many villages, sacked by Nuño's army or devastated during the Mixton war, had been abandoned. Some of the land thus left derelict had been reoccupied by Indians from New Spain, and the 'Mexican' language had spread widely at the expense of the native languages. Scattered through the *Descripción Geográfica* are many references to depopulated villages, to vanished place-names and forgotten traditions. Corroborative evidence comes from constant complaints of the decline of the value of *encomiendas*.

The decay of so many of the native village communities was not due simply to Spanish brutality. The vigilance of the audiencia served to protect the Indians from the grosser forms of ill-treatment and slavery was rare. One of the reports of the *fiscal* Pinedo, dated 1583,[2] summarises the main troubles. The first was pestilence; epidemic diseases, particularly those introduced by Europeans, wrought havoc among people who lived chiefly on maize and whose resistance to disease was low. The disastrous epidemics of 1580–1, in Pinedo's opinion, had reduced the settled Indian population in many parts of the province by more than a quarter, though the audiencia claimed to have done its utmost to provide medical

---

[1] *Recopilación de Leyes de Indias*, II. xx. 10.
[2] *A.G.I.* Auda. de Guadalajara 6: 'Lic. Pinedo al Rey. 6 de Abril 1583.'

assistance.[1] The second complaint was the interruption of Indian agriculture caused by the *repartimiento* system. The audiencia, which was responsible for authorising *repartimientos*, strove conscientiously to limit demands upon the Indians and to leave them time for the cultivation of their fields, and was particularly reluctant in Piñedo's day to authorise forced labour for silver mining; but demands for labour were incessant. *Repartimientos* were needed for the wheat and sugar estates, for irrigation and for a variety of other public and private works. Ecclesiastical bodies were among the claimants, demanding *repartimiento* labour for the cultivation of their estates as well as for church building.[2] Employers, with the connivance of the headmen, exacted unauthorised labour, or detained their Indians on various pretexts after the authorised time. Pinedo considered that the amount of labour exacted was far too great and the legal wage too small, though it had risen from 4 *reales* a month in 1550 to half a *real* a day in Pinedo's time.

The growth of Spanish *haciendas* encroached on the *ejidos*—the outlying commons of the Indian villages. The audiencia could and (when petitions reached it) did enforce the law preserving the arable land of the villages against encroachment; but *ejidos* were difficult to define, and it was impossible to preserve all the facilities for hunting and wood-gathering which the Indians had formerly enjoyed, in a country where fertile and wooded land formed but a small part of the total area. The proximity of mines and large self-contained estates also tended to draw labour away from the village fields, and in this connection Pinedo mentioned the growth of a practice which later became the curse of Mexican rural life— the practice of advancing money or goods to Indians on the understanding that the advances would be repaid in labour. This led to peonage—debt slavery, which local custom sealed as an inescapable hereditary burden.[3]

The political organisation of the village communities was changing under Spanish pressure. The traditional and religious authority of the *caciques* was declining through the activities of the mission clergy. Many villages were already governed by *regidores*

[1] *A.G.I.* Auda. de Guadalajara 6: 'Audiencia al Rey. 17 de Octubre 1582.'

[2] E.g. Orozco y Jiménez, *Colección*, vol. v, p. 155: 'La compañía de Jesús pide se le diesen cierto número de Indios del pueblo de Tuluquilla para labores del campo. 30 de Mayo 1595.'

[3] See G. M. McBride, *The land systems of Mexico* (New York, 1923).

and *alcaldes* in imitation of the custom of the Spanish towns. These native officials often sought to strengthen their position by securing written confirmation of their offices from the audiencia; and the conscientious *fiscal* had frequently to take action against notaries who charged excessive fees for drafting these confirmations.[1]

In general the *Descripción Geográfica* reveals a rural Indian community suffering disruptive change and sinking already into a sullen apathy. 'Most of the natives of Galicia are apathetic, lazy, unwilling to work either to improve their own lot or to acquire property for their children...having little or no political organisation... little given to rites and idolatries, temples and sacrifices; this being due, in my opinion, to their rude and primitive intellect, which cannot rise to seek first causes.' The bishop considered that these were the characteristics of the Indians before their conquest and conversion; but his statement does not agree with the accounts in the *relaciones* of the conquest. Far more probably, the state of affairs he described was characteristic of a conquered society which was losing its own customs and failing to acquire those of its conquerors.

The *Descripción Geográfica* goes on to state: 'The Indians who nowadays live among Spaniards behave very differently.' Frequent references indicate the existence, by 1600, of a numerous and well-defined class of Indians cut off from tribal life, wearing European clothes and living in or near the Spanish settlements. Many of these people were not natives of New Galicia; 'Mexicans', Tarascos and Otomíes were the names most often mentioned. They worked for wages in mines or ranches, or on their own account as shop-keepers, craftsmen or muleteers, and were a relatively prosperous class. Some of the muleteers owned strings of fifteen and twenty mules—a valuable property, for an unbroken mule was worth 20 *pesos* or more. Most of these Europeanised Indians kept their own horses; the law forbidding Indians to keep saddle-horses[2] seems not to have been enforced. The remuneration of Indian craftsmen is difficult to determine; but skilled workmen in the mines received up to 8 *pesos* a month—more than four times the wage legally paid for *repartimiento* labour in the same period. In addition, Indians in the mines were in the habit of taking away scraps of silver ore below a certain weight, to smelt for their own

[1] *A.G.I.* Auda. de Guadalajara 6: 'Lic. Pinedo al Rey. 17 de Octubre 1582.'
[2] *Recopilación de Leyes de Indias*, VI. i. 33.

profit. This custom had become so far recognised that *quinto* was levied on the silver so produced. Apart from this silver tax the Europeanised Indian contributed little to the royal revenue. Living outside the tribal organisation, he was also outside the *encomienda* and *repartimiento* systems, and often evaded the payment of tribute altogether. *Mestizos* were in any case exempted from all these exactions—a circumstance which must have encouraged Indian women to marry Spaniards.

The *Chichimecas*—the wild and primitive tribes of the mountain regions—remained a pressing problem and a constant danger to the more remote settlements. Both the civil and the ecclesiastical authorities nibbled at the problem by the occasional dispatch of punitive expeditions, by the establishment of missions, above all by the planting of settlements—*congregaciones*.[1] Small settlements in the troubled areas were moved and amalgamated with larger, more defensible villages; colonies of loyal Indians were planted in the unsettled country; the wild peoples themselves were induced, partly by force, partly by grants of tools, seed and stock, to settle either as agriculturalists or (like the Navajo of New Mexico in later times) as semi-nomadic herdsmen, instead of living by hunting and raiding. The author of the *Descripción Geográfica* had considerable experience of the problem, having been personally concerned in the establishment of a number of settlements in the Topia district.[2] Sometimes the *congregaciones*, owing to the authorities' ignorance of local conditions, entailed severe hardship for the people 'congregated' and for local *encomenderos*; but many settlements proved permanent and successful. Tello quotes a letter from the viceroy to the president Santiago de Vera, in 1595, informing him of the dispatch from Mexico, in the mule-train of Francisco Ramírez, of 'two hundred spades, twenty-four hatchets, eighteen ploughshares, four hundred hats and a hundred and fifty *pesos*' worth of material to make clothes for the women, so that they and their men-folk, receiving these things free of charge, may appreciate the advantages of settlement'.[3] The goods were destined for new settlements in the Acaponeta district. The *alcalde mayor* provided seed purchased

[1] L. B. Simpson, 'Studies in the administration of the Indians in New Spain. Part II. The civil congregation', *Ibero-Americana*, no. 7 (Berkeley, California, 1934).

[2] Orozco y Jiménez, *Colección*, vol. v, p. 188: 'Informe acerca de la benemérita labor del Ilmo. Sr. Dr. Alonso de la Mota y Escobar en la pacificación de los Indios bárbaros de la Nueva Galicia. 17 de Abril 1603.'

[3] Tello, *Crónica miscelánea*, cap. ccxxxiv.

locally. Fray Andrés de Medina, the saintly Franciscan prior of Tzapotitlán, appointed by the president to take charge of the Acaponeta missions, lived there for nine years, founding several churches and a school for Indian boys, and leaving at his death a peaceful rustic community. Successful settlements such as these, however, touched only the fringe of the problem in the sixteenth century, and for long afterwards great areas of mountain country remained outside the scope of the colonial administration; some of the more remote peoples, indeed, being little touched by European influence to this day.[1]

All this settlement work was part of the general policy of the Crown and the inspiration behind it was largely religious. The president was concerned with it in his capacity of governor, but though he did all he could to further its success, his concern was not personal or immediate; nor was the work inspired or originated by the audiencia. The audiencias of the Indies were not designed, either by their composition or by the nature of their authority, to inspire and originate. They were courts of professional judges called upon to administer, not administrative boards called upon to adjudicate. The nature of the courts and the training which the judges received, fostered a close attachment to the letter of the law and sometimes an ingenious pedantry in interpreting it; an appearance of dilatoriness; and a reluctance to innovate or to allow anyone else to innovate. But this legalistic conservatism, in the circumstances of the Spanish colonies, was not necessarily an evil.

It is true that in times of crisis the checks and balances of colonial government hindered prompt and decisive action. In general, however, the wide powers entrusted to the courts reflected not only tradition, but a sound instinct of authority. Successful colonial government depends on the reconciliation of two different points of view and two main sets of interests. The reconciliation was particularly difficult in Spanish America, where the conquered race was numerous, comprising tribes in many stages of civilisation, but all using stone weapons, and no match in war for armed Europeans. The action of the Crown, in replacing the destructive organising ability of the *conquistadores* by the judicial authority of the audiencias, implied the decision—however confused and hesitant—that both points of view should be considered; that Indian interests and even

[1] See C. Lumholtz, *Unknown Mexico* (London, 1903).

194

Indian customs (except in religious matters) should be upheld, except in so far as the Indians voluntarily accepted European ways. The Crown, presiding judicially over the processes whereby conquerors and conquered were to be fused into a unified and centralised society, naturally regarded the high courts of justice as its most trustworthy representatives.

It was impossible in practice, of course, for the Crown or the audiencias to maintain an Olympian impartiality. Conquest involves exploitation, whatever *quid pro quo* the conquerors may offer in the form of orderly government and technical progress. The Crown had to connive at the subordination of Indian to Spanish interests, or else expel non-official Spaniards from the Indies altogether, as Las Casas suggested. Even where they upheld native interests most conscientiously the audiencias often lacked the physical means to enforce their decisions, and the great Indian cultures—already, perhaps, past their zenith—disintegrated before the impact of European influence in ways which no legislation could prevent. Nevertheless, the Indian case was heard; legal redress was provided, in so far as the wrongs done were capable of legal redress; and in general the Indians were not slaughtered, enslaved, herded into reservations, or openly robbed. In the sixteenth century this was a remarkable achievement and much of the credit for it belongs to the royal audiencias.

A criticism commonly levelled at Spanish colonial government is that by restricting high office in the Indies to peninsular-born Spaniards, it prevented the growth of political responsibility and experience in Spanish America. The displays of political inexperience in the decades immediately following Independence support this view. Even the municipalities enjoyed but little semblance of responsible self-government, though they were the only public bodies in which Creoles normally held office. The audiencias displayed this peninsular exclusiveness in the highest degree. Even in the sixteenth century men born in the Indies became bishops[1] and in the later colonial period there were a few colonial-born viceroys; but *oidores* were almost always born and always trained in Spain. At the time of Independence the audiencias were, more than any other institutions, the hated symbols of *Gachupín* tyranny. It would have been contrary to all

[1] The author of the *Descripción Geográfica* was born in Mexico. Hernáez, *Colección de Bulas*, vol. II, p. 72.

the traditions and prejudices of the Spanish Crown to entrust high judicial office to colonists; nor, in the earlier colonial period, were there adequate law-schools in the colonies. Apart from these considerations, to have allowed any appreciable number of colonists to reach the bench would have defeated one of the first objects of the audiencias, and would have ended all attempt at judicial vigilance on behalf of Indian rights. The dilemma is a familiar one in many colonial possessions to-day, and needs no emphasis. From the beginning the *oidores* often incurred wild unpopularity among the colonists, not merely because they were peninsular Spaniards, but because they were the agents of a native policy which many colonists found obstructive and embarrassing.

In the sixteenth century the audiencia of New Galicia proved itself loyal and reasonably efficient. It was expensive, but far less expensive than a military administration would have been. Its attempts to enforce the Indian policy of the Crown were a partial failure; but in this respect it worked under peculiar difficulties; and for years the spirit of Nuño de Guzmán brooded over the scene of his exploits. The task of laying this grim ghost fell to the audiencia. To the Indians it must have appeared the least harsh, if the most incomprehensible, of all Spanish governmental institutions. To the audiencia must belong some of the credit for the planning which changed Guadalajara from the squalid settlement of the 1550's into one of the loveliest cities of the Americas. Finally, there were among the *oidores* men now long forgotten, but well worthy to be remembered: a loyal friend of the conquered race in Lorenzo Lebrón de Quiñones; and in Francisco Gómez de Mendiola a churchman whose name passed into local legend along with those of Vasco de Quiroga and Bartolomé de las Casas.

SPECIMEN TITLE OF *ENCOMIENDA* IN NEW GALICIA

Archivo General de Indias, Sevilla. Papeles de Simancas, Audiencia de Guadalajara 5. Averiguaciones del Licenciado Contreras y Guevara, sobre lo tocante a la visita del Real Consejo de Indias, fol. 157.

Por la presente en nombre de Su Majestad deposito en vos Juan Delgado vecino de la villa de Guadalajara los moradores y naturales de Teul con sus sujetos para que os sirváis dellos en vuestras haciendas y grangerías, con cargo que tengáis de los industriar en las cosas de nuestra Santa Fe Católica, poniendo en ello toda vuestra solicitud posible y necesaria, en lo cual descargo la conciencia de Su Majestad y la mía. En su Real nombre — fecha en esta ciudad de Compostela a 6 de Diciembre de 1534. Nuño de Guzmán. Por mandado de su señoría. Pedro Ruiz de Haro.

The titles granted by Cortés in New Spain were almost exactly similar. A specimen is given in S. Zavala, 'La propiedad territorial en las encomiendas de Indios', *Universidad* (Mexico, D.F., Sept. 1937).

SPECIMEN APPOINTMENT OF A *CORREGIDOR* IN NEW GALICIA

Archivo General de Indias, Sevilla. Papeles de Simancas, Audiencia de Guadalajara 5. Averiguaciones del Licenciado Contreras y Guevara, sobre lo tocante a la visita del Real Consejo de Indias (1570), f°. 144.

Nos los oidores alcaldes mayores de la Audiencia Real que por S.M. reside en la ciudad de Guadalajara del Nuevo Reino de Galicia, por hacer bien y merced a vos...; y acatando que seis tal persona que bien y fielmente haréis lo que por Nos os fuere cometido y mandado en nombre de S.M., os nombramos por Corregidor del pueblo de...y sus sujetos, que es en la provincia, por tiempo y espacio de un año cumplido primero siguiente, que comienza a correr desde el día de la data de esta nuestra carta y provisión, con la jurisdicción civil y criminal, y vos damos comisión y facultad como tal corregidor podáis traer vara de justicia en el dicho pueblo de...y sus sujetos y jurisdicción, y conoscáis de todos y cualesquier pleitos y causas civiles y criminales movidos y por mover que en el dicho pueblo y sus sujetos acaecieren y se recrecieren entre cualesquier personas así españoles como naturales, y mandamos que visitéis los términos del dicho vuestro corregimiento y sepáis y averiguéis si algunas personas les tienen tomadas o ocupadas sus tierras, y se les haced restituir y haréis relación dello a esta Real Audiencia para que en ella visto, se provea lo que sea justicia, y otrosí os encargamos mucho tengáis especial cuidado que los naturales del dicho vuestro corregimiento sean industriados en las cosas de nuestra Santa Fe Católica, y sabréis si algunos españoles tienen hijos en mujeres naturales desta tierra, y los que hallareis que padres tengan, se los hacer entregar, y los que no los tuvieren haréis relación dello para que se provea lo que convenga; y porque conviene al servicio de S.M. y de su Real justicia los delitos que los caciques y gobernadores y principales del dicho vuestro corregimiento cometieren los unos contra los otros, porque deban ser castigados, no os entremeteréis, mas solamente haréis las informaciones de los tales, y prenderéis a los culpados, y juntamente con las informaciones que hiciéreis lo enviaréis a la dicha Real

Audiencia para que en ella visto se provea lo que sea justicia; y otrosí en los casos criminales que conociéreis durante el tiempo del dicho vuestro cargo, ahora sea contra españoles como contra naturales, no procederéis contra ellos ejecución de pena de muerte ni mutilación de miembro, y en los casos que hubiere de intervenir semejantes penas, por ser, como son, cosas arduas y de calidad que para las sentenciar requieren ser vistas por personas doctas y de letras, os mandamos que tomadas las informaciones y hechos los procesos, estando conclusos en forma contra el tal culpado, los remitáis a esta Real Audiencia, teniendo preso y a buen recaudo al tal delincuente, y para que en ella visto, se provea y determine lo que sea justicia, y porque somos informados que los pasajeros que pasan por el dicho pueblo de vuestro corregimiento les toman los mantenimientos y otras cosas sin se lo pagar, y los cargan y llevan por tamemes contra su voluntad, y les hacen malos tratamientos, os mandamos tengáis especial cuidado de los amparar y defender, no consintiendo ni dando lugar que ninguna persona les haga agravio ni molestia, y a los que lo contrario hicieren, los castigaréis por todo rigor de derecho, haciéndoles pagar los mantenimientos que dieren a precios justos y moderados conforme al arancel que les pusiéreis, y de otra manera no les tomen sus haciendas ni los carguen ni lleven por tamemes aunque digan los naturales que ellos de su voluntad se quisieren cargar, haciendo guardar y cumplir la cédula de S.M. que habla sobre que ninguna persona cargue tamemes, como en ella se contiene, y otrosí tendréis cuidado que los naturales del dicho vuestro corregimiento no se ocupen en hacer obras de monasterios sin espresa licencia y facultad, por cuanto S.M. así nos lo tiene mandado, y otrosí os mandamos que si alguna persona truje vara de justicia en los pueblos de vuestra jurisdicción sin tener facultad desta Real Audiencia, se la quitaréis, y haréis información sobre ello, y prenderéis el cuerpo a la tal persona que hubiere traído vara, juntamente con la dicha información lo enviaréis preso a esta Real Audiencia para que en ella se haga en el caso justicia. Otrosí os mandamos que los estranjeros de los Reinos de S.M. y que sean casados en los Reinos de Castilla que estuvieren en vuestra jurisdicción, les prendáis los cuerpos, y con los bienes les fueren hallados los enviaréis a la cárcel Real desta corte, para que se cumpla lo que S.M. tiene provéido y mandado contra los susodichos, y tendréis cuenta y razón de las penas de cámara en que condenáreis durante el tiempo de vuestro cargo para que al fin dél déis buena cuenta con pago. Asimismo sabréis si en los pueblos de vuestra jurisdicción hay algunos bienes de difuntos, y si durante el tiempo del dicho vuestro cargo fallecieren algunos ab intestato y que no tengan herederos, cobraréis los bienes de los tales difuntos, y enviarlos eis con los testamentos e inventarios al juez de bienes de difuntos de esta Real Audiencia, para que haga en ella lo que S.M. tiene mandado. Otrosí os mandamos no entren en vuestro poder ni recibáis ningunos pesos de oro de los tributos del dicho vuestro corregimiento, so pena de privación de oficio y de 100 pesos para la cámara de S.M., sino solamente tendréis cuidado y haréis que se metan en la caja de S.M. de las tres llaves. Otrosí os mandamos y encargamos tengáis especial cuidado que los naturales del dicho vuestro corregimiento se ocupen en sus labores y grangerías y hagan así sus sementeras como las de S.M. y de sus comunidades, y crien gallinas, así de Castilla como de la tierra, y para hacer y cumplir lo susodicho vos informaréis de un buen Indio el cual ande y visite las sementeras y casas de los naturales para que vea si guarda y cumple lo susodicho, y para ello le daréis vara de justicia para que los naturales le obedezcan, y tendréis cuidado de tomar cuenta a las comunidades de los pueblos del dicho vuestro corregimiento en cada un año, y cobrar las alcances, y hacer que se metan en la caja de la comunidad. Otrosí os mandamos residáis en. . . por lo menos la tercia parte del año, con apercibimiento que no lo cumpliendo, no se os mandará pagar vuestro salario; y mandamos hayáis y llevéis de salario para ayuda a vuestra costa y mantenimiento en el dicho año,. . . pesos de oro común, los cuales mandamos a los tenientes de los oficiales de S.M. deste Reino que residen en. . . os los den, libren y paguen de los tributos que los naturales del dicho pueblo y sus sujetos son obligados a dar a S.M., ante los cuales dichos oficiales daréis fianzas abonadas que daréis cuenta con pago al cabo del dicho año de los tributos que parecieren haber entrado en vuestro poder, y que daréis residencia del dicho cargo que por nos os fuere mandada tomar, y pagaréis lo que en ello fuere juzgado y sentenciado y mandamos a todas y cualesquier personas de cualquier estado y condición que sean vos hayan y tengan por tal corregidor del dicho pueblo y sus sujetos y vos obedezcan y vengan a vuestros llamamientos y cumplan vuestros mandamientos so las penas que de parte de S.M. les pusiereis, las cuales nos por la presente las habemos por puestas, y vos damos poder y facultad para que las podáis ejecutar en las persones y bienes de los que rebeldes e inobedientes fueren, para lo cual que dicho es, y usar y ejercer el dicho cargo, vos damos todo poder cumplido con sus incidencias y dependencias.

Dada en la ciudad de Guadalajara.

INDEX

Abogados, 151, 156, 158–9
abogados de pobres, 156
Acaponeta, 193
Acapulco, 188
acuerdo, 6 n., 8, 137
acuerdo de hacienda, 8
adelantados, 9, 91
Aguascalientes, 12, 15, 17
Ahumada Samano, Pedro de, 88
Alarcón, licentiate (*oidor*), 128
alcaldes del crimen, 160
alcaldes mayores, 5, 34–6, 140
alcaldes ordinarios, 5, 33–4
alguacil mayor of the audiencia, 40, 162; of the municipality, 142
alguaciles del campo, 162
Altamirano, licentiate (*oidor*), 170, 179, 181
Alvarado, Pedro de, 28
Anáhuac, 14, 18
Arizona, 15
attorneys, *see procuradores*
audiencia, 2, 6
audiencia of New Galicia:
  administrative powers, 36, 134, 148–9
  boundaries, 35, 42, 91, 138, 151
  civil jurisdiction, 37, 125, 150 ff.
  criminal jurisdiction, 37, 50, 126–7, 160 ff.
  legislative powers, 134
  police powers, 162
  powers over ecclesiastics, 106
  president, 132
  procedure, 155–61
  promotion to Royal Chancellery, 131
  seal, 151–2
audiencia of New Spain, 6, 24, 72
  appellate jurisdiction in New Galicia, 37, 46, 125–6
Augustinians in Guadalajara, 109
Avalos, Alonso de, 19
  villages of, 19, 35
Ayala, Fray Pedro de (bishop of Guadalajara), 108, 113
  quarrels with audiencia, 110
  quarrels with cathedral chapter, 117
Ayutla, 19
Aztatlán, 15–17, 23
Aztecs, 14–15, 56–7

Barranca, 15–16
Basques, 21, 89
Beteta, Fray Gregorio de, 53
bienes de difuntos, 29, 81
bigamy, 174
blasphemy, 174, 176

Caballerías, 10 n., 11
cabildos, 5, 32–3, 124, 141–6
caciques, 56, 59, 71
caja de bienes de difuntos, 105
Caltzontzín, 21
camino real, 15
Canon Law, 2, 100, 102
Casa de contratación, 4, 5, 105
casos de corte, 37, 150
casos de gobernación, 6 n.
cathedral, 82
cathedral chapter, 110–11, 116–17, 127–8
cattle, 189
Caxcanes, 16–17, 21–2, 28
cédulas, 3, 4 n.
chancelleries, 3
Chapala, Lake, 15, 21
Charles V, 14, 97
Chiametla, 17, 86–8, 90–2
Chichimecas, 18, 28, 193
chief constable, *see alguacil mayor*
Chimalhuacán, 15–16
Chirinos, 20–2
Church, *see* ecclesiastical, episcopal, Inquisition, missions, etc.
Cíbola, 14–15, 84
Cisneros, Lope de, 112–16
Civil Law, 2, 3
Coahuila, 177
Colima, 12, 16, 19, 35, 70
Colio, Diego García de, 89
Colùmbus, 1
Compostela, 25, 28, 43–4, 47, 188
Congo, 8
congregaciones, 193
Contreras y Guevara, licentiate Miguel Ladrón de (*oidor*), 41, 66, 71, 77, 79
  averiguaciones compiled by, 120
Coras, 17
Coronado, Francisco Vázquez, 27, 30
corregidores, 7, 31–2, 26, 140
  duties and salaries in New Galicia, 122

Cortés, Francisco, 19–21
Cortés, Hernándo, 14, 20
Cortés, Martín, 80, 93
Council of Castile, 4
Council of the Indies, 4
  appeals to, 37, 150
  visita of, 120
criminous clerks, 102
cuentas, 38, 81, 124
Culiacán, 15, 17, 24, 188

Debt slavery, 55, 191
Durango, 84, 90

Ecclesiastical immunity, 103
ecclesiastical jurisdiction, 101 ff.
ecclesiastical patronage, 97
ejidos, 191
El Teul, 16, 23
encomenderos, 9, 12, 58, 62–3, 69
encomiendas, 9, 11–12, 20, 29, 57–8, 60–3
Enríquez de Almansa, Martín (viceroy), 95–6, 130
episcopal courts, 100
  appeals from, 106
  penalties inflicted by, 104
escribanos, 40, 153–4, 164–5
escudero, 9
Española, 1, 5
Espíritu Santo, 28
evidence, rules of, 158, 161

Falces, Marquis of (viceroy), 92–3
familiars, 174
ferries, 71
fiscal, 4–5, 61, 67, 103
  duties as Crown prosecutor, 154
  duties as defender of Indian rights, 154, 163
  duties in ecclesiastical causes, 106
  first appointment in New Galicia, 127
forced labour, 8, 30, 62–6
Franciscans, 108–9
fueros, 2–3
  of Inquisition, 174–5
fuerza, 106

Gobernación, 6
Gómez de Contreras, Pedro (treasurer), 81, 124
Guachichiles, 18, 85

Guadalajara, 15, 21, 25, 29, 43, 49, 196
  audiencia moved to, 82
  cathedral chapter of, 110–11, 116–17, 127–8
  'little war' of, 171
  municipality of, 142–6
  population of (in 1600), 185
Guanajuato, 12, 15, 21
Guzmán, Nuño de, 19–26

Hacienda, see treasury
haciendas, 55, 62, 191
Hawkins, Sir John, 119
hearsay evidence, 157
heresy, 174
hospital, 185
Huicholes, 17
human sacrifice, 17

Ibarra, Diego de, 29, 92
Ibarra, Francisco de (governor of New Vizcaya), 83, 89–92
Ibarra, Juan de, 92
Indian:
  alcaldes and governors, 71–2, 191–2
  craftsmen, 186, 192
  labour, 55, 62–6
  land-holding, 59
  litigants, 162–3
  risings, 27, 87–9, 139
  tributes, 32, 35, 63, 65
  village organisation, 55
  wages, 50, 68, 192
  witnesses, 159
inhibitoria, 179
inns, 71
Inquisition, 100, 173–84
  commissaries, 174
  competencias, 179–80
  conflicts with audiencia, 177 ff.
  establishment in New Spain, 118, 173
  familiars, 174–5
  jurisdiction, 174
interdict, 104
  upon city of Guadalajara, 114
interlocutory judgements, 158
interrogatorio, 156–7

Jalisco, 12, 16
jueces de comisión, 151
jueces de bienes de difuntos, 105
jueces pesquisidores, 7, 162
jueces repartidores, 10

INDEX

Kenya, 8
kinship groups, 55

Land-grants, 10, 135
Las Casa, Fray Bartolomé de, 78, 99, 195
Laws of Toro, 2
Lebrón de Quiñones, licentiate Lorenzo (*oidor*), 41–2, 66–7, 73
  trial, 74–8
  visita in Colima, 68–72
León, Calixto de, 111
Lerma river, 19, 21
licences, 78
Lobo Guerrero (inquisitor), 172
Lomas y Colmenares, Juan Bautista de, 170, 177, 181

Maceguales, 55–6
maize, 16–17, 49, 190
Malines, *Cédula* of, 31, 62
Maraver, Pedro Gómez (bishop of Guadalajara), 47–8, 108
Martínez de la Marcha, licentiate Hernando (*oidor*), 41, 46–54, 79
mayeques, 56–7
Mazapil, 85
Medina, Fray Andrés de, 194
Mendieta, Gerónimo de (ecclesiastical historian), cited, 99
Mendiola, licentiate Francisco Gómez de (*oidor* and bishop of Guadalajara), 118, 128
Mendoza, Antonio de (viceroy), 26, 52, 63
Mercado, Ginés Vázquez, 84
Mexico, 14, *and see cabildos*
Michoacán, 15, 19, 21
Mill, James, 13
mines, 28–9, 50–1, 186–7
mining camps, disorder in, 129
mining regulations, 51–2
missions, 53, 98, 194
mita, 10
mixto fuero, 104–6
Mixton rising, 27–8
Monterrey, count of (viceroy), 172
Montezuma, 56
Monzón, ordinances of, 133 ff., 149, 153
Moors, 4
Morones, licentiate Pedro (*oidor*), 74–5, 80, 86, 88
Mota Padilla, Matías de la (historian), cited, 21

Mota y Escobar, Alonso de la (bishop of Guadalajara), 185
municipal government, *see cabildos*

Naborias, 51, 57, 70
Nahuatl, 18
Navidad, 19
Nayarit, 12, 14
  Sierra de, 15–17
Nevado de Colima, 14
New Galicia, 15, 24
  boundaries, 87
  conquest, 18 ff.
  ethnography, 16 ff.
  languages, 18
  population (in 1554), 46; (in 1570), 121
  state (in 1550), 49 ff.; (in 1600), 185 ff.
  topography, 15
New Laws, 29–30, 62
New León, 177
New Mexico, 15, 56, 177
New Spain, *see viceroy, audiencia*
New Vizcaya, 89–91, 184, 188
Nochistlán, 16
Nombre de Dios, 90–2
Northern Rhodesia, 8
notaries, *see escribanos*
Nueva Recopilación de Leyes de España, 3

Oath of office, 103
oidor of the week, 106
oidores, 5–7, 20
  conduct, dress, duties, 39
  marriage, 153, 170
  qualifications, 5 n., 184
  salaries, 131
  share in administration, 148
  votes, 152
oidores alcaldes mayores, 31, 66
  duties, 37 ff.
  salaries, 40
  subordinate rank, 35
oidores visitadores, 38, 66, 136
Olid, Cristóbal de, 19
Oñate, Cristóbal de, 24, 27–30, 51
Oñate, Juan de, 184
Ordinances:
  of the audiencia of New Galicia (1548), 35 ff.
  of the audiencias, or of Monzón (1562), 133 ff., 150 ff.

203

Ordinances (cont.)
on discoveries (1573), 25 n., 91
on mines and salt-beds, 51–2, 121
on the treasury of New Galicia, 147
Orozco, Dr Gerónimo de (president), 128, 132, 138 n.
Orozco, licentiate (oidor), 128
Oseguera, licentiate (oidor), 66–7, 81

Pánuco, 20
peonage, 55, 191
peonías, 10, 11
Pérez de la Torre, Diego (governor of New Galicia), 26
personal servitude, 11, 66
personation of priesthood, 174
pesos, 38 n., 50 n.
pesquisa, pesquisidores, 38, 151
Pinedo, licentiate Miguel (fiscal), 189 ff.
plague, 58
president of New Galicia, 132
administrative duties, 158
civil patronage, 140
ecclesiastical patronage, 146
financial responsibilities, 146–8
military responsibilities, 138
municipal responsibilities, 146
prices in New Galicia, 49–50, 190
privilegios de hidalguía, 152
probate, 104
procesos, 40, 155 ff.
procuradores, 127, 155–6, 165–6
protector de Indios, 163
Purificación, 25, 52, 188

Querétaro, 12
quinto, 12, 35, 52, 91, 147
Quiroga, Vasco de (bishop of Michoacán), 99
Quivira, 14
quorum, 150

Real hacienda, see treasury
receptores, 40, 155, 158–9, 166
Recopilación de Leyes de Indias, 3
recurso de fuerza, 8, 103, 106, 113, 173
regidores, 32–3, 141–2
regular clergy, 98
relaciones, 154, 158–9
relator, 4, 40, 154, 157–8
renuncia, 142, 144
repartimiento, 9, 10–11, 58, 64–5, 70, 135

repartimiento general y perpétuo, 62
requisitoria, 155
residencia, 7, 38, 74
Río Grande, or Santiago, 15, 19, 21
ritual dances, 59
royal house, 67, 82

Sale of offices, 143–5, 186
salt beds, 121, 170
Saltillo, 177
sanctuary, 103, 112
Sandoval, Francisco Tello de, 29–30
San Luis Potosí, 12
San Martín, 85, 89
Santiago de Vera, Dr (president), 182–3
Santo Domingo, 5
secular clergy, 98
Sentispac, 17
sermons, 115
shop-keepers, 187
Sierra Madre Occidental, 14–16
Siete Partidas, 2, 161
silver, see mines
silver tax, see quinto
slavery, 30, 57, 70
solicitation, 119
solicitors, see procuradores

Tacha, 161
tanda, 10
Tejada, licentiate Lorenzo de, 29–30
temples, 16, 22
teniente de gran chanciller, 152
Tepic, 15
torture, 161
treasury organisation, 52, 123, 147
salaries of treasury officials, 40
tribute, 32, 35, 63, 65
assessment, 70 n., 136
land, 57, 59

Urdiñola, Francisco de, 177–84

Valderrama, 80, 93
Valencia, Fray Angel de la, 115
vasallos patrimoniales, 57
vecinos, 43 n., 185, 187
Velasco, Luis de, the first (viceroy), 50, 65–6, 77, 90
Velasco, Luis de, the second (viceroy), 171, 177
Verdugo, Gil, 171

INDEX

viceroys, 6, 9, 167–8
  agents in New Galicia, 129, 169
  of New Spain, 7, 9, 26, 54, 65, 77, 87–9, 93–5, 129–30, 139–40, 143, 148
  powers in New Galicia, 168–72
Villamanrique, marquis of (viceroy), 170, 172
Villavicencio, Nuño Núñez de (*oidor*), 170, 177, 179
visita, 38
  of Lebrón de Quiñones, 68–72
  of Martínez de la Marcha, 46 ff.
  of the Council of the Indies, 120

Wages, 50, 68, 192
war-chiefs, 56
witnesses, 159, 161

Zacatecas, 12–18, 29, 43, 46, 50–1, 85, 186
  civic status, 141
  corregimiento, 140
  population (in 1600), 186
Zacatula, 19, 35
Zumárraga, Fray Juan de (archbishop of Mexico), 20, 99

105

25

CULIACAN

NEW VIZCAYA

SALTI

C. de Mercado

Mazapil

DURANGO

Nombre de Dios

Nieves

CHIAMETLA

Sombrerete

Mazatlán

Chalchihuites

Acaponeta

Fresnillo

R. Cañas

San Martín

ZACATECAS

NEW GALI

R. Grande

AGUAS CALIENTES

TEPIC

Teul

Nochistlán

Compostela

Río Grande de Santiago

Etzatlán

Ameca

GUADALAJARA

R. Ler

20

VILLAGES

L. Chapala

PART OF MEXICO

OF

Zamora

SHOWING

AVALOS

L. Pátzcuaro

NEW GALICIA

Purificación

Nevado de Colima

50   0   50   100

Navidad

COLIMA

COLIMA

MICHOAC

English Statute Miles

105

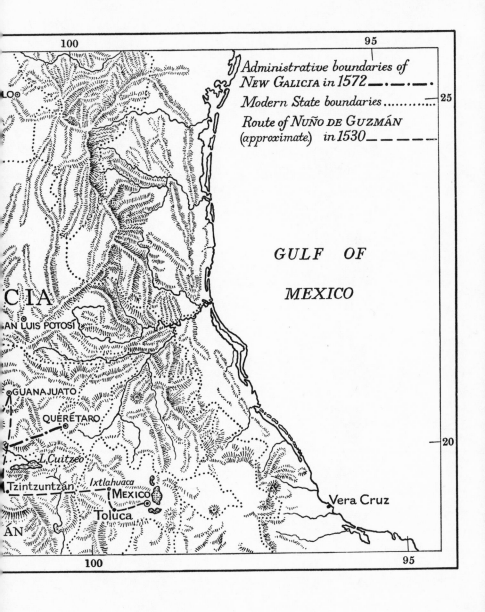

100   95

Administrative boundaries of
New Galicia in 1572 —·—·—·

Modern State boundaries ············

Route of Nuño de Guzmán
(approximate) in 1530 — — — —

25

LO

CIA

AN LUIS POTOSÍ

GULF OF

MEXICO

GUANAJUATO

QUERÉTARO

20

L. Cuitzeo

Tzintzuntzán   *Ixtlahuaca*

Mexico

Toluca

Vera Cruz

ÁN

100   95